T0029653

FSG

Also by Michelle Orange

*This Is Running for Your Life: Essays*

# Pure Flame

# Pure Flame

*a legacy*

# Michelle Orange

Farrar, Straus and Giroux · New York

Farrar, Straus and Giroux
120 Broadway, New York, NY 10271

Printed in the United States of America
First edition, 2021

Flame art on title page by Na Kim.

Library of Congress Cataloging-in-Publication Data
Names: Orange, Michelle, author.
Title: Pure flame : a legacy / Michelle Orange.
Description: First edition. | New York : Farrar, Straus and Giroux, 2021
Identifiers: LCCN 2020058351 | ISBN 9780374238704 (hardcover)
Subjects: LCSH: Orange, Michelle. | Mothers and daughters—
    Biography. | Motherhood—United States—Biography. | Feminism—
    United States—Biography.
Classification: LCC PS3615.R28 P87 2021 | DDC 814/.6 [B]—dc23
LC record available at https://lccn.loc.gov/2020058351

Designed by Abby Kagan

Our books may be purchased in bulk for promotional, educational, or
business use. Please contact your local bookseller or the Macmillan Corporate
and Premium Sales Department at 1-800-221-7945, extension 5442, or by email
at MacmillanSpecialMarkets@macmillan.com.

www.fsgbooks.com
www.twitter.com/fsgbooks • www.facebook.com/fsgbooks

1  3  5  7  9  10  8  6  4  2

The names of some persons described in this book have been changed.

*For Sophie and Samantha*

Indeed I did not think of myself as a woman first of all . . . I wanted to be pure flame.

—Susan Sontag, *The Volcano Lover*

# Pure Flame

# One

DURING ONE OF THE TEXTING SESSIONS that became our habit over the period I now think of as both late and early in our relationship, my mother revealed the existence of someone named Janis Jerome. The context of our exchange was my need for context: two years earlier I had set out to capture the terms of our estrangement, to build a frame so fierce and broad it might finally hold us both.

If not an opponent to the cause, my mother was a wily associate—allied in theory but elusive by nature, inclined to defy my or any immuring scheme. The channel that opened between us across her sixties and my thirties spanned two countries and bypassed decades of stalled communication. We pinged and texted our way into daily contact, a viable frequency. This was its own miracle, a combined feat of time, technology, and pent-up need. As she neared seventy, the repeated veering of our habitually light, patter-driven exchanges into fraught, personal territory was my doing, a response to a new and unnameable threat. Perhaps she had felt it too: that there may not be time to know all the people I had been in her absence; that I might never meet the many versions of her I had discounted or failed to recognize. That we wouldn't tell the most important stories.

If our withholding was mutual, it was part of a tradition I took from her, and she from her mother. I sought a context for this too, the narrative affliction so common to maternal lines and so little changed by a century of marked progress. If anything, the supposed release from pastlessness and isolation that kept a woman from imagining herself as universal—worthy of story and its ritual transmission—had further troubled a primary bond. "Mother-daughter relationships are generally catastrophic," Simone de Beauvoir once observed. This we knew; this everyone knows. It has been understood too that the general catastrophe of mother-daughter relationships makes them less and not more interesting, unfit for inscription.

As much as anyone, I have manifested this view. For the better part of my life, only contemplating our relationship interested me less than contemplation of my mother. As a writer the subject appeared fatal. Our catastrophe represented an absence of imagination and vitality; it was where story went to die. By the time my mother introduced me to Janis Jerome, however, early in 2016, something had shifted. Unbeknownst to her, I had spent the previous two years struggling to articulate the terms of a new project—about legacy, feminism, and failure, questions I sought to examine and refract through the prism of mother-daughter relations. In my half conception of it, the project would rest in the shadow of my mother's mortality, colored and inflected as I saw fit by the vague, theoretical specter of her loss. It would deploy specific elements of her life—our lives—to larger, abstract ends. As a matter of inability as much as instinct, it would privilege argument over plot, ideas over narrative, something else over straight memoir. When an editor asked that summer why I wanted to write such a book, I made a comment about it being the hardest thing I could do at that moment, like I had any idea.

Past seventy when she shrugged off mother-daughter affairs, Beauvoir refused to identify as a feminist for most of her life. As a product of similar if not the same confusions, I have found comfort in this. I see a heritage in it, however twisted, and heritage is what I seek. I had not turned to my mother for such things; she seemed to prefer it that way. Like her, I learned by example and lack of example not to look to the women closest to me for a sense of who and how to be, what was possible in life. Unlike her, I had a mother who had lived out a neoclassical epic of self-determination: 1970s housewife turned MBA turned CEO. Still, her example proved dim, her transformations hidden, their terms boggled. This appeared to me by design: the breach between us had not been a cost of her emancipation but its requirement. As a child I stopped seeing her clearly; in adolescence I stopped wanting to. I charged forth into an old and new kind of catastrophe: despite a near-complete failure to know my mother, my own becoming was both guided and thwarted by a determined effort not to become her.

Standing on the far side of that calamity, I began coaxing our relationship toward disclosure, background, dimension—a shared line of analysis. It was my habit and my handicap: inquiry as an act of love. If she saw it that way, my mother remained a slippery subject, too cool-minded and wildly individual to suffer grand unifying theories, or to share space with the dominant social movement of her time. I respected her resistance even as I weighed its consequence. Early in this

process, her lack of interest in feminism interested me most:
What was more feminist, I thought, than the purity of its confusion? I found her attitude perverse but not unfamiliar. I had
sent at least one of my selves into the shadow sisterhood made
up of women who learn to live for themselves, pretending a discrete existence, hoarding their petty freedoms.

I may have met my mother in that lonely place. I would not
have known.

MY MOTHER MENTIONED Janis Jerome as though I might recognize the name. She had popped up that early spring evening—
texting, per usual—with questions about that class, my puking
dog, Mercy, and an outstanding payment for one of the contract
gigs I used to slap together a living. When I complained, again,
about the missing money, she urged me, again, to follow up,
keep on it. She took a reliable interest in career and financial
concerns, but I recognized her advice as an act of mothering by
the way it reached one arm back toward the woman who had
had to figure these things out for herself. Be persistent until
you understand what's happening, she went on.

When I started at Canada Trust
almost 40 years ago, they were
underpaying me

I pointed it out and my boss
accused me of thinking only
about money

Can you imagine

It was their mistake!!!!!

It made me furious

So wrong

> How did you figure out they
> were underpaying you?

I did the math

My salary was supposed to be
10,500 and they were basing
deductions on 10,000

I had the letter!

1977

But I was made to feel small for
asking

> Right

It's a thing with me

IN THE BEGINNING, they made her a clown. They had her bake
cakes. At thirty-three, with a six-year-old and a toddler at
home, she had answered an ad in the local *Pennysaver*: assistant
coordinator of branch promotions for a national trust company

that functioned as a bank. The job was her entry into full-time work. On Saturday mornings she would blow balloons and hang streamers while standing on check-signing podiums. She orchestrated "birthday" parties for branches opening around the city. She baked sheet cakes in our kitchen, wrapping nickels in foil and dropping them in batter-filled pans. Sometimes the cake paid a penny per slice. She would dress in a clown costume: rainbow wig, painted face, floppy shoes. The idea, I suppose, was to make customers feel at home, to promote the bank as another member of the family, with occasions to celebrate and a mother willing to make a fool of herself.

She felt too old for grunt work, to be hustling between warehouses and wearing jeans on the job. Within a year she had agitated for a promotion to product communications and a desk in the head office. I have no memory of my mother the clown. From this period I recall only the texture of white crusted icing giving way, the crumble of burnt yellow cake and beguiling tang of money in my mouth.

It was a thing with her: being underpaid, undervalued, undersold. Part of a new generation of girls educated as a matter of course, she had spent four years submerged in the grammar of a failing language, studying the epics and great myths. She earned a Classics degree in 1966 and entered an unreconstructed world, marrying three months after graduation and picking up teaching work where she could find it. Five years, a first home, and one baby later, it appeared she might repeat the course of her own mother's life: raising children, following her husband's career, adding tick after tick to a thousand-page cookbook. She feared channeling her mother in other ways: a darkness visited. Sitting in her perfect new dining room with her brilliant husband and precious baby, she would fall to sobbing. But this was hormones, stress, exhaustion. This was not her mother's life.

Earlier that same year, an event advertised as a Dialogue on Women's Liberation took place in New York City. Germaine Greer, Diana Trilling, and two other women joined Norman Mailer at Manhattan's Town Hall for a much-anticipated debate. D. A. Pennebaker leapt through the aisles, collecting footage his codirector, Chris Hegedus, would eventually help shape into the 1979 documentary *Town Bloody Hall*. Gloria Steinem and Kate Millett had declined to join the panel. Adrienne Rich, Elizabeth Hardwick, and Susan Sontag sat in the audience. Greer, then thirty-two, gave a dazzling performance, dispatching Mailer with ease. He was made to play the glib, shabby fool; she emerged as a new kind of empress.

Only one moment rattled Greer's command. Handed the mic where he sat in the audience, the poet John Hollander began by paraphrasing the first half of an Oscar Wilde quip: "All women come to resemble their mothers—that is their tragedy." From there he asked Greer "how the transformations you envisage [for women] might result in a transformation of that theatrical down-curve." Visibly irritated, Greer dismissed the question: "I can only say that I don't resemble my mother *at all*," she replied, "and [the question is] based in a false premise." Diana Trilling, then sixty-five, filled the awkward, intervening silence. In fact she thought it a marvelous question, with far-reaching implications. "Who will a daughter identify with if not her mother?" Trilling wondered. "If women are not to grow by identification with their mothers, what are they to grow by?"

WHEN, AT THIRTY-SIX, my mother decided to leave Canada Trust and pursue a business degree, her boss jeered. Who did she think she was? He stood in her office doorway at the close of her last day, arms folded. Even with an MBA, he told her, you might find yourself back in your kitchen, eating bonbons.

She had also applied to law school. A professional income was the goal, enough to survive on her own if need be. At thirty she feared the marriage at the center of her world was beginning to unmoor. The sense of being undervalued as a partner crushed her before it made her furious. She would rise, still married but divided from that self, well-protected by a fat salary and her own place in the world. The law school's rejection letter settled it: she would get an MBA.

Business schools were growing commodities just then, the new sure thing. Their share of total graduate program enrollments nearly doubled between 1975 and 1985. You might call it a movement, a dazzling mesh of systems, ideas, and aims; a culture unto itself, resolved in its vision of the value, order, and operation of things. My mother understood both her world and the wider one to be changing, and demanding change in turn. What was a woman to grow by? Who could even pretend to know? It was necessary—basic, urgent—simply to grow.

No part of this directive drew her closer to the thing called feminism. From my mother's vantage, the movement then at hand was chaotic, excessive—opposite the secure, empowered, self-sustaining existence she sought. Its mission was overwrought, ill-defined, its promise too diffuse. Feminist identity was limiting, more pigeonhole than portal. Above all, it seemed to her, a feminist was an imprecise thing to be. Radicalized on first contact with a male-dominated profession, even as she seeded her independence my mother failed to see what all those shouting women in bigger cities had to do with her.

One of a handful of women in her section of sixty-some

MBA students, in the program's early months she panicked. The business school's acceptance letter had expressed concern over her high school math transcripts, recommending a summer prep course. Management science gave her nightmares. When her economics professor made sadistic work of handing back test results, she would fume: *I've got a house, a car, a husband, two kids—why am I taking this shit?* Anger bore her down at her desk, each night and every weekend. By the second semester she was acing exams and collecting scholarship checks.

Midway through the program, she was hired as a financial analyst at a life insurance firm. She wore skirt-suits, not jeans, to her new office. She convinced a florist to waive delivery fees for a standing order, letting people wonder who sent the weekly bouquets. Fresh flowers on the desk, she thought, seemed like a female-executive kind of vibe. After a year on the job, shortly after her graduation, she was assigned to train a new hire, a man with the same title and position as her but no MBA. Asked to review an internal budget, she discovered this new hire was making a lot more money than she did. She went to her boss, then to HR, asking for parity. Both times the answer was no.

As we texted, my mother continued filling in the details of a story she'd never told me: another job came up, consulting work—well-paid but outside her domain. It was also in Toronto, a two-hour drive from our home in London, Ontario. Aware of my mother's unhappiness at the firm, a visiting consultant had floated the offer. "Sounds tricky," I wrote her. "Do you still know him?"

It was tricky

I do still know him

He certainly changed your life

He put the opportunity in front
of me

Do you remember I mentioned
Janis Jerome?

No

There's a business case about
that whole story

It's called Janis Jerome

But it's me

HOW MUCH had gone missing between us? To what version of
me had she introduced this other version of her? I spewed
questions. She made clipped replies. We kept doubling back
over each other. A former professor of hers had written up my
mother's signal career decision as a business case: Beginning
in the mid-1980s, MBA students at her alma mater considered
the facts and decided whether "Janis Jerome" should leave
her family and take the better job. A parallel case describes
"Jack Jerome," whose situation varied from Janis's only in first
name and gender pronoun. When they teach Jack, everyone
votes for him to move for the great opportunity, she told me.
When they teach Janis, they don't think she should go.

But what's the point of the exercise? Do schools still teach
it? Where can I find it?

"I think the case was sold to Harvard," she wrote.
"Google it."


I DID GOOGLE IT, and within a few clicks had purchased "Janis Jerome" from the *Harvard Business Review*, seven pages for $8.95. An MBA pedagogical tool, business or practice cases often present real or lightly fictionalized scenarios to illustrate best and worst practices, elicit discussion, incite debate. "Janis Jerome" presents my mother's dilemma with alterations to certain identifying details. Some minor edits have been made since 1984, notably to update the salary numbers at stake, but most of the case remains as it was. Written in high narrative style, it opens with Janis at a coffee shop, "scribbling furiously on a pad of paper" as she waits for her sister, Denise. We learn that forty-year-old Janis and her medical researcher husband, David, live in Montreal. A mother of three, Janis "would have described herself as having had a pretty normal childhood." A personal history unfolds over two pages: Janis the consummate student, then young bride and mother; Janis the devout but bored housewife, deciding to enter financial services and discovering that she is not content to simply fill a job. Janis grows hungry, forever wanting more, "more responsibility, more challenge, more recognition, more advancement." The case presents Janis's drive and perseverance as functions of her nature: high-achieving, competitive, a workhorse and born leader.

On the advice of a vice president at the bank where she works ("It's the MBAs and CFAs who have the fast track now," he tells her), "depressed but determined," Janis decides to go to business school. She tells David she's done her bit for the family, it's her turn now. Bewildered but ultimately supportive, David has "little idea what had happened to change [her] outlook on life." Janis worries about her age and about being surrounded by people with more exposure to the business world. The case makes no mention of how she feels joining the program's single-digit percentage of women.

Early on, Janis can't keep up. Nothing makes sense. David is miserable and her youngest daughter cries a lot, "claiming that Mommy [doesn't] love her anymore." Janis works late at the university library evenings and weekends. Soon she is tutoring other students. By second year she is confident and in control. The same pattern plays out in her postgraduate life: fear and struggle followed by mastery and success.

By the time the economist "without much experience in business, no business degree, and little knowledge of the company's operations" joins her department, Janis is bored with her post-MBA job. She trains the economist—referred to as "this new person," "this newcomer," and "the new hire"—then discovers a nearly 50 percent discrepancy in their pay. A single pronoun in the following paragraph betrays the economist's gender: HR tells Janis "it was necessary to offer him a high salary because of the difficulty attracting financial services executives." Janis comes to believe the company is under-paying her—"relative to this newcomer"—because they saw little chance of a woman with a young family relocating for a better job.

Five pages in, the case returns to Janis scribbling in a café, ready to unload on her sister the pros and cons of the decision at hand: a job offer with an Ottawa consulting firm. Topping the pros list is the "terrific" money, almost double what she makes in Montreal. Although consulting doesn't excite Janis, she likes her prospective new boss and sees opportunity to move ahead. The whole thing, Janis tells her sister, "represents a major upward movement in recognizing my worth." Denise is skeptical: Where would she live, what would it cost? Did Janis really expect David to give up his work and follow her? What about the kids?

"You know, it's funny. I love the children," Janis tells Denise. "But I see very little of them now . . . I know that I'll miss seeing them, and I won't be there sometimes when they need me. But there will be the weekends. Actually, I'll probably end up spending more time with them at the weekends than I do now! I think that I've been in the office the last three Sundays!" Besides, it might be even worse for the kids if she stays, stagnates, never realizes her potential. "Wouldn't I be bitter?" Janis wonders. "And what kind of role model would I be? Wouldn't it be good for them to see their mother as a successful, independent individual rather than as someone tied to her [crappy] job because of family?"

Making its classroom debut in the mid-eighties, "Janis Jerome" was devised as a primer on the concept of "fit," the influence on performance and satisfaction of the interplay between an individual's characteristics, those of her job, and the circumstances of her life. It was also intended to prompt discussion of dual-career families, navigating career crossroads, and the role of HR in better managing high-value employees. Although the case treats it as incidental, Janis's gender dominated class discussions. Sitting in the same rooms in which my mother had studied a few years before, a majority of MBA students were disgusted by Janis Jerome. She was out of line and out of control, a "hysterical selfish bitch," wrote one student, "who doesn't know what she wants." Splitting the vitriolic difference, another student described Janis as "self centered with high power needs," a woman "who knows exactly what she wants."

In addition to asking whether Janis should take the job,

a worksheet asks students to predict, using a four-point scale, whether Janis Jerome will be successful in her career; successful in marriage; and successful as a parent. Finally, they are asked to indicate their feelings about her. Where does she fall on a seven-point scale between *selfish* and *sharing*? *Cold* and *warm*? *Submissive* and *dominant*? *Bad spouse* and *good spouse*? *Caring* and *uncaring*? *Ambitious* and *unambitious*? *Good parent* and *poor parent*? Shortly after introducing the case study, its co-authors reimagined the exercise to harness the extremity of student reactions. They changed Janis to Jack and began teaching the two cases in parallel: two sections of the program went home with Janis, two with Jack—each group unaware of the other. The next day all four sections would gather to share their responses.

The contrast stunned faculty: Janis was a cold, calculating, self-involved bitch; Jack was an ambitious guy with a difficult problem. Janis should stay where she is, lower her expectations, be happy with what she's got. Having changed course on the cusp of middle age, Jack seemed poised for a professional breakthrough. And bravo to that: what's best for Jack is by definition best for his family.

AFTER A FIRST SPRINT through "Janis Jerome," I read and reread. The layout is simple and—despite a glut of Britishisms and exclamation points—the language plain. If the facts were clear enough, the story kept slipping out of view. It was a familiar sensation, a sort of narrative blindness that focused me on the margins, the things left out. I associate this feeling most with my mother, whose elisions had beguiled me long before her story did. That "Janis Jerome" rests so fully on omission, I thought, helps explain a determinedly private woman's agreement to dress her life in a wig and funny nose and offer it up for judgment. If the situation is complex, its framing is clean and context-free, a matter of variables and outcomes, success and satisfaction ranked on a numeric scale. The case reduces an existential, gendered dilemma to a purely professional, gender-less one. A broader version of this transformative promise had drawn my mother into the world of business. She mastered its concrete terms and structuring principles with what must have been tremendous relief. Told in a different language—the bland jargon of marketing clichés—its stories describe a realm of knowable systems and achievable goals. "Janis Jerome" was designed to be one of them.

My mother didn't imagine the exercise jumping its rails. The invention of a male twin surprised her. Though it elided the discrimination that had marked her early career and helped change the course of her life, "Janis Jerome" wound up telling a story of gender bias. In 1989, the study's co-authors published "Confronting Sex Role Stereotypes: The Janis/Jack Jerome Cases," a paper that describes early reactions to the case and presents data from a more recent Janis/Jack Jerome exercise involving 224 MBA students. The 1989 respondents were more encouraging of Janis, less ruthless in their appraisal. Calling the later results counterintuitive, one of the paper's authors told me they may have been tied to the growing number of women in the program across the late 1980s, the school's increasingly rigorous anti-discrimination policies, and the corresponding tendency of male students to self-censor.

All down the line, my mother turned down invitations to visit the classes debating her life. The 1989 respondents got an update to the case: the real Janis took the consulting job but was fired after one year due to "lack of person-job fit." She got another job without much delay, they learned—along with a 50 percent salary bump—and had achieved her goal of vice presidency of a major financial services company within five years of earning her MBA. "Her marriage is intact," they were told, "however she finds it difficult to leave her children on Sunday evenings."

It is, of course, the case's most conspicuous gap: What happened to Janis between the ages of eighteen and thirty-six? Where had her fearsome ambition hidden itself? How are we to understand its sudden reanimation? Janis's marriage is a blank space. The case depicts David as both tolerant and priggish. He agrees to become the primary caregiver and helps with tuition but finds the business world trivial, treating Janis's MBA friends with "impatience or contempt." The case concludes with Denise's perspective: worried about her sister, she wonders how she can help with this decision. Then comes a vague note of duplicity, the suggestion that even those closest to Janis don't know her heart. Having spoken to David in recent months, the final sentence reads, it was clear to Denise "that Janis announcing that she would be taking a job in Ottawa would come as a tremendous surprise to him."

My mother was already gone when she clipped a 1985 op-ed titled "Women Must Focus on the Big Dream." Written by Kati Marton for *The New York Times*, the piece suggests women "aren't doing nearly enough to combat" a post-second-wave resurgence of sexism. Marton urges women to bend the tricks of men to suit their own needs: "One of these things is self-centeredness. To our detriment, we have grossly underrated this quality. By self-centeredness, I mean learning to isolate a goal—something you want so badly everything else pales in comparison . . . Women must learn to focus on their dreams at the expense of other, lesser commitments." My mother glued the article to a sheet of 8.5 x 11 paper, filed it carefully, and transported it from home to home over the next thirty years.

"We must banish forever the notion that ambition is unfeminine," Marton writes. "Ambition is a sign of self-respect. It carries no gender connection of any sort."

When my mother announced she was leaving the insurance firm—and London, Ontario—her boss and his boss invited her to breakfast. She was thrilled. She imagined the extension of respect and congratulations, her good-faith induction as a peer. Instead, the boss's boss seethed, berated, warned of her mistake. They didn't want her to go but offered no reason to stay. It was the last time she bothered to ask twice for equity, the raise, or a big promotion. From then on she saw the signs and simply left, kept moving. No one ever tried to stop her.

The boss's boss, an American, had ordered the steak. He wore a massive school ring with a blood-colored stone. My mother trained her eyes on it and waited for the meal to end.


"JANIS JEROME" IS A RELATIVE of numerous late twentieth-century texts purporting to reckon with a woman's prerogative to work, foster a sense of independence as well as—or instead of—a home and family. Occupying a vast spectrum of honesty and intent, they are as apt to exploit as address seriously the various terrors bound up in the near-doubling of women's participation in the American labor force (in Canada it tripled) across the century's second half. A subgenre of those writings sought to pathologize a woman's will to self-determination, drawing a direct connection between a rise in female self-sufficiency and the proliferation of ways and degrees to which a woman might be considered sick.

Published in 1984, *The Superwoman Syndrome* is a self-help manual for a certain kind of working mother disguised as a more sober work of social science. The book capitalized on a then-popular theme: in trying to "do it all," women risked "feeling desperate, harried and miserable because we're letting down the people and things we care about." Written by Marjorie Hansen Shaevitz, a psychotherapist and mental health consultant, the book opens with a multipart diagnostic test—"Are You a Superwoman?"—followed by a symptom breakdown of the attendant "syndrome."

Having been imprinted with the idea that they must serve at the altar of home and family only to age into an era of greater opportunity, Shaevitz writes, women born between 1930 and 1950 are prime Superwoman Syndrome candidates. Shaevitz is herself such a woman, worn down by her efforts to be the perfect wife, mother, and worker. "I had no role models to follow who were successful at meeting all these new and multiple demands," she writes. "My mother couldn't help me; in fact, like many other women her age, she probably thought I was crazy to be trying." Shaevitz draws on first- and third-person anecdotes, including one about an MBA in her early thirties who passes out in the middle of a morning run. The fainting woman's male doctors find nothing wrong with her, but Shaevitz and other women recognize it straightaway: classic Superwoman Syndrome.

"More and more I hear about women pushing themselves to the point of physical and/or psychological collapse," Shaevitz writes. Though the book itself is fairly innocuous, the blaring title supports the very 1980s attitude, as noted by Susan Faludi in her 1991 book, *Backlash: The Undeclared War Against American Women*, that women are not meant to be super, that "the triumph of equality . . . has merely given women hives, stomach cramps, eye-twitching disorders, even comas."

In 1989, five years after her move to Toronto, my mother the executive VP took her first trip to Japan. By then, the concept of *karoshi* had permeated Japanese culture. Roughly translated as "death by overwork," *karoshi* was said to afflict Japan's working and professional classes, those men (and it was still mostly men) powering what turned out to be the close of Japan's "economic miracle" and the middle of a bubble economy. As millions of Japanese workers logged sixty-hour workweeks, the rate at which otherwise healthy men in their thirties and forties suffered strokes and heart attacks began to rise. Suicide related to overwork was a subset of the crisis, which in 1987 prompted Japan's Ministry of Labor to begin publishing *karoshi* statistics.

My mother had learned to look to Japan early in her financial services career, as the rest of the world's major economies had done. Theirs were the models in vogue, the ideas to borrow and schemes to replicate. In Tokyo she was struck by the number of gray-skinned men passed out on the subways, slumped in their fancy suits like discarded puppets, masters of the universe in a sleep so deep it looked like death.

She left Japan with a cold. She brought it home, and there it made a sort of home in her: lingering, persisting, changing shape. It established residency, a squatter with whims and a personality of its own. To ignore this new guest was to indulge it, to stuff it with lobster and fine liqueurs. In the enigmatic way of such things, a bad cold became bronchitis, became something else, became nothing. Became much worse.

Having been treated for pneumonia at forty, she told her doctor a few years later the infection hadn't slowed her down. At forty-five, she believed her post-Japan malaise to be just another stubborn virus. She rested when she could, pushed through; felt a little better, felt way worse. She was trying to stay nimble, keep her footing as the economy loosened and a new decade began. It was not the time to take a leave, or even a few days off. So she lived with her guest, unable to shake it free.

It hid behind her breastbone, fatting itself on regular supplies of stress and exhaustion. Months passed. She could beat it, she thought, if she just kept moving: uptown, downtown; home, office; London, Toronto. After about a year of this, she collapsed.

Admitted to St. Michael's Hospital in downtown Toronto, she was diagnosed with acute pneumonia. Though the infection was treatable with antibiotics, my mother was told her lungs would not be the same. The severity of the pneumonia and its prolonged hide-and-seek incubation had left her with permanent scarring: a coterie of new guests that together formed a welcoming environment for even the most errant viral and bacterial intruders. Come in, they said, sit down; let's see what we can make of you. A respirologist warned she needed to take better care, slow down, pay attention to her body. From here on out she would be the same but different, someone more prone to lung infection—to sickness—than she was before.

It must have sounded like a dare.

MY MOTHER'S MOTHER, Rita, turned five years old in 1920, the year by which most American and Canadian women had been enfranchised to vote. She had been dead for half a decade the night I learned about Janis Jerome.

Another of my mother's selves loomed that early 2016 evening, awaiting proper introduction. I had come to know her only obliquely. For as long as she could, she had held this most embodied version of herself even farther from view than the rest. But the attic wife was restless, ready to be free, and my mother's powers of restraint were fading. In the months that followed I would finally meet her, the woman who for twenty-five years had returned to the same hospital, sometimes by appointment and other times by ambulance, but always alone—spent and sick again—to be poked, injected, prescribed, to suffer scopes down her throat and to puff her hardest into brilliant machines. Her disease had a name, but I didn't know it yet. What good are names anyway? What is a name but a useless badge, a story you can't control?

From my mother I learned that storytelling is a treacherous business, best left to the professionals. I came to resent this as a chef might resent having been raised on gruel. It was not stories but their want that shaped my sensibility. And I did want them, even as I came to distrust their role in organizing and defining a life, a self, a family, a race, a gender, a nation. In my work an instinct toward story has always competed with an impulse to question and dismantle, to work through and around narrative terms. It was some time before I discovered there was a name even for this, one of the things I became: an essayist.

The bones of my mother's story hold my attention the way any writer's attention is held: with the promise of marrow, something essential to feed on, from which blood might flow. Yet I resist their assembly, the prospect of building from them any one of the cunning designs spread out before me. It may be a matter of inheritance, my sense of those stories that demand telling as the most dangerous sort. Of course a story makes no demands without a teller in its midst.

I am that teller, and I am in danger.

IN ONE OF MY EARLIEST MEMORIES of her, my mother is installed behind my father's desk. In the half-buried den at the far corner of our split-level house, behind a door she sits in shadow. On the desk a fan of papers reflects the yellow lamplight. It is evening. Perhaps I meant to say good night, perhaps to check on her, or to present myself for checking on. I am aware of the trespass: she is studying and I have interrupted. Her expression is calm, her presence expansive but firm, one with the desk. Bare against the red shag carpet, the soles of my feet prickle. There is pleasure and embarrassment in standing before my mother. A private light seems to emanate from her, fearful and alluring. It hovers between us, shedding no warmth. A warning, a raised finger; a thin white flame.

# Two

THERE WERE NO STORIES at Rita's memorial. The summer gathering in the ground-floor lounge of my mother's Toronto condominium had the feel of a cocktail party short on points of intersection. The rewards for longevity are as few as the peers who remain to tell an old woman's tale, to tilt her portrait where it hangs. Most of the people grazing and cradling smudged glasses in the parlor that afternoon didn't know Rita, my grandmother, who had died two months before, three weeks shy of ninety-six. We honored her at our convenience.

As Rita's eldest, my mother was bound to play host and designated mourner. It was in both capacities that she proposed a toast midway through the gathering. Positioned by the door, I drew my chin up and my elbows to my ribs as my mother moved to the center of the room. Her bond with Rita had appeared to me neither close nor contentious, a thing with standard, sturdy dimensions but all the guts scooped out. Even its network of live wire complications was well-maintained, properly bundled and grounded. As a result, I never gave much thought to their relationship, having absorbed in part from its example the idea that, in the story of a modern woman's life, the mother-daughter attachment didn't—and maybe couldn't—amount to much. The foundations of this attitude began to fracture in the years preceding Rita's death, when a brutal depression brought two decades of dynamic widowhood to a halt. The onset of her decline was as sudden as its duration was prolonged. It was a period of sorrow and revelation: for five years I watched mother and daughter navigate to its end a free fall with a secret history.

I shared the nerves that seized my mother as she began to speak. Surrounded by expectant faces, she appeared not just spotlit but alone, exposed. Having rarely heard her talk about Rita, I was less curious about what my mother might say than grossly aware of all that she could not. She touched on Rita's origins and her love of golf; she alluded to her struggles in a manner both pointed and vague. Her voice unsteady, my mother seemed eager to finish, step back from this strange precipice. Or perhaps the moment's overwhelming sense of regret and privation was mine alone. The confusion posed its own questions: What did we share now? What in this world belonged only to us? Rita's death had drawn the matter of inheritance close, invoking the forces that had helped shape our maternal line, leaving gouges and fissures where a strong heritage might be. It was a predicament that marked us simply as women, existing without and outside of history, severed from our own past. Born across different quadrants of the twentieth century, we were marked as well by that century's movement to rectify and restore, to empower and connect women in the fight for equal rights. In the name of that connection, the movement's second wave had emphasized certain forms of severance: from the old ways, systems, and mythologies and perhaps especially from one's mother.

Gloria Steinem has described separating from her mother, Ruth, as a matter of survival. Ruth's debilitating nervous depressions began when she left the workforce to become a housewife and mother to two girls. Steinem spent decades obsessed with the fear of repeating her mother's experience, which she characterizes as the breaking of a human spirit. "Like a lot of daughters," Steinem wrote in a 1983 essay, "I suppose I couldn't afford to admit that what had happened to my mother was not at all personal or accidental, and therefore could happen to me."

"It is hard to write about my own mother," Adrienne Rich admits in *Of Woman Born*, her 1976 critical history of motherhood. Rich describes herself as "a woman who, born between her mother's legs, has time after time and in different ways tried to return to her mother, to repossess her and be repossessed by her, to find the mutual confirmation from and with another woman that daughters and mothers alike hunger for, pull away from, make possible or impossible for each other." Rich cautions against the modern impulse to sever with the past, in all its forms. For her, "a belief in the necessity to create ourselves anew still allows for curiosity about the artifacts of written history . . . The desire for a clearly confirmed past, the search for a tradition of female power . . . springs from an intense need for validation." The cathexis between mother and daughter—so essential, distorted, and misused—Rich writes, "is the great unwritten story."

Rich recalls her mother as a creature of myth. Her name, Helen, "had a kind of magic," even before Rich made the connection, after reading Greek mythology as a girl, of her mother to Helen of Troy. She saw Helen's beauty reflected in the image of Botticelli's Venus that hung on the wall of her childhood home. If Rich still looked to her mother's body for hints of what she might become, by adolescence a more general doubt set in. I will marry and have children, Rich thought, "but *not like her*. I shall find a way of doing it all differently." She yearned for a son, having long identified more with men than women: "The men I knew seemed less held back by self-doubt and ambivalence, more choices seemed open to them. I wanted to give birth, at twenty-five, to my unborn self, the self that our father-centered family had suppressed in me, someone independent, actively willing, original . . . If I wanted to give birth to myself as a male, it was because males seemed to inherit those qualities by right of gender."

What had Rich inherited from her mother? What was hers by right of gender? Where once the Eleusinian Mysteries organized a civilization around the mythic adventures of the goddess Demeter and her abducted daughter, Persephone, today the mother's loss of the daughter, and vice versa, remains unrecognized as tragedy. It has no Hamlet, Lear, or Oedipus, a lack Rich connects to the systematic unmooring of an essential female relationship, the forces that conspire to refuse the transmission of "a kind of strength which can only be one woman's gift to another, the bloodstream of our inheritance. Until a strong line of love, confirmation, and example stretches from mother to daughter, from woman to woman across generations, women will still be wandering in the wilderness."

At Rita's memorial, an old friend of my mother's approached me with a bothered look. Fifty years earlier, when she first met my mother, her radical opinions and the freedom with which she shared them marked her from her peers. I later learned that as a university student this friend had lectured my father's mother on the subjects of class and privilege. My grandmother, a former schoolteacher, had married a doctor, and with six children afoot employed a live-in nanny. Her family hailed from the same north Ontario mining outpost as did the young woman; her husband's father, a grocer, had left Calabria on a boat, part of the previous century's mass peasant migration. The young woman had sought to check my grandmother, remind her that to live in such comfort is cause for embarrassment. She succeeded mainly in leaving everyone present embarrassed on behalf of everyone else.

Now she suffered a few pleasantries before getting to the point: a Canadian with something to contribute had a duty to stay home, enrich her own nation, honor her debt, not get any funny ideas about herself. To resettle in the United States, as I had done, amounted to filial treason. And for what? Purchase in the land of flaming vanities? The woman's flesh had the softness and shine of the chronically ill, the polish of decades spent up against the world. I stood in half admiration, slow-blinking above my flattened champagne. The ease and directness with which she spoke was, of course, wholly un-Canadian. Squinting up at me, at once solid and glassine, she mentioned a former student of hers, a musician and national radio host who had done right, stayed home. She would not live to see him disgraced by allegations of sexual violence. In a few months she would call to inform my mother of her final illness, then ring again with less expected news: *Guess who's back in the Catholic Church?*

The woman's death followed Rita's rather suddenly. Since then I have recalled often and with a certain fondness my final vision of her, the hot blast of skepticism, her determination to be heard. As a child I had known her as one more ambassador of my parents' former lives, and of the more robust friendship to which their biannual visits paid faithful tribute. Our sole exchange as fellow adults was the truest thing I heard that afternoon. Still squinting, she had offered a parting thought: "I see a great deal of your mother in you," she said. "I wouldn't have said so in the past: but there it is."

THE NEXT DAY we traveled west out of Toronto and down the 401, toward London. More than the burial itself, our return to the city had a ceremonial cast. We had all once lived there and, one by one, we had all left: myself, my mother, brother, aunt, and cousin. Rita was the last to go, and not by choice. Alone in her apartment at ninety-one she had begun to feel unsafe. The nights grew endless; her body began to waste. Her thoughts turned habitually to the balcony, the obliterating earth below. The next year, my mother and I made the same trip down the 401, from Toronto to London, to pack up Rita's apartment in preparation for her move to an independent living facility on the east coast, near her youngest daughter, Jeannette. Though she made no protest as the two of us inspected, trashed, and boxed up her belongings, we understood the move to be her greatest nightmare. Having first tasted it only in her seventies, for Rita independence was life itself.

The portrait set out at her memorial, taken in Rita's would-be debutante years, testifies to a beauty even her daughters never knew. Born in Montreal and raised one of five in Toronto, Rita grew up in the home of her mother, Blanche, on River Street, downtown. Blanche was a French Canadian Catholic with a strong will and bawdy good humor. Abandoned by her husband, a gambler and World War I veteran, Blanche found work in a bakery. When the Depression hit, Rita left her freshman year of high school to work as a typist and help pay the rent. She kept working through her twenties, and in early photos models impossibly stylish, bespoke overcoats, striking poses with her girlfriends against glossy, whale-shaped cars. Blanche remained at the bakery, developing party bits about her coworkers, like the one with the weak bladder who spent her shifts standing over a heating grate. She served her grandkids icy Cokes in glass bottles and saved the plastic straws. She was always asking them to pull her finger and they always did. Despite marrying a charismatic Irish Protestant named Latham Boyle, Rita would raise her kids Catholic. She enjoyed her single, working years: having put off marriage, she was just shy of twenty-nine when she gave birth to the first of two daughters, Jacqueline Claire, on June 1, 1944.

Stationed on Canada's west coast at the time, Latham, then thirty, had volunteered for service in the hope of avoiding a draft into active duty. With Blanche's help, Rita tended to her newborn; by the time Latham returned for good the baby was old enough to question this stranger's presence in broken sentences. He resumed work at Texaco, a sales gig he had lucked into while golf caddying almost a decade earlier. It was solid but itinerant work, meant to secure his family's entry into the middle class. They had a second daughter, Jeannette, left Toronto, then moved again.

Somewhere in this time, Rita suffered her first depression. Away from her mother and alone with two young children, her life had narrowed to the point of suffocation. Even-tempered and chatty when well, her presence now grew ominous. Rita's pain suffused the home, bewildering Latham and cowing her two girls. A lifelong pattern took its first form: illness and respite, hospitalization and release. Silence entombed Rita's predicament, the blackness that trailed her from town to town, room to room, task to dull task. By her late thirties she had begun to seek and receive treatment—some of it, including electroshock, quite effective. But the matter remained one of great shame.

In 1953, the year *The Second Sex* was published in North America, Rita was mother to two girls under ten. She took little interest in books, saving herself, always, for the movies. A good musical or screwball comedy seemed to answer a hunger whose frustration sat at the center of Rita's life. She sought story—plot, drama, resolution—where she might reliably and painlessly find it. With their blighted, world-beating army of women, I have to imagine the movies of that period also offered Rita entry into a larger tradition, an idea of what a woman could be. The bargain was dual: for every magnificent, rampaging Stanwyck or Dietrich heroine, there were ten nameless, marvelous, creaturely Others, the sort of inhuman entity Beauvoir decries, who with no religion or poetry of her own is forced to "dream through the dreams of men."

Elizabeth Hardwick published a long review of *The Second Sex* on its release. In it she questions Beauvoir's assertion that women are capable—physically and otherwise—of living the kinds of lives the great myths exist to ratify, valorize, and warn against. Where Beauvoir insists that woman's physicality should not "condemn her to remain in the subordinate role forever," Hardwick wonders: *Why not?* In her view, "This poor endowment would seem to be all the answer one needs to why women don't sail the seven seas, build bridges, conquer foreign lands, lay international cables and trudge up Mount Everest.

But forgetting these daring activities, a woman's physical inferiority to man is a limiting reality every moment of her life . . . Any woman who has ever had her wrist twisted by a man recognizes a fact of nature as humbling as a cyclone to a frail tree branch. How can *anything* be more important than this?

Weakness and the potential for rape preclude a *Larissa* of Arabia. But then Hardwick doubts that women possess any of the measures of fortitude required for achieving greatness. She goes on to claim that women put a price on sex because they don't enjoy it; that women can pass on the gift for musical composition but never manifest it; that some women have written well despite their gender's "'natural' and inevitable" literary limitations. "Women have much less experience of life than a man, as everyone knows," Hardwick writes. "But in the end are they suited to the kind of experiences men have?" She lists male artists who dared, who suffered, who *experienced*, and who produced great work, and wonders if any of her kind could do the same. What woman could persevere through syphilis like Flaubert, or epilepsy like Dostoyevsky? Perhaps she should rather be grateful for the vote, access to education, and the opportunity to publish occasional pieces, under her own name, that please her chin-stroking editors at the *Partisan Review*.

Hardwick came to regret the essay. Certainly, despite its glibness and solid burns, it carries a strong whiff of the internalized Otherness Beauvoir describes: a woman unable to see herself, or any woman, as subject, capable of adventure, heroism, greatness; worthy of the favor of the gods. Though her description of "that most extremely doomed and chained being—the mother who must bear and raise children" is half in jest, a reader might reasonably assume that Hardwick saw no connection between the kind of experience she credits—the privilege of enduring real hardship—and that of her own mother, who raised eleven children. For her the housebound mother's lifetime of chores amounts to "bad luck."

Twenty-six years after her Beauvoir essay, Hardwick's prismatic roman à clef *Sleepless Nights* countered in form and substance some of the poses struck by her younger self. Via her novel's narrator, Elizabeth, Hardwick centers herself as subject; a dreamlike mosaic of impressions and reflections challenges bedrock notions of whose perspective and which experiences might be considered monumental. Especially notable is the novel's fond, ambivalent portrait of Elizabeth's mother, a woman who had "in many ways the nature of an exile . . . I never knew anyone so little interested in memory, in ancestors, in records, in sweetened back-glancing sceneries, little adornments of pride." The narrator considers her mother's femininity, finding in her memory of it a simplicity, even a deterministic quality that now feels bygone, less possible to entertain:

> My mother's femaleness was absolute, ancient, and there was a peculiar, helpless assertiveness about it. Not the assertiveness of opinion, for she seemed to have no opinion about it . . . The assertiveness was merely the old, profound acceptance of the things of life . . . Without plan, without provision. All of that comes later as the body and even the soul go about the daily caring for the results of this seemingly natural acceptance.

The mother's passivity, in Hardwick's description, her "seemingly natural acceptance" of her sex, appears to have resulted in a quantity of children the novel shaves down to nine. Vexed by their mother's "tidal," "ineffable" femininity, those children settled on "a singularly low birthrate for themselves."

Hardwick, who left her native Kentucky for New York City in her mid-twenties, had one child, and published eight books.

IN THEIR EXPERIENCE of gender and a gendered world especially, Rita and Hardwick—born a year apart—might be considered products of the same time. I see some of Hardwick's contradictions in Rita, who likewise appeared divided between a sense of femaleness—her own and that of her mother and daughters—as absolute, and a mortification that it should be so.

A 1955 move to Windsor, in the very south of Ontario, marked a shift for Rita: for the first and last time, her family would rent a freestanding house, brand-new, with front and backyards. The girls got a black cocker spaniel they named Queenie. Latham's travel slowed and Rita began to speak again. Detroit, just next door, was booming. Rita would take the girls to Hudson's for shopping and big American hot fudge sundaes. In Detroit the department stores sold *pink* shoes—not just brown, black, and blue. When my mother got a pair, with a purse to match, the world felt right in a way it never had before.

Rita became a Brown Owl, a Brownies den mother, and Jackie joined the Girl Guides. She adored the uniform—light blue with a blue tie—and would have eaten rocks for a badge. Rita taught her girls the Brownie Law: "I promise to do my best, to do my duty to God and the Queen, to help other people every day, especially those at home." My mother founded the Wacky Jacky Club, an elite society rife with rules and plans, mostly about new membership, which never opened beyond Jeannette. She won the citywide spelling bee, losing the regionals on "spaghetti." In the face of all this flourishing, her parents offered neither disapproval nor encouragement. She passed her happiest Christmas, a high-yield event: full stocking, new skates,

and a white bolero sweater with silver snowflake embroidery—
with one to match for Jeannette. Knit by an aunt who designed
professionally for a Toronto factory, the sweaters were easily
the loveliest things the girls owned.

After three years, Latham's work uprooted the family from
Windsor. He told the girls they were moving to a penthouse
with a balcony, high on the mountain in the nearby town of
Hamilton. They discovered it to be a basic two-bedroom in a
six-floor building, a block from the mountain, with a three-by-
four terrace. Queenie vanished without ceremony. Their dad
was a salesman, and he sold them.

He was also an athlete, a hockey player who nearly turned
pro. The winter of my mother's favorite Christmas, Latham
took his daughters skating on the frozen Canard River. He
brought his old hockey stick, and raced down the ice gripping
the top end while his girls clung to the bottom. When he hit
the right speed and a clear stretch of ice, he hollered for them
to let go. A moment's hedging, a propulsive crack of the stick,
and off the girls flew like cartoon animals, their screams wild,
mittens and uvulas waving. Sucking wind where they landed,
they glimpsed their father cutting and gliding upriver, a figure
transformed. The pair of them filled with pride and apprehen-
sion at the sight: the raw beauty of his strides, leg over leg; the
spitting trails of ice. They watched him go, each with a gathering awareness of the distance between that fleet, free-stroking
body and her own.

As their daughters came of age, in the mid-1960s, Rita
and Latham settled in London, Ontario, renting another two-
bedroom apartment. If they never fully exited the working
class, they lived well enough, finding community at local golf
and social clubs. On retiring, after forty years with Texaco,
Latham's pension funded a Tampa, Florida, mobile home.

The girls would almost certainly do better: Jackie was poised to study classics on a university scholarship; Jeannette was touring Europe with her high school band. They had swiftly out-educated both genders on either side of the family. As her daughters neared their launch into this new world's mirage, Rita suffered her worst breakdown yet. Hospitalized again, she was granted early release to attend her eldest's wedding.

AT TWENTY-SIX, my mother stood on the tobacco field where her new home was to be built, looked its builder in the eye, and asked if he was honest. Red-faced, the man mumbled something about doing good work. For my mother, the gambit included sticking the leap her parents had not. Though she had marched her honors degree almost directly up to the altar, marrying earlier than her mother, she would have what Rita never did: home ownership, her name on a deed. It was the backdrop against which she might come into better focus— clarified, rooted, whole. A home and family of her own were the antidote to a life of constant challenge and change. Even as she sailed headlong into it, my mother doubted the bargain's integrity. Was it honest?

They had wed in London four years earlier, and from there followed my father's academic ambitions first to Rochester, New York, then Ottawa, then Toronto. She found teaching work—elementary and adult ESL—wherever they landed. In 1967, a change in my dad's draft status hurried them out of New York and back over the border. Three years later, he accepted a tenure track position teaching English literature back in London. They set about looking for a home, eventually settling on a plot of land on the outskirts of town. The city was growing, suburb by suburb and annex by annex. In 1971, their planned subdivision marked the city limits; there were tobacco fields where the houses would be. Before that, before the farms beyond the city limits finally gave way, the land was home to Iroquois and Anishinaabe peoples. An Attawandaron village had stood on the London campus where my father began a decades-long career, and where my mother would eventually join him as a graduate student.

One thing was certain: the house my mother imagined would need some Norman Rockwell. She searched in vain for prints, seeking out art dealers and local exhibits. Undeterred, she wrote the artist himself, mailing a letter off to "Norman Rockwell, Stockbridge, Mass, USA." Rockwell replied, suggesting she query his Canadian publisher. Ultimately she tore a few pages from a coffee-table book for framing, and hung them in the laundry room. The largest and most prominent of those was *The Discovery*, in which a young boy stands in front of his parents' bureau, each hand clutching part of a Santa costume spilling from the bottom drawer. The boy wears an expression of comic shock, accusation gathering in each clenched fist.

For decorative and functional items alike, my mother developed a taste for local estate auctions, drawn to the deals but also to the entrée they provided into other lives. It felt right to salvage from dismantled homes the most beautiful things, revive and borrow from the dreams they held. At auction she found a green-and-white arca rug for the living room, and the oakwood rocking chair in which she would nurse her two babies. For the kitchen my mother chose a tomato-red suite of brand-new appliances: fridge, stove, and dishwasher. Sitting alone in her newly furnished house, the refrigerator's electric hum seemed to intensify, following her from room to room, a vibration that settled in her bones. Each night her husband indulged her complaints with a mix of bemusement and annoyance. He heard no buzzing, or whirring, or whatever she was talking about. Eventually he agreed to replace all three appliances with a different make and new color—avocado green—for good measure.

In those years, my mother's tastes turned from Rockwell to a local artist named Jack Chambers. London born in 1931, as a young man Chambers moved to Europe, where he scaled the walls of Picasso's French villa, took the master's advice to study in Spain, and there converted to Catholicism. At thirty, Chambers was back in London, starting a family, painting heady abstracts, then all in silver, then not at all. A few years passed. Then, during an eastbound drive on the 401, toward Toronto, a glance in his rearview broke the painter's heart. The moment triggered an aesthetic shift toward what Chambers called "perceptual realism," and inspired the first of what would become his most famous paintings: faithful renditions of domestic and landscape scenes. *401 Towards London No. 1*, a vast canvas of green, sky, and highway, bears the hallowed, backward quality of its inspiration. A strangely gradient, disembodied view captures a horizon of unlikely convergence, a vision of home available only in floating, reflected hindsight.

*The Hart of London*, Chambers's only full-length film, opens with actual 1954 news footage of a gorgeous, high-kicking deer loose in London's downtown. Passersby and then the police gather on the winter scene, images that bleed habitually into white. The deer is soon killed and displayed, a kind of suburban sacrifice. Later, Chambers's sons are depicted feeding more local deer. On the soundtrack, their mother's voice hisses caution.

In the master bedroom, my mother hung *Diego Sleeping #1*, Chambers's 1970 graphite portrait of his sleeping son. The scene is shadowy and unsentimental; the square, slightly elevated perspective suggests that of a parent at the foot of the bed. The boy sleeps on his back, his head turned to the left, to the wall. A blanket dominates the foreground; the boy's lower half appears swallowed up by the ridges and valleys of its woolen maze. The tension of the image—between innocence and menace, stillness and encroachment—unsettled me as a child. From a position of safety in my parents' bed, I would turn to the Chambers without really wanting to, bypassing the boy to fix on the blanket, the leering faces hidden in its folds.

THEY CALL IT THE FOREST CITY. Before it was tobacco fields and planted orchards, London was all trees. Not long after the city's European settlers razed its woodlands to build a downtown, Londoners vowed to replant, to line the newly cleared streets with elm and maple. So the alias refers to an act of restoration that itself suggests a stubborn, malign innocence; there is affection and a certain pride in the nickname's refusal both of what was and what is. It may be the nature of cities to spring from paradox, and from the collective nurturing of that paradox to ever greater heights. I imagine this paradox growing tall enough to cast a shadow, one that offers shade to those laboring to keep it alive.

My mother's second child lingered in her womb. Three weeks past her due date, she agreed to be induced. Three hours after the first contraction, things began to move too quickly for an epidural: to escape the pain she went under general anesthetic shortly before delivering. In the years that followed she would attribute her reaction, on regaining consciousness, to a strong dose of nitrous oxide. She would remember laughing uncontrollably after being told she had given birth to a baby girl, like it was the funniest thing she had ever heard.

It may have been the resistance I met, in seeking further details of my birth, that first set me divining. My need for more—a better, fuller story—seemed to bore my mother. *I wasn't really there*, she would say. *I woke up and laughed my head off.* What more could be said, I wondered, and looked elsewhere. Born on schedule, I would have been a Gemini—twinned, like my mother. Had I waited? Did her body hold me back? When I got old enough to read the paper, I would scan the horoscopes for clues not about the future but the past, checking my own sign first, then the sign I was meant to be.

Archaeological digs of my mother's drawers grew bolder in direct relation to her growing absence. One yielded a palm-sized notebook, its white cover illustrated with a young girl in profile, her face hidden inside a bonnet. The notebook contained my mother's account of my birth and the ensuing week or so spent with her newborn in hospital. It was the 1970s, it was Canada, and a week was standard even for uncomplicated deliveries. The details are spare, a list of proper names and feeding times, arrivals and departures. My own name appears on day two. On a back page, my mother practiced it in print and cursive, drafting a birth announcement.

The notebook mentions none of the following: My mother wrinkling her nose when a nurse asks if she wants the baby to sleep in her private, air-conditioned room. Making three ticks per menu item, as instructed, and receiving three servings of everything. The view of the park and the phone hot from use. The baby thriving and her milk coming in. The reaction to his daughter's birth of the husband who brings roses from their backyard garden. That she is pleased but distracted, eager to resume her life. That two weeks after giving birth, she begins a professional development course at the community college where she works.

I would linger over the notebook details involving my father, how often he visited, what treats he brought. I would study my mother's inventory of her newborn's "dark hair, beautiful skin, long, narrow fingers + long nails, short forehead—wide eyes but almost closed." On a separate page was preserved under yellowed tape a curl of baby hair, dark as described. I claimed the notebook as my own, a rare prize. I tucked it into the baby-pink jewelry box I had also repossessed from a back corner of my mother's closet, confident that neither would be missed.

Looking through the notebook recently, I was struck by a detail that had meant nothing to me as a girl. Three days after giving birth, my mother noted having begun a new book: *Lives of Girls and Women*, "by A. Munro." A gift, almost certainly, from my father. Directly under that title there appears another name, a woman's name. Like Alice Munro's, the name is familiar to me now, in a way it was not when I first held the notebook in my hands. The name figures. I feel a pang for my mother at the thought of her placing a call to this woman, perhaps with an offer of thanks. I think of her laughing and wincing and laughing some more: *A girl, you say?*

WE GOT LOST on the way to Rita's burial. London's only Catholic cemetery sits in a part of town none of us knew well. I was twelve when we buried my grandfather there. The choice was perhaps a first assertion of Rita's will: Latham's family had refused to attend their wedding service, which her Catholic parish confined to a church vestibule. Rita asked me to write a poem commemorating the first anniversary of Latham's death, and submitted it to the local paper for publication with the obituaries. I don't recall her mentioning him again.

St. Peter's Cemetery is an arboreal refuge in London's

desolate east end. We gathered by the family plot, at the foot of a stout maple tree. I watched my mother place the box of Rita's ashes against the Boyle headstone, then step back, hands folded at her waist. She wore low heels and a light-colored dress, her face a mask of sorrow. She appeared to speak, but I couldn't make out the words. An unwelcome instinct, a blade of mistrust, pressed again at my throat. I felt as I had the day before: unable to step forward, stand at her side, complete the tableau.

At some farther perimeter stood my father, whom I had invited over my mother's faint objection. After Latham's death, she had purchased the plot of land where we stood, intending it for the two of them. My father had arrived from the house built on the old tobacco field, where he still lived. Our mock Tudor split-level no longer marked the city's western border; London had pushed well beyond it. The waves of suburban development continued, despite the city's steady decline, the closure over recent decades of its signature manufacturing plants—Ford, Kellogg's, McCormick, Electro-Motive. The population had more than doubled since my birth. If the various suburban clusters expanded, they never quite combined, forming a porous kind of metropolis, both big and small enough to be the city one makes it. Perhaps because most come to London to raise children and establish a middle-class lifestyle, the results of this experiment have been limited. The parents of a high school friend told me that despite spending their entire adult lives there, London had left no mark on them. They retired to a spot on Lake Huron without glancing back.

Rita's inurnment ceremony trailed to its finish following the placement of her ashes by the family headstone. We must have trusted some phantom officiant to come remove them, that a later disturbance of the dried, even grass would take place without us. The next time I visited, many months later, the plot appeared sealed, pristine, a silent mouth.

MY MOTHER WAS FORTY-THREE when her father died, a year older when she purchased a burial plot alongside his. She had left London by then, mostly. No doubt she loathed the city that remained the seat of her family: mother, sister, kids, and the husband whom she still imagined by her side in death, if nowhere else.

No matter how often she returned—as she did most weekends through my early teens—I understood her to be gone for good. The rest was just a story someone told. Often that someone was me: I became a skilled rhetorician on the subject of my mother's choices, pacifying concerned adults and explaining to confused friends that my mother was actually up to something really cool. I had a Dictaphone to prove it, identical to the one spotted in my mother's briefcase. I had imagined recording my own important musings on cassette after tiny cassette, but once in possession of a Dictaphone, I became more interested in secretly taping and decoding the conversations of others, beginning with the ones taking place in our house.

I never recorded Bets, the towering Dutch woman my mother hired to watch us after school. Bets (whom I called Mrs. H—, and never Bets) lived nearby with a husband and two kids of her own, a boy and girl who came to our house most days. I liked their company, but preferred having their mother to myself. On those days, I didn't have to pretend to want to do anything but trail Bets from room to room, basking in her worried cheer. She had chapped red hands that smelled of bleach and a bigger imagination than most kids I knew. At eight, my limited meal-prep repertoire outdistanced hers. Warm but mildly frantic, she told stories so well that I soon begged her to write them down, and from there we launched a devoted correspondence. I left fat, intricately folded missives under a padlock on my dresser each morning, and every night I pulled from beneath my pillow a delicate, fantastical note, often appended—often by request—by a sketch of an anonymous, slender-necked princess. Even Bets's penmanship thrilled me, the way it wove like lace across the page, each character scalloped and fine.

She had the body of a warrior. I loved to see her standing just a bit taller than my father in the foyer. The times I recall really angering her all involve my succumbing to a primal impulse to grab hold of her body—a flexed arm or passing leg, a handful of her behind. In time the clinging, obsessive, explicitly maternal bond I sought became one more thing overwhelming Bets, an already overwhelmed woman working to support her own family.

Among her duties, it was clear she hated light cleaning the most. Because I hated it too, I apprenticed myself to her tasks. Together, Bets and I crashed through the house swiping at counters and lassoing vacuum cords, waggling feather dusters and zooming the iron up and down the board. They were things to be done, not cared about. Still, I began picking up slack where I saw it when Bets was not there. I started worrying in earnest about getting dinner ready on time. And each night, I wrote tortuous letters to the woman I loved, occasionally with my mother across the table, giving me the same appraising look she did when, as a younger girl, I burrowed into my father on the mornings he slept late.

Division reigned and replicated between us. My mother was two women, at least—in a way, it seemed clear to me, that Bets was not. I wondered if this was the price of entering the world as she had. I kept a safe distance from the woman who built up her body with shoulder pads and heels, drawing closer when my mother wore a clean face and nightgown. These two versions of her shared little beyond an air of suffering that made the one appear vulnerable and the other a figure of shimmering rage. The mystery of that affliction filled the house, making everything in it suspect, a potential coconspirator. It manifested in lipstick and flannel a tenet of Catholicism I was stuck on: that someone else's suffering should make me feel loved.

IN OUR KITCHEN, a row of fan palms and philodendron lined the wall behind my father's chair. Above them hung a row of ferns and spider plants. To the left, on top of the fridge, sat a raft of modest planters full of succulents with smooth or velvet leaves. Under the sink was stored an ancient jug of half-inch-thick glass, in which water sat to distill for at least twenty-four hours. The kitchen garden's care involved many tools and implements, and I came to loathe them all: the spritz bottle, the pruning shears, the leaf polisher—the latter a bamboo wand topped by a furry beige orb. It looked absurd, I believed, because it was. But my mother was entirely serious about the plants, and in her absence their survival became my domain. I was to check each one twice a week and water on a discretionary basis. I would haul the big mamas into the kitchen sink basin; for the hanging plants I balanced on a chair, stretching to reach through tangled foliage and push a finger into soil. Mist, trim, repeat.

Briefcase set down, her perfume beginning its slow, punishing saturation of the room, on Friday nights my mother would move to the wall. Assuming a skeptical physician's pose, she would address each plant in turn, palpating, caressing, seeking an answer of some sort. I would stand aside, leaking tolerance for the scene, aware my efforts would not yield the desired result. Inside the house, little seemed to please my mother. Disappointment met her at the door and cut a path in her wake. Her impatience with its particulars sharpened my allegiance to our home, the things it still held. The kitchen garden seemed to me another of the arbitrary things to which my mother assigned inordinate value. I resented and relished my enlistment in the rituals of its upkeep. It may have been the question she asked me most in the commuting years—*Did you water the plants?* A test it wasn't possible to pass. Some weeks I lied, others I spent an hour taking waxy, palm-sized leaves in hand and tenderly buffing each one.

Quick to dispose of the weak and to replace them, my mother seemed least surprised to find that a plant had simply died. Her attachment to each one was impersonal: maintaining the whole was the thing. Passing through the kitchen at night, I avoided the wall. It felt especially alive in shadow, insatiable; a set of proxy lungs. In behind the plants hung the painted image of a baby. A portrait in olive and crimson tones against a black background, my mother had sought out the print after receiving a Christmas card with its image in 1970, shortly before conceiving her first child. Painted in the early 1800s by an unknown American, *Baby in Red Chair* has a flattened perspective and pseudo-medieval cast, its dark, sooty finish suggestive of incense and candle smoke. The baby—pearly white, generic—appears seated on a throne that is actually a high chair, its enormous head tilted and eyes closed. A small, sublime smile hangs on its lips. The image has the feel of a stylized neo-icon: the child but no Madonna. I always understood this sweet, smiling baby to be a girl.

When the plants were thriving, they seemed to merge with

the baby, claiming its subject as their own. The infant's feet would disappear into the reach of fingered leaves from below; her forehead might recede behind a spider fringe touching down from above. The smile, though, remained intact, unobstructed, the mysterious center of a mysterious, compromised world.

# Three

THAT MY MOTHER AND I DIDN'T TRAVEL well together never stopped us. Across my teens and twenties especially, we spent the bulk of our time alone in far-off places. The mother-daughter trips were in part the product of an absent parent's magical thinking: the rough equivalence of a few days in Mexico to as many years at home. If we began each one in good faith, these excursions rarely went well. Yet every few years she would propose another destination, and I would agree to go.

Travel represented something particular for the women in my family. Rita's prospecting began in her seventies, following Latham's death. Where previously she had journeyed only to Florida and back, she cast her sights farther and wider with each trip, testing this new freedom's limits. At eighty-eight she was exploring India and posing atop some poor elephant; she had seen Alaska and Australia. The rest of us championed Rita's travels, which retained a certain mystery. There were no souvenirs, no photographs, no postcards, no adventure stories beyond her quality report on this or that cruise line's buffet.

The doing of the thing was the thing. The satisfaction of her desire for the world was a private endeavor, no elaboration required.

My mother's hunger wore a more outward face. To travel was as exciting and necessary as to have traveled, to be one who travels. Having first seen Europe as a newish bride, through her thirties it was the discoveries she made traveling on her own and with close friends—in France, Mexico, Colombia—that shaped her appetite. She worked and saved hard for her trips. She filled travel journals with things seen and done, making notes to her future self on where to eat and what to pack when in Tokyo, Venice, Caracas. She was most faithful to Paris, the city that stood as a monument to what she most wished to be: refined, perfected, built for beauty and good taste. She returned always with two suitcases, the second full of linens, perfumes, romantic prints and postcards.

She sent a telegram from Interlaken on my ninth birthday, during a trip my mother recognized then as pivotal. Traveling with a friend through Switzerland and France, just shy of forty, she was flush with gratitude. Her travel journal hums with the bounty and confidences of each new day. She ended the trip feeling freer, knowing more, and more sure of what she knew. In those weeks she had learned to drive on autoroutes, read French maps, tell good wine from bad. She wrote about raising her standards for clothes and food, but also for love.

I don't recall a French doll among those my mother brought home. Occasionally I would petition for an audience with my international doll collection, stowed on a high closet shelf. Laying them out on my bed, I would admire and deliberate, confirming my favorites. First of the bunch, always, was the Spanish flamenco dancer with pearl earrings, a fan, and a finely ruffled pink dress, the skirt flared up at one side. There was a Dutch girl with thick beige braids, a lace apron, and a sidelong expression. A Venetian with the same expression wore a fringed black shawl, a glass pendant, and pins in her hair. A girl from Barbados had blinking eyes, brown skin, hoops in her ears, and three massive strawberries piled on her head.

Like everything my mother gave me, the dolls were never fully mine. Strange, splendid, and mute, more than a wider world they betokened her worldly appetites. A generous source of souvenirs, my mother held close the essence of her travels, modeling adventure without quite embodying it. Her hunger for new frontiers was passed on anyway, distilled to a sharpness I carried into a lonely and somewhat compulsive relationship to travel. In early adulthood I worked and saved as my mother had, planning entire years around a few weeks away and returning often to Italy, in search of the paternal heritage that had beguiled me as a girl. My roaming amounted to a performance of freedom that only occasionally pierced the real thing. It was enough to keep me hounding, sniffing out the life, the sense of home it seemed my mother, her mother, and I could only attain—and only briefly—in the outermost corners of the world.

AFTER RITA'S DEATH, my mother proposed a trip in her honor. Her mother's estate amounted to a few thousand dollars; my mother's portion would fund a joint excursion. We had not traveled together in the eight years since her second marriage, at sixty, to an economist named Frank. Their match had triggered an unlikely release: my mother retired within a year of remarrying, ceding her CEO-ship to paraglide, delighted, onto the powdery beaches of leisure and domesticity. Trying to make sense of her global transformation from a distance, over the years that followed I entertained various theories: astral conversion, psychotropics, body-snatching. Who was this easygoing, absurdly relaxed person shrugging off carpet spills and ferrying her new step-granddaughters to Paris? When could we meet?

If our relations improved post-Frank, there was a limit. Alone in the same space, we reached it quickly. No matter how well we imitated normal interaction or how frequently we sparked a few genuinely good vibes, our bodies maintained a blood feud neither of us understood. My body in particular kept up the fight. In time I had to accept as genuine this loosened, more even-tempered version of my mother. Across the marriage's early years, I came to trust her newfound interest in my life. But some animal disagreement persisted, especially when we tried to pretend it didn't. Although we had both evolved to feel most comfortable in the state of transience that things like travel plans and hotel rooms enacted, we couldn't do it together without raising the specter of a more profound sense of rootlessness—one we shared, and for which at different times each of us had blamed the other.

So we planned to do it together, again.

I RECALL MY MOTHER walking through the Toronto airport more clearly than anything that happened in the week that followed. Her stride is clipped, with a slight, sharp bounce. She walks ahead of me; I refuse to match her pace. A couple of times she almost disappears from view, passing through a veil of bodies. I am in her path and pretending not to be. She believes we need to rush, and I do not. Across a bleach-blue terminal I watch her from behind, the trim cut of her shoulders, the light bump of her hair with each step. The collar of her black knee-length coat is turned up; her boots have high, wide heels. She does not look back.

It rained our first day in London. It was late spring, close to the first anniversary of Rita's death. The U.K. was our compromise between my wish for something simple and my mother's push for a proper adventure, something she could plan. It was to be my first time in London. Waiting in the rain for the last of the buses we had ridden all through our first full day of her itinerary, I watched my mother's face turn pale and her expression drain. At the hotel she took to her bed, shivering with the beginnings of a cold. Close and damp, our room opened onto a brick wall. Finding the scenario I feared coming to pass on day one, I struggled to muster sympathy, hating the sound of my voice: flat, airless, immodest. It was such an old sound, and so tiresome to me. The sound my mother made in London was new, or at least recent, or more plain. Rita's death had opened unwelcome frontiers, removed a set of protections for which she had not received credit. On this new horizon stood my mother, wide open and more reduced, it seemed, each day. The sound came from deep in her chest: dark, shredded, *productive*. If I had heard it before, I never heard it so well as I did then, in our room, where each time my mother fell to coughing it seemed she might never stop.

THE NEXT DAY I left my mother to rest, riding one of London's oddly miniature subway cars to Trafalgar Square. From there I wound up in the National Portrait Gallery, having walked through its doors the way I tend to open the classics: less hungry than seeking a restoration of appetite.

In her book on the museum, Lara Perry describes a concern of the gallery's early trustees—about the kind of people who would visit, and why. They worried, especially, about women: those idle bourgeois who might add a sweep through the Portrait Gallery to an afternoon of shopping and social calls, making one a rough equivalent of the others. They worried these women would miss the point, treat their visit as another well-appointed act of consumption, imbibing the sober faces on the wall like so many cups of tea.

Founded in 1856, the Portrait Gallery was conceived with something more in mind. Following the reformation of British Parliament, Philip Henry Stanhope, Thomas Babington Macaulay, and Thomas Carlyle sought to build an institution that would "address a newly imagined nation on behalf of itself," Perry writes, tracing "the lineaments of the political nation through which the Gallery itself was constituted." The idea was to do this through portraiture, a strategically curated selection of images that personified England's late-nineteenth-century ideal of itself. Which meant the gallery was founded on something of a contradiction: though it was designed to collect and display works of art, by its own mandate, "art" was of secondary concern. A portrait's subject was of primary interest, above the work's quality or its creator.

The idea of a portrait gallery as a portal to the past, in nineteenth-century England, would inevitably treat history as a matter of genealogy. Royalty was the museum's organizing framework, along with Parliament and the Church. Though the so-called Chandos portrait said to depict William Shakespeare was the gallery's first acquisition, trustees treated literary figures as supplementary, pleasant additions to a full meal. For the most part, the gallery embodied the idea of history as self-selecting: to be the subject of a portrait, pre-photography, was to already enjoy elevated status, a level of power known to shape how stories of the past are settled and retold. The gallery's trustees wielded an ultimate version of that power, including and discarding portraits according to their ability to further a revised, aspirational legacy, one the educationist Sir Joshua Fitch described at the time as "a rational patriotism founded on . . . the preciousness of the inheritance which [our ancestors] have left us."

Women had a particular role in the establishment of that legacy. That is to say, women who were also portrait subjects. (The Portrait Gallery had by the end of the nineteenth century acquired work by female artists in the relatively high proportion of 2 percent.) Most of the women whose images hung in the gallery were royals, but the trustees further selected for criteria and codes that upheld certain Victorian ideals of femininity, and erased from its account those images that failed them. Queen Victoria herself was the full expression of this standard, a mature and virtuous woman, Perry writes, represented as simultaneously "head of state, wife, mother, and later, widow."

The ideal Victorian woman was learned and modest, lovely but not unreasonably so. One preferred composition for her portrait involved a lace cap and a book at hand. If a famous courtesan made the cut, it was in part because she could be construed as a figure of caution. If a portrait depicted a woman in the style of a goddess, it was Minerva, the wise and arty virgin sprung whole from her father's brain. Influence over a powerful man was perhaps the most consistent criteria for a female portrait under consideration by the trustees.

I LOST MY BEARINGS in the Portrait Gallery. It was a familiar feeling: all museums demand of the visitor a certain level of purpose, a plotted course—that one should at least pretend to know what one is doing. We're going Ancients to Modern;

we're starting at the top and working down; we're just here for the Rembrandt. In the Portrait Gallery, I found myself without strategy or purchase, standing dully here and there, in a graceless slide from room to room, outside the human flow that moved in a somatic rhythm bent on eventual expulsion. I stood apart from the visitors peering at the walls and the strangers on the wall staring back. There seemed no way to join in, narrow my gaze. At some point I remembered Jane Austen—the tiny, unfinished watercolor-and-pencil portrait by Jane's sister, Cassandra, housed somewhere in the museum. The only credible likeness of Austen, it shows her seated in what appears to be a rocking chair, arms folded, her head covered and face framed by a half dozen spit curls. Austen's large brown eyes cast a cool, judgy gaze to the left; her tapered nose and small, discerning mouth allied in their distaste. A much-softened engraving of Cassandra's portrait of her sister now appears on England's ten-pound note.

Standing in front of the palm-sized Austen, I tired of the Portrait Gallery. I would take a quick look at the Brontës and be on my way. Is it necessary, is it possible to give history a human face? Is it imperative not to? Thinking back to that visit, nothing, not even the images lining the halls, is nailed down. The countless heads drift free, arranging and rearranging themselves, some floating through a window, some turning to the wall. The portraits are faceless, or wear one face, as does the crowd. As do I.

BRITAIN'S SUFFRAGISTS had a particular interest in the female artist. She was a figure of skill, creativity, and independence. She refused the commonly held idea that women were incapable of creative genius, and therefore undeserving of equal standing. "How many times have women been reminded . . . that their sex has produced no Michael Angelo, and that

Raphael was a man?" wrote Mary Lowndes, who helped found the Artists' Suffrage League in 1907, which became a production studio for the banners, posters, and other propaganda that British suffragists used in service of their cause.

The suffragists also made targets of London's museums. In July 1914, a woman named Margaret Gibb, alias Annie Hunt, entered the National Portrait Gallery and headed toward the painting she had selected on the previous day's visit. When she reached the J. E. Millais portrait of Thomas Carlyle, its gray-bearded subject's hands folded below a look of unsettled reproach, Gibb pulled out a butcher knife and started chopping. Having shattered the protective glass, she slashed the painting in two places. The act was a protest, Gibb claimed, of the detention of Emmeline Pankhurst, the much-arrested figurehead of women's suffrage in England. Mrs. Pankhurst, as she was known by her followers, had encouraged the movement's turn to militancy, after leading decades of peaceful marches and lobbying to little result. By 1914, a faction of Britain's suffragists operated as radicals, their rallies frequently ending in brawls between ankle-skirted women and the police, who circulated to London's premier art galleries a collection of surveillance photos identifying known offenders.

Earlier that spring, a Canadian-born woman named Mary Richardson hid a knife up her sleeve and entered London's National Gallery, next door to the Portrait Gallery. She was also angry about an arrest of Mrs. Pankhurst, this time in Glasgow. Richardson believed Mrs. Pankhurst was being held in an underground cell, where she might catch a fatal Highland chill. At that time, several years from the first of a series of suffrage victories in England, one of the movement's numerous fractures was best evidenced by a split between Mrs. Pankhurst and two of her three daughters: Sylvia, the middle sister; and the youngest, Adela. Although they started out working along-side their mother and older sister, Christabel, Sylvia and Adela came to see the feminist mandate as a subset of the socialist one, and disagreed with the movement's turn to violence, arson, and the resulting cycle of imprisonment and hunger strikes. Where both daughters opposed the First World War, which broke out two weeks after Mary Richardson slipped into the National Gallery with a meat cleaver up her sleeve, the conflict made patriots of Mrs. Pankhurst and Christabel, who through those years took a dramatic pro-government turn. Sylvia and Adela eventually disavowed communism, as happened with that significant number of twentieth-century feminists who mistook it for a vehicle to their salvation.

At the National Gallery, Richardson sought out Diego Velázquez's *Rokeby Venus*, a seventeenth-century oil-on-canvas depiction of the Roman goddess of love—nude and in repose, gazing into a mirror held by winged Cupid, her son. The colors are jewel-toned, the composition spare, and the style sensual, almost humid. The faces of both figures are smudgy, indistinct. Though it's clear that Venus's gaze, via her reflection, looks to the viewer, the cut of her eyes is masked in shadow. Decades later, Richardson suggested she found the painting obscene. She remained proud of having got "five lovely shots in" before the guards intervened. At the time, she released a statement explaining her actions: "I have tried to destroy the picture of the most beautiful woman in mythological history as a protest against the Government for destroying Mrs. Pankhurst, who is the most beautiful character in modern history."

OTHER THINGS HAPPENED in London. On leaving Westminster Abbey, I ran into the queen. She appeared in the street, part of a full-court procession on its way, it turned out, to opening Parliament. Like me, many of the people lining the barriers along Parliament Street had wandered into the scene. Together we welcomed further joiners, exchanging few words, excited to be excited. A carriage holding the Imperial State Crown passed by. Shortly after came the queen, perched inside a gilded, red-wheeled carriage, surrounded front and back by Household Cavalry on white horses. Dressed in icy, bridal white, even behind glass she drew the eye. A perfect miniature of herself, she was a vision in diamonds, pearls, satin, and furs. A massive gothic tiara made more plausible the snow-white bouffant in which it sat. One was in fact impossible to imagine without the other. Queen Elizabeth II's face is embossed onto every Canadian coin and appears on the nation's twenty-dollar bill. Watching her pass, her head angled to match perfectly the image I had thumbed a hundred thousand times, I found restored my childhood sense of the queen as not just our obscure, pretty mommy, but the patron saint of flushness, and of want.

As I stood waiting for the queen, my mother left her sickbed to purchase a bouquet of flowers for the room. For the rest of our stay, the pursed mouths of a dozen pink tulips presided over the silence that surrounded my mother's cough, which seemed to tear out of her body and into mine, sucking muscle to bone. After two days on the antibiotics that were now a fixture in her travel kit, she felt strong enough to rejoin the trip and venture out. I bought her a Pimm's Cup at Claridge's that arrived with a six-inch spoon to match its sterling platter. She humored me with fish and chips at Rules, the setting for a pivotal scene in Graham Greene's *The End of the Affair*. We remained unsure how best to honor Rita, except by doing exactly what we wanted to do. And so one night we stayed in to watch

*Cabaret*, my mother for the first time. Propped up in the bed a handshake away from mine, she clamored for Joel Grey. When he and Liza sang the song that delighted her most, my mother twitched and shimmied in the dark:

> *Money makes the world go 'round,*
> *It makes the world go 'round!*

Whenever we tasted or saw or bought something especially wonderful, my mother would slap her palm to the table and propose a toast to Rita.

*To Rita!*


IF EMMELINE PANKHURST MADE DAUGHTERS of many women, few were as devoted as Mary Richardson. Richardson never left the U.K., where women won partial suffrage in 1918, and full voting rights a decade later. From time to time, when she wanted cheering up, she would visit the *Rokeby Venus*, which despite repair still bore her faint mark. Shortly before she died, in 1961, a BBC reporter asked Richardson why it took so long, why women's suffrage was such a vicious fight. "Prejudice," replied Richardson, "and men's love of tradition—they're much more hidebound than women are."

Richardson was one of many suffragists, including Sylvia Pankhurst and Harriot Stanton Blatch, to write a personal history of the movement. Pankhurst wrote several books, the first of which, *The Suffragette: The History of the Women's Militant Suffrage Movement*, was published in 1911, while the fight was still in progress. Part gilded family history, part manifesto, the book puts the current moment into context, ranking "the militant struggle in which this woman's army has engaged . . . among the great reform movements of the world." In her preface, Emmeline also strikes a martial tone, invoking a legacy of grateful yet envious daughters:

> Perhaps the women born in the happier days that are to come, while rejoicing in the inheritance that we of today are preparing for them, may sometimes wish that they could have lived in the heroic days of stress and struggle and have shared with us the joy of battle, the exaltation that comes of sacrifice of self for great objects and the prophetic vision that assures us of the certain triumph of this twentieth-century fight for human emancipation.

*The Suffragette* asserts the movement's generational character, describing the cause as one passed—literally in the case of the Pankhursts—from mother to daughter. Sylvia's assertion of her mother as patron matriarch of suffrage is both necessary and uncomfortable: the movement needed to imagine itself. Hungry for a face, it found apt reward in a mother figure who ordered her offspring to starve.

Perhaps it couldn't last. Women's suffrage, Susan Faludi argued in a 2010 *Harper's* essay, marks the end of "the old maternal feminism," and a turn toward "a feminist culture much more matricidal." In the 1920s, the simultaneous peak of modernism's call to dispense with the past and the rise of a mass consumer economy eager to tell this newly liberated demographic of young women who they were—and, more important, what they should buy (i.e., not your mother's petticoats)—disrupted the generational transmission of power, stalled the movement's momentum, and began a cycle that transformed the very idea of how feminism worked. "Liberation was no longer an intergenerational collaboration but a fight to the death between generations," Faludi writes. The result is "a generational donnybrook where the transmission of power repeatedly fails and feminism's heritage is repeatedly hurled onto the scrap heap. What gets passed on is the predisposition to dispossess, a legacy of no legacy."

By the 1990s, the matricidal feminist culture Faludi laments had merged with a more general suspicion of narrative, especially historical narrative. Having inherited no persuasive, unified feminist story, a new generation of scholars began issuing principled refusals of story itself. In her 1995 essay "How to Satisfy a Woman 'Every Time' . . . ," the gender and feminist theorist Judith Roof critiques the extent to which several influential second-wave texts rely on structuring metaphors of generation, reproduction, family, sisterhood, and maternity. One of these is *Of Woman Born*, in which Adrienne Rich reasserted the mother and motherhood as primary to feminist narrative, an idea that cut against the movement's conflation of progress with maternal amnesia (Rich cites one slogan of the day: "I am woman giving birth to myself"). Roof is skeptical of Rich's emphasis on "the liberating character of a hidden tradition" of maternity, whereby "knowledge of an origin—the great goddess—becomes inspiration for change in the present." The problem, Roof writes, "is in imagining that the values attributed to matriarchy overcome the generational and authoritarian structure in which they are embedded. Matriarchy is patriarchy with a different cast."

The problem, as well, is that familial, reproductive narrative models confirm certain ideas about how time works, and how change occurs over time. In generational paradigms of history, time is linear, "elements that come first appear to cause elements that come later . . . the past produces the future as parents produce children." But progress is never linear, Roof argues, and feminist progress especially feels vulnerable, in its retelling, to the deceptions of story that would make it so. The familial metaphor of feminism's conception of itself, in which we're all mothers and daughters and sisters "pitted against a figurative father," reverts to an Oedipal mode, erasing differences of position among women—of class, race, ethnicity, and sexuality—that are in fact central to the issue at hand. Roof rejects "the overt feminist link between history, narrative, and liberation," asking instead that "we narrate feminism not as a family affair or generational history, but as a partial story with no beginning and no end and no structuring binaries. If this sounds like . . . the end of the story itself, it is because *no* story is the point."

Reading Judith Roof is like reading a genre thriller about my own murder. The effect is dual: dread and refuge, horror and exhilaration, rage and supreme relief. I find myself as in thrall to the predicament she describes as I am to the workings of my body, over which I do and do not have command. Is this how it feels when the Great Mother demands that you starve?

OVER OUR WEEK IN LONDON, I found myself regressing in the usual ways. On the bad days, sullen withholding occasionally gave way to slightly less sullen engagement. Even my posture turned preteen, round-shouldered and furtive, until the strain sat in my ligaments. No longer built for this dance but unable to fully give it up, I limped through a few of the old beats. My mother plowed forward, refusing to notice. Open displays of her anger had been scarce in recent years; I had not feared her in decades. Perhaps I missed both: What else did we have?

As she showered one morning, I picked up the notebook in which I had seen my mother writing and shook through the pages—looking, I suppose, for evidence of my own despair, some record of the smashing into a thousand broken rooms every room we shared. I found instead a spare outline of the trip, things seen and done, the day's accomplishments. The style was anonymous, the text without plot or protagonist. It made no mention of illness or miserable daughters. It was clean, like her hand.

SEVENTY-FOUR YEARS before Mary Richardson got her lovely shots in, the first World Anti-Slavery Convention took place in London's Exeter Hall, a few blocks from Trafalgar Square. A refusal to admit women onto the convention floor briefly overtook the convention's agenda. Only a handful of women were in attendance, some having traveled from America. Two of those women, Lucretia Mott and Elizabeth Cady Stanton, met for the first time at Exeter Hall, and talked of organizing a convention of their own back home.

White American women had a particular interest in the antislavery movement. For them, Paula Giddings writes in *When and Where I Enter: The Impact of Black Women on Race and Sex in America*, "abolitionist activism was primarily a means of releasing their suppressed political energies—energies which they directed toward the goal not of Black liberation, but of their own." White women who took part in abolitionism often did so out of a sense of unhappiness with their own position, and were further radicalized in the process. For Black women, Giddings writes, "it was the issue of race that sparked their feminism." The difference in how each cohort ordered the primacy of the two issues complicated relations already beset by racism.

A pervasive ideal of womanhood imported from Victorian England further divided mid-nineteenth-century American women. Industrialization and the birth of an American middle class also gave rise to an obsession with status, moving up in the world. For women, that obsession found expression in what Giddings and others have called "the cult of true womanhood," which saw the well-established feminine ideals of "domesticity, submissiveness, piety, and purity" elevated to markers of elite status. Real women, in this construction, were mothers, housewives, models of moral and social grace. As Giddings points out, the cult made womanhood synonymous with privilege: only women of leisure could honor its terms. The cult of true womanhood excluded those women "who worked outside the home, or whose race had a history of sexual exploitation." For white women, the cult "was used as a means to circumscribe, and make dependent, the very women who had the education and resources to wage an effective battle for their rights," reducing them "to an image of frailty and mindless femininity . . . If the cult caused Black women to prove they were ladies, it forced White ladies to prove that they were women."

Though it helped undermine crucial alliances in the mid-nineteenth-century fight to end slavery and enfranchise women, the cult of true womanhood arguably helped radicalize the next generation of American women, which included Ida B. Wells, Frances E.W. Harper, and Harriot Stanton Blatch. The latter, daughter of Elizabeth Cady Stanton, eventually moved to England, where in 1889 she joined the Women's Franchise League, the first suffragist group founded by Emmeline Pankhurst. If the league proved too radical for Blatch, she resolved to use her newly acquired organizing skills to help revive the suffrage movement in the United States, to which she returned in 1902, the year her mother died.

All three women would find purchase in the nation whose ideals had operated to such deleterious effect in their native country. Both Harper and Wells made pivotal lecture tours of Great Britain in the early 1890s. Aware of U.S. sensitivity to British judgment, and of Britain's role in the abolitionist movement, Wells, a journalist and activist, recruited Members of Parliament and British aristocrats to join in the formation of the London Anti-Lynching Committee. Her work led to a steep decline in American lynchings, and to the formation of the National Association of Colored Women, which would play a key role in the fight for women's suffrage and civil rights.

After a day of debate at Exeter Hall, in June 1840, it was agreed the Anti-Slavery Convention would seat women after all—with limited access, out of sight of the men. An oil painting commissioned to memorialize the gathering depicts those stubborn women on the margins, a few bonneted faces claiming their place in the crowd. It hangs in the National Portrait Gallery.

SOME YEARS AFTER our London trip, I stumbled on a photo my mother snuck of me there. I am seated at the small table in our hotel room, hunched at my laptop in a hotel bathrobe. My mother's tulips form a pink smear behind my head. She chose a high-res close-up of one of those tulips for her iPhone's lock screen, and kept it there for the next six years.

Early in the post-tulip era, our devices opened a portal between us. We were both new to smartphones when I shared a texting app we might use to stay in touch. The app showed me when my mother was there, if not available, and when she was last online. I responded to this information as to a kind of overture. In time, it began to feel almost natural to float a line in her direction, see where it landed. It was once pointed out to me that my voice rose two octaves when speaking to my father; with my mother it had always dropped at least three. Over text I found a lighter, more flexible register than any I had managed in person. My mother's voice also acquired dimension in this flattened space. It was looser, more playful. It held my interest. At home in New York I began to ask questions; in Toronto she deflected, demurred, ghosted. It was in large part a reconstructive effort, made possible by the discovery that being together and separate at once might be our relationship's most viable mode. The effort continued even when it paused, a collaboration in which words, unpunctuated sentences, and tiny, repeating icons appeared to solder and stack like rows of red brick. Our exchanges quickened when one of us waited alone at an airport, as though travel, action, adventure—but also limbo, boredom, loneliness—were vital to whatever we were building.

On a spring morning in 2014, my mother sent me an article from that day's *New York Times*. Titled "Who Is a Feminist Now?," the article featured images of female artists including Taylor Swift, Beyoncé, and Lena Dunham. The headline question had an evergreen appeal, reliable bait even for those weary of debates surrounding feminism and feminist identity. I thought my mother an unlikely target for the article's recycled provocations, but in her email she expressed an old irritation in newly expansive terms:

> Why do we have to categorize people with the term feminist? For my generation it had a negative and radical connotation of bra burning, being pushy and not being able to work with others, men and women. Now I read it means simply gender equality. Well, who wouldn't believe in that?????

She went on, describing her early belief in working within the system. She wrote of finding that system hostile to women, and refusing to accept that she should be paid less for doing the same job as a man. She had left jobs because of it:

> In fact, I left a city over it. That cost me and our family dearly. Maybe I shouldn't have done it. But I was MAD. I had worked so hard to get an MBA. I will never stop counselling women to ask for what they are worth. You must know your worth in the marketplace.
> SO, I believe in gender equality. Am I a feminist?

Within spitting distance of seventy and still confused, for my mother the answer was beside the point. I sent one anyway: "YES YOU ARE A FEMINIST, IT'S A REALLY EASY QUESTION."

Did I believe either of those things? Did it matter? Perhaps my mother's sense of having operated according to her own anger and her own beliefs, absent a larger context, is simply one part of a story that can only be partial. Perhaps to be a daughter of Pankhurst, today, is to negotiate between the drive for a settled history and the sense of its injustice, if not its impossibility. Thinking through these questions, I am conscious of the need to consider them through the lens of daughterhood. Must I? I have never felt myself to be a mother's daughter. I have never even wanted to—any more than my mother believed herself a feminist.

But I am; and she is.

EMMELINE PANKHURST eventually moved to Canada, where she claimed to find a more enlightened, gender-neutral society.

The winters got to her after a few years, and she went home. All those ocean crossings, convictions and reversals, allegiances and disloyalties, estrangements and rapprochements. History is a scribble, a mess of furious, obliterating strokes where a face might be. Somehow the straightest line I see in Emmeline Pankhurst's story is the one that runs from her Toronto apartment to one over on River Street, where a fatherless seven-year-old named Rita was a few years away from entering the workforce, part of the first generation of Western women to come of age with the right to vote.

SOON AFTER wondering if she was, in fact, a feminist, my mother returned to London, England, on a historical errand. Having traveled to Greece the previous year, she was in search of the missing caryatids, those female figures carved in stone and used to hold up the Erechtheion and other Greek temples. The caryatids represent the women of Caryae, a city whose male population was murdered and its female population enslaved during the Peloponnesian War. At the beginning of the nineteenth century, the British ambassador Lord Elgin removed to England several caryatids, and much else, from the Acropolis. The acquisition and display of the treasures at the British Museum remains a source of debate. Far from home, the caryatids endured; my mother spoke of them with awe. She brought me two gifts from London: a National Portrait Gallery tote bag and a small notebook with a cover image of two caryatids, their faces hidden, their furrowed braids similar but not quite the same.

I lifted the cover with one hand, a pen with the other, and started writing.

# Four

FOR MY MOTHER, mastering emojis was largely a matter of finding them on her phone. Early in our texting life, my frowny faces and fiery meteors had irked her: "What is that? Where can I get those things??" A hyper-finite language with endless semantic possibilities, once she unleashed the emojis my mother developed a fluency that far outpaced mine.

She knew intuitively the value of a well-timed red balloon. She had an unlikely way with kimonos and mallard ducks. I admired most her emoji-fied embrace of non sequitur, the line of thought that could only resolve in a huge pig nose. I understood her to prefer answers to questions, brisk solutions to knotted problems, next steps to the current moment. Either something had shifted or I had missed all along my mother's capacity—in any language—for betweenness, meandering, conversation as play. Each random icon expanded the dimensions of the thing growing between us; it shocked me how much. I was charmed by each appearance of one of her favorite emojis: the twin ballerinas in black leotards and bunny ears, their toes stretched in perfect parallel.

Nearing seventy, she confronted the milestone as she did most things: with a bullet-point list. Since mastering five-year career plans in business school, she had relied on them to parse out a life. Items on her next half decade's agenda: ceding her last board position; more time with family; fewer but bigger trips; building physical strength. Owing to equal parts principle and laziness, I had never made such a list. A thin but sticky generational residue clung to me, a legacy of the feudal sellout wars of my youth. If this stubborn microbiome offered no protection from an age of mass, corporate consumption—if I took my place at that table with minimal fuss—it had helped ensure that near forty I had no job, no spouse, no savings, equity, or assets, and no kids. I had spent the bulk of two adult decades grappling for basic equilibrium: creative, financial, and otherwise. My mother's success—the grueling battle for it, the low-six-figure income, and the closet full of beige and gray skirt-suits it entailed—occupied another planet, one that held no interest for me. I had other, better options, did I not? I was more and not less free, wasn't I?

For a little while, anyway, a lack of overt pressure to replicate my middle-class upbringing hid the fact that I probably couldn't if I wanted to. In my late twenties I finally put into motion the only plan I ever had: move to New York City, *make it*, or at least pursue a clearer sense of what *making it* might mean. A decade later, the river was flowing both ways. Reflecting on the determined shapelessness of my adult life, if not of my life as a woman, I turned more and more to my mother. Which is to say to my phone.

She spent the early part of 2014 in Florida with Frank, golfing, suppering, and catching matinees. Having returned to

Ontario to report on three alleged homegrown terrorists, on a February evening I was sealed into my childhood bedroom by a quantity of snow the city hadn't seen since the late 1970s. That afternoon I had attended Friday prayer at the London mosque the alleged terrorists used to frequent. Crowded into a back room with the rest of the women, I watched the imam via closed circuit on a mounted TV screen. A man fainted up front. Lying in bed that night I thumbed out messages to my mother. She didn't like the thought of me in a headscarf. That's going too far, she said, for a goddamn story. We were texting rapid-fire, moving from subject to subject in nectar-sipping bursts. Though it allowed me to slip questions in sideways, my mother's pivoting, whiplash style tested my appetite for digression. Talk of the mosque turned to the raiding of my father's candy supply, the cupboards stocked with his favorite: milk chocolate, supersweet. My mother sniffed.

His palate is not tefined

Refinef

                    Refinef

Refined

Peter Pan

                    I don't know if that's true

                    What age do you feel like
                    you are?

45

Why 45?

Not sure

Does it sometimes surprise
you that you are not 45?

40s are amazing

Loved my 40s.

Came into my own. Took back
my power

Lost it in my 30s

I can look around the house
for it if you want

Haha. Not there. A sweet
trusting person is there.

Have i seen Lego movie ?

I don't know, have you?

??

———

EVEN MORE THAN MOST, it seemed to me, my mother's attempts at personal myth-making rested on omission. But what if I took her at her word? I hadn't considered her forties to be particularly amazing, but what if I quieted my reflexes, bore down on floaty turns of phrase like "found my voice" and "took back my power," tried harder to see things as they were? What if I considered more coolly the idea of my mother's thirties, which kicked off in tandem with my birth, as a decade of disempowerment? I found myself straining, now and then, in the role of covert interlocutor. The pleasure I took in our increasingly freewheeling exchanges was genuine, but a pretense lingered. The act of writing to my mother was now bound up in the prospect of writing about her, viewing her as subject, a source. Among the many questions this raised: What if my truest, freest self—my writerly self—was more limited than I knew? Was I engaged in a form of deceit, and did it matter, if the project drew us closer? How much did I really care? What was going too far for a story?

TWO OF THE YOUNG MEN I was reporting on had taken part, the previous year, in a terrorist attack that killed thirty-nine foreign nationals, including three Americans. The Al-Qaeda assault on a gas facility in Algeria also killed Xris Katsiroubas, twenty-two, and Ali Medlej, twenty-four, from London, Ontario. Raised Greek Orthodox, Katsiroubas had converted to Islam in high school, together with his friend Aaron Yoon, a Catholic of Korean lineage. In high school and beyond, Aaron and Xris were tight with Medlej, a Muslim of Lebanese descent. All three traveled to North Africa in 2011—to learn Arabic, they assured their families, and to study the Koran. Arrested, tried, and convicted on terrorism charges, Aaron had been in a Mauretanian prison for almost two years when the January 2013 news of the Algerian attack broke, and Xris and Ali were identified among the terrorists. Yoon's family learned of his situation when headlines about the trio began leading Canadian papers, accompanied always by their senior yearbook photos. Six months later, Aaron was abruptly released from prison. The details of his exoneration unclear, Aaron returned to London a free man, in time to celebrate his twenty-fifth birthday.

Tracking down leads and stitching in the details, I struggled most with the London parts—the role in this story, if there was one, of what struck me as the city's essential placelessness. Blocked at my desk that spring, I texted my mother. My confusion confused her: What is there to say about London? But that was the problem: the any-town quality both locals and exiles invoked reflexively and insisted upon if pressed. The refusal of character is its own character, nonentity its own entity. If they reverted to the same roster of clichés in describing their town, Londoners often appeared startled by the question, alert to a mystery in which they may or may not have some part. Over text, my mother humored me:

Big fish in little pond

People from Woodstock thought
London was a big city

Hilarious

But London is also not the
small town people claim it
to be

Small town mentality?

Boring?

No opportunities for women in
business

Country club

Wasp

White

                     Very white

                     But less so all the time

I know people moving there

                     Lots of people move there

                     No one can say why

Retirement

Good place to raise kids

Was childhood a good
experience there?

When I say I often dream of London, I mean that I dream of
the house where I grew up, that my mother loved and left, and
my father kept. My dreams are rarely set anywhere else. Even
the most extravagant set piece or visionary pastiche eventually

opens onto a familiar hallway or scrap of wallpaper. As if to let me know, exactly, where all of this is really taking place. When I say coming home is a little like stepping into a dream, I mean that I broach the possibility of having never really left.

In his London works, Jack Chambers's landscapes and domestic spaces have an interchangeable, mutually suggestive quality. Together they form a portrait of memory, attachment, an enveloped and enveloping context. My unconscious seems to work at something similar—a semblance of home, portable but transporting, strictly defined and utterly capacious, where anything and all the same things are possible. Still, I struggled to find the room in that house in which young men dream of dying in the desert, taking with them as many infidels as they can. I wondered whether there was such a room, or if this new dream resided in a house all its own, with London its latest annex among many.

Aaron refused to see me. His will was strong: for almost two years he remained in regular phone contact with his family while incarcerated in the Salafist wing of a North African prison; on each call he assured his mother everything was going well. In 2012 he turned away the Amnesty International delegate making a routine visit to the prison, hoping to do his time with no one the wiser. Later, when the death of his friends made his whereabouts public, Aaron claimed his confession was elicited through torture. He was not a warrior but a victim—of injustice and misunderstanding. All he wanted was a ticket home.

I was looking for Aaron at the mosque the day I attended Friday prayer, having heard he had returned to services there. I may or may not have spoken to him on the phone. My former high school, where Aaron had spent his freshman and sophomore years, refused to let me in. Visiting Xris's family parish church, I made a wrong turn into the gloomy hall that had hosted my senior prom. The route to the bathroom, of grave tactical importance that night, lit up inside me like an old battle instinct. I sat in front of the town-house complex where Aaron had returned to live with his mother and brother, across from the mall parking lot where I heard my first Nirvana song. On the way there, passing the tall white apartment complex where Rita lived for many years, it seemed possible she might still be there, safely tucked inside. At another glance the building was opaque, anonymous, a monument estranged from its ghosts.

Aaron never emerged from his family's town house; it was Xris I found. Xris, who had detonated a suicide vest inside a vehicle carrying British and Filipino hostages. Xris who loved his grandmother, his family's Orthodox priest told me, very much. I knew well the cemetery where his grandmother was buried in 2009. Through my early twenties, I spent mornings running almost from the moment I woke up. In London I ran along the Thames River, out of Byron and into the downtown, past the university, out to Masonville, the last and most extravagant of London's malls. Alternate days I ran down Oxford, past the London Muslim Mosque, the McDonald's where I held my first job, back up to Springbank, into Woodland Cemetery. It was a way to be good. On the best days, I returned home with shoes and socks covered in bright red coins of blood.

Near the end of my London reporting, I drove my father's car through the Woodland gates. Snow enwrapped the city in fold after suffocating fold, making some suburbs impassable. An obituary suggested Xris's grandmother was buried at Woodland; at the front desk I asked for directions to her grave. Setting aside her bag of pretzels, an elderly clerk turned up in the database a more recent burial under that name, fairly close to the first one. I asked for directions to both, and she traced them out on a cemetery map. The newer grave still had a temporary marker, she told me. It might be tough to make out in the snow.

In fact only the tip of the small cross was visible. Xris's was the last of several temporary markers I excavated in the section containing his grandmother's remains. Lodged in a drift that passed my knee, I cleared the snow by hand, digging to reveal a dove of peace above Xris's name and a sleeping cherub below it. A garland of red plastic flowers and a gold Christmas ornament appeared, hung from the cross's neck. With my phone I snapped picture after picture, unsure what else to do. Beyond the fence along Wonderland Road, a line of traffic thickened. Daylight waned. A headstone later replaced the marker, engraved entirely in Greek.

Back in the car that afternoon, I sat for a while. No other visitors came. A pair of deer appeared farther down the path, barely credible, but true; then three more, and another. They lingered near an abandoned snowplow with no particular plan. This was their home—to whom else could it belong? And so calmly they turned, black eyes shining, to watch a gold sedan roll by.

BACK IN BROOKLYN, I pinged my mother later that same winter. I enjoyed testing her allergy to idle bitching, a disinclination which among other things gravely limited her messaging repertoire. With me she resisted not just complaints but any form of debate. She would grow more placid and remote the harder I worked to draw her out, provoke a reaction. Often I grew frustrated not because we disagreed but because she showed so little interest in argument. It was with this in mind that I texted her about Sheryl Sandberg's announcement of a public service campaign to ban the word "bossy." The Facebook CEO and author of the corporate feminist manifesto *Lean In* believed "bossy" to be a kind of slur, too often used to undermine "a girl's ability to see herself as a leader." Her campaign comprised an ad launch, a press blitz, and a website selling "ban bossy" merchandise. I think it's fairly harmless, my mother wrote. "Asshole" is more descriptive.

Descriptive of whom?

You just let it roll off and keep
your eye on the prize

If bossy is banned, asshole
should be too

The point is that only girls
are called bossy

When they exhibit behavior
that is encouraged in boys

Hm

Did anyone call you bossy?

I was more concerned when
people called me ambitious and
it was negative

Who called you ambitious?

Men, trying to give feedback
and be "helpful"

Esp. Re being intimidating to
men

Ie you couldn't be ambitious
and attractive to men

Such horseshit

You are who you are

What did grandma say?

We didn't discuss. I would tell
her about all the interesting
people i was meeting and she
would ask if there was a man in
my life

I mean when you were little

Don't think she ever called me
bossy but I was

What about feminist

Was that a bad word?

Sort of conjured up a bit of a
hysterical image back then

Never thought of myself as one

I believed if you had the skills
and experience you should
proceed

>But you must have realized
>you had opportunities
>grandma didn't have

>Regardless of skill or
>experience

Absolutely.

Many factors account for that
though. Not just feminism

Economics, politics
Technology, medicine (pill)
Rise of service industries

>You see those factors flowing
>into feminist movement, not
>out of it

>Or parallel to

Maybe parallel in some cases

I think you could argue
feminism hastened some issues
that were afoot for economic
reasons

Good points to consider

Have you seen any Sherlock
Holmes with Benedict
Cumberbatch ?


THAT SPRING I WATCHED MY MOTHER watch *Grey Gardens* for
the first time. Wrapped in a red velour blanket on a couch in
Sarasota, she suffered loudly through every show tune, each
raccoon sighting. She frowned as Little Edie Beale declared
herself to be a staunch woman. I was introduced to the movie
as a university student, the year my father taught it for the first
time. Shot in the vérité style he sought to showcase, *Grey Gardens* documents the relationship of an elderly mother and her
middle-aged daughter living alone in a crumbling mansion on
the tony shores of East Hampton, New York. Big Edie and Little Edie are Bouviers—aunt and cousin, respectively, to Jacqueline Kennedy Onassis. At the time Albert and David Maysles
began filming at Grey Gardens in the early 1970s, the derelict
estate and its eccentric owners had already been subject to public exposure and a subsequent cleanup effort funded by Jackie
O. The Maysles approach the situation as a sort of mystery, the
terms of which their observation must reveal.

My father was dismayed by his students' response to *Grey
Gardens*: They laughed. They howled. They covered their
mouths and guffawed. They thought everyone involved must
be joking. Here was a popular myth in the flesh: the old bag
and her spinster offspring, crazy cat ladies festering in the ruins
of their womanhood, warbling show tunes, mourning lost suitors, and spooning ice cream in bed. What was the point of this
plotless, invasive exercise beyond the spectacle of two widely

loathed and laughable archetypes caught on film in their ne plus ultra habitat?

Big and Little Edie lack irony the way a beetle lacks a spine. They live for themselves, dress for themselves, declaim their love of freedom, and litigate the past in mid-Atlantic accents. Even their airs have a perfect sincerity. They are straightforward and suspended in time, at once too modern and too archaic for their moment. The viewer senses the filmmakers' struggle with their own tendencies toward irony on the one hand and a pure fascination with the Edies on the other. Who could turn away from the invalid mother shrieking orders from her bed, the daughter bashing from room to dissipated room, feeding intrepid vermin, reprising old dance routines, and muttering about finally leaving her mother, moving to New York City, living her own life. But how to turn a camera on them?

Ultimately, the Maysles included themselves in the film, breaking a basic vérité rule. If it doesn't eradicate ironic distance, the decision indicates a sincere desire to do so. The freighting of this portrait of cloistered mother and daughter with irony, in other words, occurs almost entirely on the side of the viewer. The movie attracted a cult following, especially in outsider and queer communities. For several decades, a mainstream audience was disinclined to accept as a rare form of tragedy a story with subjects it knew only as agents of repulsion, and of farce.

To be viewed as a love story, *Grey Gardens* would first have to qualify as any kind of story. The Edies themselves struggle to view their own lives as ongoing: clearly wedded to their independence and to each other, in attempting to narrate their stories they return habitually to the men who left, the repressive patriarch (they call him "Mr. Beale"), the rejected proposals from titled millionaires, the chances at a real story gone wrong. To watch the pair alternate between praise of each other's beauty and accomplishments (Big Edie's as a singer, Little Edie's as a dancer) and recrimination involving fathers and suitors driven away is to recall the confusion reflected even in the language of what inheritance might be shared between women: where "patrimony" denotes the concepts of succession, heritage, and handing down, "matrimony" describes a specific act—a bond but also a sort of breakage, a handing off.

"Did the family know this was going on?" my mother asked, referring not to the squalor but its documentation. The apparent abjection of the Edies mortified her, if only on behalf of her fellow Jackie O. I imagine more women than men watching in furrowed quiet, wishing to turn away: for us, the pair enact a horror scenario more horrible for having no narrative quarter. My mother's sense of exploitation is a not-uncommon response to *Grey Gardens*. I see the film's potentially troubling terms as part of what make it essential: the actual existence of the Beales insists on the story being told, beyond the absence of story they seem to represent. They propose a new kind of myth, more plausible for its embrace of ambiguity, its accommodation of the many worlds we now know to make up the one. Late in the twentieth century, Vivian Gornick proposed mother-daughter constructions as a more apt vessel for the ideas and themes that were for millennia bound up in the drama of father and son. The historically male story of what Gornick calls "the struggle to be in the world" is not just remade but revitalized by the complexities that attend the modern mother-daughter contest of oneness and twoness, duty and agency, separation and becoming.

*Grey Gardens* belongs to Little Edie. Visually and otherwise, her confusion flits against her mother's immovable frame. "When I go to New York City I see myself as a woman," she says. "But in here I'm just, you know—mother's little daughter."

Unable or unwilling to exist as one or the other, Edie seems to thrive within her ambiguity, to inhabit it fully, almost wild with the knowledge that her refusal to choose is in fact the only possible choice. As the credits rolled, my mother stood with a shudder. "That's it for me," she said, tucking her discarded blanket around my feet. She had coughed a lot that night. I knew not to look or stir when her thin shoulders folded together. I knew not to ask if anything in *Grey Gardens* had moved her, beyond the appalling fact of its existence.

THAT SUMMER, the day after my fortieth birthday, my mother ate chocolate cake and cherries for breakfast. Sitting in her den and plucking from a glass bowl full of them, she asked if I liked cherries. I said I did not, recalling how often in our recent conversations it seemed my mother and I were on a first date. The rapport built over text had begun to color our real-life dynamic; conversation between us grew lighter, more agile. Perhaps more striking was the growing ease with which we shared the same space. Something about the informal picking up and dropping of connections, fostered by all that texting, had opened for each of us the possibility of the other's receptivity. To sit in comfortable silence, two people must trust foremost in the ongoingness of whatever it is they are doing. I was spending more time in Toronto. Especially on weekend mornings during my visits, we chatted for hours over a newspaper-strewn table. That Sunday, I watched her spit another cherry pit into a napkin.

"Did I ever tell you about Uncle Ken and the cherries?"

She had not: Ken was her father's brother, a navy pilot who had flown North African missions during World War II. Growing up, I knew him as a figure of affluence and mystery: in his prime, he flew via Concorde and threw lavish dinner parties;

he once gave me a rubellite taken from his father's ring. I know it's a rubellite because my mother had it appraised, having fumed over the passage of a family heirloom to a little girl.

My mother rested her head in one hand. The other held the stem of a cherry still in the bowl. She received a call one night: toward the end of a long illness, Ken had asked to be taken to an ER, believing he was dying. In fact, a hastily consumed pound of cherries had brought on a bad case of what my mother called "the shits." Between illicit shrieks of laughter, she described the phone relay between herself, her sister, the hospice, and the ER, the truth of the situation slowly clarifying. Ken died several years later at eighty-nine, having spent his last decade in a Montreal home for people living with HIV and AIDS. To the end he remained curiously flush, occasionally sending money to Rita, a few hundred dollars here, a couple thousand there. I told my mother to keep eating.

"Did I ever tell you what he said to me?"

"When?"

"When I visited him."

"No."

" 'Oh, you'll be here soon,' he said. 'How old are you now?' "

"You'll be here soon? Where was he?"

"On his deathbed!" She made a high-pitched sort of hooting sound, the push of a wrong button, then growled at Ken's memory: "Bugger off! I came here to *visit you*."

"Why would he say that?"

" 'Give it twenty years and you'll be right here.' " She shook her head. Her face cleared. "I'm stopping now," she said, rising from the table with the front closure of her robe in one hand and the half-full bowl of cherries in the other. Before dinner the previous night, she had mentioned a recent bout of planning— for her and Frank's old age. Getting old in Toronto, she feared, was beyond their means. Frank had joked about moving back to Woodstock, where his mother had lived past one hundred. Or there was always London. My mother rolled her eyes. "The only way I'm going back to London—"

"Is in a casket," I said, rolling mine.

"Well, it will be in a little urn, just like we did for Rita," she said. "You'll hold me there just like we had her."

She looked well that night. In those years especially, her loveliness often took me by surprise. If the talk of old age and incapacity had a theoretical sheen, certain questions loomed: not just why she was ill, but how ill she might really be. Even Frank had no clue. She had withheld from him the series of midlife hospitalizations; none of us knew her disease by name. She would insist she had it under control if a cold brought her low or her thinning arms drew notice, whenever a violent coughing fit silenced the room. *Bugger off.*

What from one angle looked to me like the same old hubris in another light reflected artless courage. In fact, her attitude toward sickness was consistent with a larger refusal of all those names, terms, and conditions that might pin a person down. A favorite teacher described my mother at fifteen as "living proof that beauty and brains can mix to good effect." A woman learns—first from her mother, often; then from the world— that it is not so easy for her to be seen as more than one thing. She who chooses wisely might be wiser not choosing at all. Raised Roman Catholic in a nation often defined by its lack of identity, though she contemplated joining the sisterhood in her teens, a decade later my mother had effectively left the Church. Soon after that, "wife" had come to feel like a con. To be white accorded certain privileges but little understanding of what, if anything, it meant to be white. Raised in a working-class family, she was set on being anything but working class. Although possessing great beauty was ideal, being a great beauty held striking disappointment. "Mother" was overrated. "Woman" posed an obstacle to her ambitions. "Feminist"? No. And to be sick was to be a sick person: fixed, limited, identified.

If she never claimed them as ruling identities, other identifiers had mattered very much to my mother: MBA, vice president, CEO. But the promise of an embossed business card alone doesn't carry someone that far. Status and security meant a lot, but the fire that won them was its own entity: what it defined with light and shadow it also threatened to consume. That the fire was not entirely under my mother's control made it all the more hers, more clearly and fully *her*.


LATER THAT SUMMER, on a return visit to Toronto, I watched a photo of Catherine Deneuve ruin my mother's morning. Working the red carpet, a great beauty of her generation was aging, my mother felt, in a particular way—the way of feminine caricature. "Like one of those Fellini women," she said, pointing to an image on her laptop screen. I found it innocuous: bad dress, bad hair, so what. "Oh my *God*," my mother cried, dropping her head into her hands.

The obituaries scanned and travel section discarded, sitting in her den we had reached the point in the morning when my mother turned from the paper to a popular gossip site where famous women are advertised "flaunting," "flashing," or "showing off" various body parts in photos snapped without their permission. One of the women pictured that morning had lived much of her life as a man. Unbothered by gender transition in practice, my mother admitted confusion over the premise. What did it mean, after all, to feel like a woman, to be a woman? Did those amount to the same thing?

For the female-born, did a lack of protest equal acceptance? We sat for a few moments, scanning ourselves for an inclination either way.

"I suppose," I announced finally, "I feel most like a woman when I am treated like a woman." My mother widened her eyes. "With all that entails," I added, widening mine.

A little later another item, on the same website, inflamed her further: "This Erica Jong—she did *Fear of Flying*? Now she's got one called *Fear of DYING*! What does that mean? We have to fuck in the coffin now?" Her left leg was jiggling the way mine had come to do. She frowned. "What are they doing to me? First there's Catherine Deneuve looking like . . . a hooker."

"A hooker now."

"Well!"

"I thought she was a Fellini grotesque."

"A Fellini grotesque *hooker*."

She muttered something about Deneuve staying home.

I set down my phone.

"Are you really saying she's too old to show her face in public?" My mother frowned. "That's not very feminist of you."

"Well, it's not," she replied.

A few nights later my mother dreams she is working in a fire station filled with men. She wears only a bikini. Nearby, the firemen interview another woman, considerably overweight, for a job. "I didn't think she'd be so fat," my mother hears one fireman say. And standing alone, off to the side, in her bikini, in her dream, she has a private thought: *That's not very feminist of him.*

A POPULAR EARLY-TWENTY-FIRST-CENTURY SLOGAN, branded on T-shirts, onesies, mugs, and other surfaces where popular slogans go: The Future Is Female. Despite its neat, declarative thrust, the phrase contains all the old questions: of identity and essentialism; what it means to be female, and what it should mean; and perhaps most critically the question of transmission. What gets carried into such a future, and what must be left behind? What stories does a female future tell about the past?

Simone de Beauvoir used ancient mythology as a portal to these questions, arguing that the bedrock of all human narrative was and had always been bad for women. The ancient myths, she claims in *The Second Sex*, almost invariably present woman as adjunct, exotic, Other. Beauvoir's position connects to a larger convulsion with regard to myth, perhaps epitomized by James Joyce's *Ulysses*, the modernist linchpin that both honors and explodes Homer's *Odyssey*. Led by Beauvoir, mid- and late-century feminism especially stood in rejection of the foundational stories in which, when they figured at all, women appear as goddess or fury. By the new millennium, the word "myth" was synonymous with "lie."

Toward the end of his life, Beauvoir's contemporary Joseph Campbell lamented mythology's dwindling influence. Transmitted down the centuries from antiquity to modern civilization, myths have provided instruction on nothing less than "how to live a human life, under any circumstances," Campbell said in a 1984 interview. Particularly attuned to that life's various passages, "childhood to adult responsibilities . . . the unmarried state into the married state," the great myths often hinge on feats of becoming—male becoming. Campbell's description of a girl's path to womanhood invokes the Othering tendencies of myth Beauvoir saw as endemic. It turns out there's not much to it: "In primary cultures today the girl becomes a woman with her first menstruation," Campbell said. "It happens to her. Nature does it to her." In primitive cultures she might "sit in a little hut for a certain number of days and realize what she is . . . She sits there. She is now a woman. And what is a woman? A woman is a vehicle of life. Life has overtaken her." Woman's destiny is not to enter the world but to succumb, revert, become one with the earth. She is "what it is all about—the giving of birth and the giving of nourishment. She is identical with the earth goddess in her powers, and she has got to realize that about herself."

For Campbell, the future of myth was not necessarily female. He believed no new mythologies were possible "for a long, long time to come . . . Things are changing too fast. The environment in which we're living is changing too fast in order for it to become mythologized." The myths of the distant future will primarily concern the planet, "not the city, not these people, but the planet, and everybody on it . . . And what it will have to deal with will be exactly what all myths have dealt with—the maturation of the individual, from dependency through adulthood, through maturity, and then to the exit." It was a prediction made in the face of prediction's impossibility: "You can't predict what a myth is going to be any more than you can predict what you're going to dream tonight," Campbell warned. "Myths and dreams come from the same place."

I found *Fear of Flying* in my father's library during the mid-teenage period in which I sought out and read books almost entirely with my body. At fifteen, a final gasp of childish pride in my own growth concentrated itself in my feet, which I willed to sasquatch proportions. Massive feet struck me as not just bad-ass but a solid omen, such that I took to buying shoes at least a size too big—ten, ten and a half, bigger than my mother's. I imagined others finding huge feet as cool as I did, being as impressed as I was by their swagger, and barely noticed when they most certainly did and were not.

A few shelves up from *Fear of Flying* and a few years earlier,

*The Joy of Sex* had been fun to pass around with friends, but according to the magazine in which I'd seen it mentioned, the Jong offered something more: a well-imagined woman's actual, embodied sexual experience. Persuasive evidence of the female orgasm, I thought, might help mitigate my sense of slippage, of a diverse set of powers having been reduced, externalized, made bodily but no longer mine to control. Nothing I had done or knew to do, partnered or alone, had eased this predicament. If the pursuit of carnal knowledge via literary text was destined to fail, *Fear of Flying* proved a particular letdown. Born two years before my mother, the novel's protagonist, Isadora, is well into a second marriage at twenty-five. In fact her life mostly concerns men and her attachment to them; she wonders about that now and then, in the helpless sort of way Isadora wonders about everything. I found her corny, even tragic, her attraction to crudeness and fondness for the word "cunt" not just passé but suspect, tuned to an appraising male ear. The "zipless fuck," Isadora's fantasy of sex free of power games and gendered bullshit, left me cold. She complains of measuring her own orgasms against those of Lady Chatterley "until I was twenty-one." Isadora has lots of the wrong kind of orgasm, and I experienced each one as a betrayal: even here, what interested and eluded me most is described as incidental, understood. *Fear of Flying* left intact my belief that the legend of the female orgasm persisted to keep women buying movie tickets, perfume, and "irreverent" books.

A new class of popular feminist texts emerged in that same period, led by Susan Faludi's *Backlash*, Camille Paglia's *Sexual Personae*, and Naomi Wolf's *The Beauty Myth*. I noted their presence but looked elsewhere for instruction on my own experience: music, magazines, my friends. If the idea of my face appearing in full color above the front-page fold of the city paper, as my mother's did at sixteen, filled me with horror, so did the fact that

I wasn't front-page material. I liked beauty, if not power, and wanted my share. My mother liked it better, and even then had so much more. In the picture, her face is surrounded by yellow and orange calceolaria blooms. Her smile is full but modest, radiant, compliant. She had been stopped by a photographer while visiting the indoor gardens near her home in Hamilton. The caption reads like an ad, complete with lineage and home address: "Miss Jacqueline Boyle, daughter of Mr. and Mrs. L.C. Boyle of 921 Concession Street, makes an attractive picture at the Gage Park greenhouses."

The first-edition cover of *The Beauty Myth* features a detail of *Angelica Saved by Ruggiero*, a nineteenth-century painting by Jean-Auguste-Dominique Ingres. Ingres based the image on a scene from *Orlando Furioso*, a sixteenth-century epic poem by the Italian Ludovico Oriosto. Writing at the height of the Renaissance, Oriosto sought to align his epic with the classics: *Orlando Furioso* combines chivalric elements with those of ancient mythology. There is a hero knight and his hippogriff; a worldwide quest; an errant and fatally desirable pagan princess; a Christian emperor who warmongers to avenge his father's death; an island of women; a quantity of bloodthirsty orcs. There are endless exiles, metamorphoses, concealed identities; and duels, duels, duels.

Ingres depicts the knight Ruggiero atop his hippogriff, armor glinting and cape a-billow as he drives a spear into the mouth of a sea monster at the naked princess Angelica's feet. Angelica stands chained by the wrists to a rock overhead, the frontal length of her body exposed to the viewer. Her wavy, bejeweled blond hair falls past her hips; her head and neck bend unnaturally to the left, toward Ruggiero. She looks to her savior with distrust and mortification, her eyes rolled back. In Oriosto's tale, once rescued from the orc, the beautiful and much-pursued princess must then escape Ruggiero, who demands sex for his trouble.

Angelica appears alone on the cover of *The Beauty Myth*, her rolled eyes cast toward the title. Her predicament is severed from its context: if her chains are no longer visible, Angelica's condition remains clear. She has been reclaimed as evidence, a symbol of the thing, and the thing itself.

"GLORIA STEINEM IS EIGHTY," my mother wrote me the day Gloria Steinem turned eighty.

> I know

Wow

> How old does she have to be before you'll call yourself a feminist?

. . .

Maybe 95

> 95?

Maybe

> Well, she seems stubborn.

My fixation on my mother's relationship to feminist identity across those years now seems obviously misplaced, like fussing over what we might wear to the apocalypse. It was an easy heckle, a sore spot for each of us not because we were sure of the implications but because we were not. It's true I found her general lack of allyship odd, even perverse, but on the subject of feminism my mother and I were doomed to a series of canned exchanges, neither of us knowing or caring much about Sheryl Sandberg or Gloria Steinem, but having absorbed the idea that we should. Neither did my growing interest in the core texts, conflicts, and principles fuel a more purposeful dialogue; I had no desire to educate, much less convert. The feminist question was a cheap alternative to the ones I kept seeking new ways to ask: *Who are you? Where were you? What do you believe?*

The subject of her health was a more direct route to those questions, and to what remained of my mother's immortal wrath. The constant check-ins had drawn the concept of mutual accountability out onto an open plain between us: she tended to hang back, keep to the present, accept answers about my general welfare with little follow-up. Certainly with no threat of drumming up old business, the trouble I have caused myself and my own body. I took a less elegant approach. That winter, she mentioned feeling better—having said nothing, in any of our daily conversations, about feeling ill. "I am getting some energy back," she texted one night. "Had a huge choc cupcake for dessert [winking tongue-out emoji]."

                                    Where did your energy go


   Have just finished antibiotics for
   low grade chest infection

   Reason for no/low energy over
   holidays

Saw doc end Jan. in TO

> As in bronchitis?
>
> Or pneumonia?
>
> Why did it take so long to treat it?

Nothing dramatic like that

Insidious

Should have gone to doc earlier

> I don't think you're proactive enough
>
> Why didn't you??

Holidays

> Isn't that precisely why you're in this position?
>
> I don't get it, honestly
>
> You would be so mad at me if I had a chest infection and it took me a month to treat it

Well, i have lived with this for
25 years and not done too badly

But I do admit my appt was 4–6
wk too late

But isn't it true that
you've lived with it at all
because you didn't pay
close enough attention to
your health

I'm not trying to yell at
you, but for the people who
care about you it's very
frustrating

You seem to make excuses

Many factors

Excuses

I think this should be your
top priority

I got run down trying to keep
a marriage and family together
while trying to earn income to
support myself should it all fall
apart

Extremely stressful and my
body quit

It is my priority

                              That was then, what about
                              now

You need some history

                              I've heard the history

Then why would you say I didn't
pay attention to my health

                              Because you didn't

I did. I left the marriage.

                              I'm not saying there weren't
                              other factors

                              There always are

Damage was done

                              But you've said yourself,
                              you were working too hard
                              and stressed out and you
                              let lung infections progress
                              too far

My point is at THIS point,
I can't understand why that
pattern would repeat

And why you can't see it
repeating

You need to put your health
first

We all need you to do that

I AM

OKAY

OK

Then let's not wait over
a month to treat a lung
infection

I didn't know I had one!!!!!

Uh, cause you didn't see a
doctor

That's what I mean by
priority

Proactivity

Are u quite done?

Are u???

[lady with hands up emoji]

[squinty tongue-out emoji]

[picture of Mercy's paws
folded up like origami]

[pawprint emoji]

Early the next morning, my mother texted to inform me, "re: proactivity," that she would not be flying to Montreal for a five-hour board meeting, and would take part by phone.

DURING HER 2016 APPEARANCE on his talk show, Bill Maher asked Gloria Steinem, then nearing eighty-two, if younger, freer generations of women fail to recognize the debt owed to their forebears. Among other things, that year's Democratic primary had revived larger discussions of gender, identity, and allegiance. "Gratitude never radicalized anyone," replied Steinem. "I did not say thank you for the vote. I got mad on the basis of what was happening to me." And why were these same young women favoring the presidential candidacy of Bernie Sanders over that of Hillary Clinton? "Men tend to get more conservative be-cause they gain power as they age, and women get more radi-cal because they *lose* power as they age . . . The women will get more activist as they get older. And when you're young, you're thinking—where are the boys? The boys are with Bernie."

"What a dopey comment," my mother texted me, echoing most of the interested world. "Isn't it the opposite? Women gain power and men lose." I said it depends on how you define power. "Voice," she replied. "I never had a voice or a real opinion until my forties. Now it's hard to shut me up sometimes." I suggested her example tends to support Steinem's comment, that perhaps as a voiceless young woman she deferred to loudmouthed men.

Did you assume I would grow up knowing how to think for myself and voice my opinions?

Yes. You had many more role models than I ever did.

[I thought this over.]

You mean like Madonna?

My mother named my paternal grandmother, my aunts, and herself as women whose example I had benefited from and she had lacked. Rita too, she added, presumably referring to Rita the swinging senior and not the frustrated, miserable woman who had raised her.

"I didn't really think of any of you as role models," I wrote airily.

"Maybe not consciously," she replied.

# Five

WE ARRIVED IN MEXICO on a late spring afternoon, under a banner of limitless sunshine. Having touched down at the San Diego airport shortly before my mother, I watched her emerge, looking drawn in her traveler's black, into the terminal depot where we were set to meet. I wondered if she had used oxygen on the flight, as was now her custom for longer hauls, but decided not to ask. Four years after our London trip, we were bound for Rancho La Puerta, a spa retreat set on three thousand acres in the mountains of Baja California. She had proposed the trip the previous fall, in part to mark her retirement from a board directorship, and the effective end of her professional life. I agreed, never having visited such a place. Within a week of our booking, gnomic emails began seeding my inbox: "Creating a better body is part of The Ranch experience, but it's so much more," read one. "Originality is reborn here." Erica Jong had recently led a ranch workshop: "How to Write the Story of Your Life." My mother expressed regret at having missed it. "'How to turn your personal life into a captivating story,'" she texted me, quoting from the website schedule. "Who wouldn't want to learn how to do that?"

At the airport we boarded a coach-style bus. Border protocol, we learned, shifts according to whim. That day, several dozen of us were required to de-board on the American side, collect our baggage, form a pink-skinned line, and enter Mexico on foot. In Tecate we climbed into one of several small white vans, and within a few minutes passed through the ranch gates. Hoping to ward off a reversal of her decision, my mother had scheduled our stay during her board's annual meeting, but soon changed her mind anyway. She would give it one more year. Seventy-five and only semi-retired, Frank had been skeptical of the initial decision. What would she do with herself? "Whatever I want!" exclaimed my mother. She never imagined still working at seventy-one, or seventy-one in general. Her seventy-second birthday would fall in the middle of our stay.


OUR CASITA WAS MODEST: two double beds, a fireplace, and a master bath. The first night, I stayed in bed while my mother checked out the vaulted dining hall, where a bell heard throughout the compound announces each of the day's three meals, and where guests eat organic vegetables grown on the property and learn about those foods, like quinoa, which taste of education. The ranch grounds featured natural abundance in perfect measurement and proportion. Navigating this strictly curated, impossibly casual aesthetic, I found myself holding sudden fields of wildflowers suspect, mistrusting the unruly rosemary bushes that scented our patio. The ranch's pseudo-rustic cross of stringency and indulgence piqued our respective tendencies: where my mother reveled in luxury—turning childlike with wonder in its presence—pleasures that take a too-decadent form made me massively uptight. I wanted to give in to the ranch experience, whatever that might be. Or at least not spend the week in a defensive crouch.

Kicking back at the ranch, it turned out, required superior decision-making skills. Each day's schedule was filled with dozens of possible activities: hikes, fitness classes, nutrition seminars, wellness workshops, sound-bath therapy, and on and on. There were also a host of beauty treatments—scrubs and facials and massages and manicures. At the group dinner tables where guests gathered each night, discussion consisted mainly of scoring that day's activities, and gaming out tomorrow's. Most of the people we met had made multiple trips; some visited annually. Everyone agreed: things were better at the ranch. The only problem was fitting it all in. "I take the same class at home," I heard one woman pant as she bounded between gymnasiums, her frame of corrugated muscle on bone so fierce and brittle that each sight of her filled me with a sense of doom. "But it's just *better* here." Her voice leaped an octave: "*Everything is better here!*"

Women come to the ranch in predictable configurations: middle-aged pairs of friends or relatives; solo seniors; young professional girlfriend cliques; and, of course, the mother-daughter combo. The novelty of the latter attracts special appreciation from other ranch guests, a good number of whom walk the grounds in replica pairs, the same body rendered in poignant contrast. It's always a little embarrassing to fulfill a consumer pattern, to find your crudest or most inchoate desires packaged, priced, and retailed back to you. To enjoy special status as a mother-daughter unit at the ranch is to represent both that unit and its unique market value. I imagined our joint outline as especially desirable in a setting that exists to show women in particular who they are and what they like, generational transmission being a white whale in the business of buying and getting sold, paying and being the product.

Partaking of various exertions and organic tomatoes grown on-site, the privileged enact an extreme version of the modern struggle between the free person and her freedom. I came to wonder if everything was better at the ranch—if women especially found themselves so at home within its exaggerated biome of choice and confinement—in some measure because it concentrates and makes accessible an elusive tension at the center of their lives. In his *Ethics of Authenticity*, Charles Taylor describes the modern struggle "between higher and lower forms of freedom." In a free, inward-looking society, there exists always the temptation to slide into anthropocentrism, a crushing self-centeredness. To hold one's own interests above all others is to flatten the world beyond the individual; the fewer the horizons of meaning beyond the self, the more attractive the freedom to determine one's own life appears.

This wheel of self-justification often spins in the name of authenticity. "Self-determining freedom is in part the default solution of the culture of authenticity," the ideal of our time, Taylor writes, "while at the same time it is its bane, since it further intensifies anthropocentrism. This sets up a vicious circle that heads us towards a point where our major remaining value is choice itself." On one side of this struggle are those who might describe the women alternately depriving and indulging themselves at a Mexican spa as exemplars of narcissistic blight; on the other are those, like Taylor, who truly believe in authenticity, but acknowledge the ways in which our quest for it can run aground. Women's access to self-determining freedom remains new, and is subject to limitations that disproportionately affect women marginalized for reasons of race, class, creed, and sexual or gender identity. Some version of the struggle Taylor describes feels particular to the experience of those women flash-flooded with choices, waist-deep in a predicament as exhilarating as it is immobilizing. Women also come to know intimately the extent to which the freedom of consumer choice can distract from how little actual freedom there is to be had.

Whenever quiet settled on us back in our room, my mother and I reached for the ranch activity schedule, resuming a faithful study of our options for that day, or the next. We weighed them all week, cross-referencing schedule items with their catalog descriptions. We chose carefully—or, in my case, hardly at all. We leaned heavily toward spa treatments. During one of mine, a gentle, middle-aged woman named Rosario with fleet, hummingbird fingertips spent forty minutes flicking various potions and serums across my brow. The ritual culminated with a geyser of warm, diffused rose water sprayed directly into the center of my face. After positioning the steamer nozzle, Rosario left the room. Bound in cotton blankets, my body was inverted on the table, arrowed toward the floor. Gravity held me fast. Choking on the ambrosial blast, I refused to turn away.

THE RANCH'S FEW MALE GUESTS were often spotted scratching their heads and looking lost. They wandered alone through the finely veined network of asphalt paths connecting the many villas, casitas, gyms, spas, and auditoriums. Men were once plentiful at the ranch. Founded in 1940 by Edmond and Deborah Szekely, in the early years it functioned as a sort of working commune. Europeans came to wait out World War II—the Szekelys themselves were forced to leave the United States at the same time that Edmond, a member of Romania's reserve army, was called up to fight for Hitler. The odd Hollywood type showed up for a week or two of vegetables and physical labor. Aldous Huxley had a favorite casita; Johnny Weissmuller and Burt Lancaster were regulars.

A guru in the style that by the late twentieth century came to define the term, Edmond Szekely wrote over eighty books, including *Cosmos, Man and Society* and *The Essene Way: Biogenic Living*. Personal health, wellness, and a pure and sustainable diet were his mantra; he claimed to have discovered Vatican documents that proved Jesus was a vegetarian. Time having smoothed down the rougher bits, Szekely's biography suggests a cult figure who wasn't entirely wrong. During his reign, people at the ranch referred to him as "the Professor." Although Deborah took over the compound when the couple divorced in 1969— Edmond died ten years later—people at the ranch still do.

Under Deborah Szekely, the ranch began to cater primarily to women. She recognized her most promising client base in the same years that women were encouraged to consume in the name of their own independence. In keeping with a more general turn toward consumption as destiny, as Susan Faludi observed in *Backlash*, by the 1980s, "The passive consumer was reissued as an ersatz feminist, exercising her 'right' to buy products, making her own 'choices' at the checkout counter . . . The feminist entreaty to follow one's own instincts became a merchandising appeal to obey the call of the market—an appeal that diluted and degraded women's quest for true self-determination."

My mother grew attached to the idea of the ranch as matriarchal concern. With the help of her daughter, at ninety-four Deborah Szekely still owned and ran the business. She addressed guests once a week with an evening talk. My mother returned from Deborah's talk on a cool early evening, inspired by her vigor yet already grieving the elder's death. It's going to be so sad, she said. Some big corporation will buy this place and ruin everything.

FOUR DAYS IN, we plotted a birthday escape. Despite trudging to the dining hall for every meal, we were losing weight. Only alcohol was more elusive than refined starch. During her sparsely attended talk, a ranch employee of over fifty years named Manuelita acknowledged the spa's heritage as a "fat farm." Guests were weighed on arrival. She recalled the early days of beautiful, overweight girls sent to the ranch by their rich parents for slimming down. "They would sit right out there," said Manuelita, pointing to the lawn behind us, where the girls would eat potato chips and cake they bought in town. Eventually, a passing trainer would drag them all into the gym. Wearing thick glasses and a white cotton blouse, Manuelita spoke with a younger woman's cadence, curling up her sentences at the end. She referred often to "Professor," his wants and wisdom. She remained scornful of those gorging, opulent girls.

We decided on dinner outside the compound. Seated at La Misión in Tecate, my mother and I fell on our margaritas and basket of greasy, thick-cut tortilla chips. Housed in a former mission church, with its small dining room of dark wood, oxblood tablecloths, and gray-haired waiters monitoring the soccer game on the TV mounted behind us, La Misión held bleakness and warmth in a fragile balance. We had maintained mostly separate schedules. Several times that week I spotted my mother at a distance, crimped forward at the waist, walking in slow, determined steps, one or both hands on her hips. That evening we struggled to maintain a convivial spirit. I began to feel sick before the food arrived; she asked for the check at the first opportunity.

Santos, our shuttle driver, had a strong nose and deep reddish skin. His van had broken seat belts and sale info painted on the window. On the way to La Misión, he had told us his story: born in Sinaloa, at eighteen he had crossed the border into Arizona, where for over a decade he made good money building pools. Too much money, he said, for a young Mexican. He met a woman and got into drugs. He met another woman and things got even worse. Santos moved home to get clean, met a better woman, had kids, found Jesus. He hardly knew his father, Loreto, who had died not long ago. Santos believed himself the eldest of twenty-three children. Only one of Loreto's women came to his funeral, and it wasn't Santos's mother.

Santos grew thoughtful on the ride home, his story loosening at the seams. If his time in the United States was mixed, it was hard to regret the money. Too good then, maybe, but think of it now! My mother was quiet, holding her remaining energy close. We sped under a piglet-colored sky, the town turning to desert scrub. I heard my mother tell Santos in a faint voice that he was alive, and that's what mattered most. "I was just going to say that," Santos replied, glancing in the rearview.

A splendid bouquet of lilies and roses had appeared in our casita earlier that day. On discovering the flowers, my mother flushed with pleasure and opened an envelope bearing my name, assuming some mistake. When I returned to the room a half hour later, I found her sitting on the couch with a curious look, amusement and annoyance playing across her brow. In fact the bouquet was meant for me.

In the hour or so before dinner, my mother retold the flower story several times: the innocent entrance and joyful discovery; the honest misunderstanding and complex chagrin. She had not yet heard from Frank, who was traveling overseas. Frank: the love of her life, the man her friends called Prince

Charming. Frank, who appeared like a forgotten, final puzzle piece and transformed my tense, demanding mother into someone who made thoughtful, contented noises to herself—the very same noises, it turned out, Frank was always making to *him*self. Watching her morph through those early years into someone more wifely yet more distinctly *girlish*, I didn't know whether to blame Frank or thank him.

Having smiled at my mother's first performance of the flower dance, I squirmed through the following two. She began revising in real time—juicing the pathos, playing up her haplessness. A long silence had settled between us when she launched a fourth rendition. "So here I am: open the door, walk in the room: Flowers—*for me!*" She once puzzled over being told she was funny. I'm *zany*, she told me. Not funny. I learned this was true. She could be mischievous, coquettish, game—qualities that begged for a straight woman, the role I happened to perfect over my time spent courting adolescent queen bees. Via text and then in person, humor had become a reliable point of access, though some core of our dynamic endured: my mother remained the star and I the audience. If I performed it was with and not for her. One effect of having muted myself for so long—determined she not get the best of me either way—was a residual sense of proportion, of keeping even displays of pleasure in check.

During her fourth retelling of the Great Flower Caper, though, my mother found a rhythm, and the whole thing—the bit and her commitment to it—started to get to me. If it had something to do with me, her displeasure wasn't my fault. Finding it safe to laugh, I felt myself swan dive into hysteria. Watching me seize on the bed, my mother frowned, unsure what, exactly, was so funny. Another fifteen minutes, half an hour passed. Talk turned elsewhere; quiet settled over the room. My mother dressed for dinner, pulling on a pair of hot-pink capris. Reading, scribbling, I paused, glancing up at the bouquet. Perched at the end of the bed, she was right on the beat: *So I walk in the door . . .*

Back at the casita, after dinner, I lit a fire less for warmth than to cut the room's floral haze. Of course, the bouquet mortified me too. Flowers sent by a man to a woman are meant to be received and understood in a specific way, and to particular effect. I had long struggled to divorce the gesture from its impositions; in high school I asked my date to the prom and insisted he skip the corsage. Earlier, between performances, my mother had blurted a warning: the flowers will stop coming. That's how they get you. The words struck out like a lizard reflex. She remembered Frank, early in their courtship, showing up with one bouquet for her and one for Rita. That's all it took, she said, to bring her mother on board.

"That's it?"

"Sure: *All right, let's go with this one.*"

That my mother is chronically undersupplied with bouquets feels like something I have always known. Even their occasional presence seemed to remind her of a larger absence. That first executive gig kicked off a habit of buying flowers for herself. A reliable portion of her travel photos comprised lavish close-ups of this or that iris, lily, azalea. As a girl I found her emotion over peonies in bloom embarrassing on several levels. Their beauty—all beauty—impassioned her in a way it was clear to me I never had.

When we were settled in our respective beds for the night, my mother returned to the subject of flowers. Perhaps her high school boyfriend, Jerry, had sent her some. She can't remember. But he must have. She had recently found Jerry's death notice in the paper. As a sophomore I wore the ring he gave her at sixteen, a gold band set with a single cream-colored pearl. I had pilfered it from my mother's pink jewelry box, into which I stuffed notes from my own teenage boyfriends.

"What did you like about Jerry?" I asked.

She thought for a moment.

"I thought he was an *in* person. He was kind of cute, and he seemed like an *in person*. He hung around and seemed available."

"He seemed available?"

"He was a good person."

Perhaps it was on her birthday that my father had first sent my mother flowers. She can't remember, but it might have been. It was the summer after her first year of university, anyway, that yellow roses arrived at her parents' London apartment. My mother kept the letters my father sent that summer and the summers that followed. An attempt to reread them in recent years had ended almost straightaway.

I wore Jerry's ring all through grade ten, along with my father's father's well-preserved fedora. Like everything else my mother left behind, I assumed the ring was mine to mistake and mishandle. At some point the pearl loosened from its setting and fell away. It was awful to look down and find the setting empty, hanging open like a grasping, horror-movie claw.

Ranch nights were fresh and cold. My mother was turned on her side, facing me, eyes closed but not yet asleep. We had run out of wood for the fire. In the mornings, barefoot on chilled Saltillo tiles, I would stand at the tiny sink in the corner of the room and prepare my mother's cup of filtered coffee. In her sleep she sounded as though she were struggling not just to breathe but to communicate, her airways speaking in tongues.

The first night I lay frozen. Later, when I couldn't take it anymore, I would hiss her awake. I was grateful for my mother's
lack of interest in the flower sender, not knowing where to begin. She observed what seemed to me a customary abstention
on the subject of my love life, as though talk of it was beneath us
both. So it surprised me that night when, edging into sleep, she
mentioned a man I used to know, about whom she had read in
an essay I once wrote.

"Whatever happened to him?" she asked. "He wasn't a
deadbeat."

I turned my head on the pillow.

"Does he still live in Toronto?"

"I imagine so," I said.

"What was wrong with him?"

Lacking a real answer, I said something about how he
seemed to know, at twenty-three, exactly how his life would
turn out. My mother nodded, eyes closed. Some years had
passed since she broke her long silence on the matter of my
work. More than anything I wrote, it appeared my persever-
ance had earned her respect. Whether as a matter of principle
or real affinity, she became an avid and generous reader, offering nothing but praise. She bought up stacks of my first book,
distributing it freely, recommending always an essay about
Rita, which she reread once a year. I stared into the space in
front of the lowering flames.

"He also thought I was a goddess."

"Oh? What's wrong with that?" She stirred under the
covers. "Sounds good to me."

"You think that ends well?"

"I don't know. I never had it."

"No?"

My mother's reply was faint, on the point of vanishing. "Don't think so."

IN THE EARLY 1990s, having seen his work in a hotel south of Mexico City, Deborah Szekely visited the studio of a sculptor named Victor Hugo Castañeda. Born in Michoacán in 1947, Castañeda renders the female body according to various formal ideals—sometimes classical, sometimes surrealist, sometimes folk abstract. Szekely commissioned several Castañeda maquettes during that first visit, large-scale versions of which are now installed across the ranch compound. Over the years, the addition of a new Castañeda became a celebrated event at the spa. Most of the figures are seated, crouching; all of them intertwine a sense of determined inwardness and that of an essential femininity. Miniature versions are sold in the gift shop. Each sculpture's evocation of stillness and self-containment feels of a piece with its female form. That is to say: they photograph very well.

The sculptures—lone, unexpected—sneak up on passersby. I first discovered each one with the startled pleasure they are there to elicit. Over our week at the ranch, I wearied of passing them, then of resisting them, still later of wondering why these faceless emblems of "modern" womanhood bothered me so much. "Castañeda pays homage to the significance of women," reads the ranch's website, "and to the beautiful as opposed to the ordinary." Positioned like mascots across the compound, the Castañedas mostly uphold the idea that there is something called "the significance of women," to which homage is due. With their eyes closed and heads bowed, buried, or gently turned away, they propose the entirely ordinary idea of internality as a source of female power, woman's self-rule as a sentimental, private, ultimately recessive affair. The anti-goddess points only to herself. On a patch of lawn near the Mercado, a naked woman cast in gleaming black bronze folds from the waist over crossed legs, her arms stretched forward, toward Mount Kuchumaa, her long hair poured into gentle sine curves, her face hidden. I later learned that what I saw as the figure's refusal of the world, especially her immediate surroundings, the artist intended as a posture of worship. Her I photographed from every angle.

AT AN "INNER FITNESS" TALK, my mother found her attention drifting. The self-described life coach leading the session used personal stories to make his points, then invited audience members to share stories of their own. Perched at the edge of her bed that night, my mother recounted to me a woman's description of making broccoli soup for her husband, even though her husband hated broccoli soup. The woman felt he should be grateful that she cooked for him; the husband wondered why she kept serving something he didn't like.

"I'm sitting there thinking, *Why am I listening to this?*" my mother said. A vague sense of obligation had drawn her to the session. Perhaps it was time, she told herself, to give such things a shot. "There was no pedagogy, no outcomes," she complained. "It was all anecdotal." There was, in fact, a handout—a flowchart that organized emotions according to their authenticity, where "expansive" emotions are deemed authentic and "constrictive" emotions are not. "Can you make sense of that?" My mother held the sheet out. "I spent so much of my life teaching," she sighed. "I guess I like things a certain way."

Inner fitness had no official place in my mother's previous

ranch stay, fifteen years before. She made that first visit alone, in the year before she met Frank. She packed her new hiking boots and a few opera CDs—*Tosca, Aida, Carmen*—which she listened to through headphones on her casita's patio. The challenges of that stay were mostly physical: she soldiered through trail hikes, tried yoga, resolved to take up skiing. She had a tennis lesson and recorded in a tiny notepad the various weights she pressed, legs and biceps. "In tai chi," she noted, "the *slowest* is the winner."

The plan was rest and rejuvenation but also a kick start. Having confronted in her late fifties the idea that she had a body, my mother set an agenda. She vowed strength and endurance, to max out her insurance allotment for massages and take every holiday. She pledged to keep her clothes fitting and not hide her figure; she resolved to listen to more opera and break ninety on the golf course. In her notebook, she wrote bullet-point sketches of various women she met. There was the San Francisco publishing burnout on her first vacation in five years, who had devoted herself to her job but in the wake of a layoff lost her relationship and got into drugs. The mother of four confronting an empty nest; the librarian and single mother of a teenage girl; and the rich wives from Westchester, Connecticut, and Beverly Hills, each of whom managed several households and focused on their kids while their husbands worked.

For women of my mother's means and rough demographic profile, to seek a way forward at the turn of the last century was often to wind up at a place like the ranch. Not as cushy as some spas and less medicalized than others, it attracts those women looking for, in addition to all the usual things, a sense of themselves as seekers—of a better body, naturally, but also "so much more." The ranch experience evolved alongside a movement toward a more therapeutic cultural vernacular, a shift embodied by the rise of Oprah Winfrey, who visited the ranch at the height of the media scrutiny of her body, its size and changing dimensions.

Almost as a rule, this new language of the self lacked poetry. Like prayer and branding exercises, it is incantation-friendly: tell your truth, live your best life, be your most authentic self, amen. The vocabulary used to describe the search for authenticity in an age of irreality is itself a symptom of the predicament. Charles Taylor describes the struggle for a language of "personal resonance" undertaken by certain post-Romantic figures—those artists no longer operating within a publicly defined order, a sense of convention and common reference. Forced to rebuild a world, the path to solipsism was "all too readily open." But the modern poets offer proof "that the inescapable rooting of poetic language in personal sensibility doesn't have to mean that the poet no longer explores an order beyond the self." Listening to the poets, Taylor suggests, may be the best hope we have. It affirms a modern paradox: the work of being true to yourself enfolds you in a larger whole.

I took heart in my mother's allergy to ranch jargon. Having come from opposite poles, our refusal brought us to the same place. One evening she described an early-morning meditation workshop she had attended. The leader was tolerable but the room far too cold. I went to no classes or talks that day. Instead I wandered the grounds, read by the pool, and waited for the dinner bell. I'm leaving out the hour of the day I spent reclined on the bed, after lunch. It was a Sunday, mellow and warm—a perfect afternoon, I thought, for sex. I felt all of the ranch's three thousand perfect acres and four dozen daily activities pitched against this thought—which became a wistful thought, the kind one thinks about an old friend on a faraway continent. Maybe I'll see her again someday.

One of the guru's formulations piqued my mother: Life = events + story. He asked the group to consider what they tell themselves about the things that happen to them. If you get a flat tire, do you blame yourself, do you blame someone else, or do you get on with fixing it? My mother asked the guru to list the core benefits of meditation. He tried, and she tried to listen, but the cold was going right through her. Meditation can help you control your thoughts, he said, which helps you control your words; and if you control your words you can control your life; and to control your life is to control your character. I said it sounded like the last two were probably reversed. The guru quoted Marcus Aurelius, Oprah, Deepak Chopra, and Willie Nelson—twice.

Love in; peace out.

*Breathe.*

One woman in the workshop told the group that she uses her mantra to further relax during spa treatments, and in unison the two dozen women in the room went: *Ahhhhhh.*

Unhappy with her meditation performance, my mother had no interest in trying again. She spent most of the session thinking of the warmer clothes she would buy at the Mercado once it was done.

IT WAS AFTER NINE when an unhappy porter appeared at the door. Our plumbing had given out, but the golf carts were retired for the night. We would travel to our new casita on foot. As it became clear that we were headed to the remote top of the compound, the silence between my mother and me stretched taut. The porter barreled ahead of us. I made my steps slow and methodical enough to match hers. At lunch the previous day, I had been surprised to hear her tell a stepmother and stepdaughter that her lungs "aren't great." The disclosure was presented not as the beginning of a story, or the end, but something in between. She was asked for and offered no further details. She planned her schedule around the temperature, which often broke one hundred at midday. Over dinner at a group table, a strapping blonde from Dallas appeared bored by her fragile seatmate. From across the table I saw my mother through this woman's eyes—meek and gray—and hated all of Texas for it.

"Does she need a nurse?" the porter snapped at me. He was far ahead when I asked him to slow down, a shadow in solid darkness at the base of a steep incline. "Her lungs aren't great," I said. "This is difficult for her." The porter looked at my mother, bent forward under a lamppost, both hands on her hips.

"*Does she need a nurse?*" he repeated.

I turned to my mother only once, when I could no longer bear not to. Her breathing was shallow and strained. "Are you okay?" I asked finally. My mother looked past me, up the mountain, and resumed her slow march.

The villa was our reward. Three times the size of our casita, it had a king bed and a huge patio overlooking the hills. We hated the villa. We needed a drink. Settled inside, my mother mocked a ranch pamphlet left out for guests; I writhed at full extension on a cot designed for a small child. "But I thought we could sleep together," my mother said.

"I thought we could not."

That night I dreamed of moving from one apartment across the street to another, in a Brooklyn that wasn't Brooklyn. A woman and several men entered the new apartment, all waving kitchen knives. They taunted me when I picked up a knife of my own, said I didn't know how to use it. I said I did, but I didn't. One man—blond, a brash, American type—invited me to try. I pointed the knife tip at his heart and pushed it into his chest, which was firm, like brick cheese. He remained still, then calmly stabbed me back. I had the sense of being tricked. We continued this way for quite a while. At some point I looked out the window, at my old building across the street, and wondered at this new place having been here all along, closer than I could have imagined.

In the king bed my mother dreamed she was giving a dinner party in a house that wasn't any particular house. There was a river beside the house that, as the dinner party continued, began to overflow— with shit. The river, the shit, began to fill the house, until there was more river and shit than house, and everybody agreed the dinner party was over.

# Six

WE WERE LOOKING FOR THE TENNIS, propped up side by side in my mother's Toronto bedroom. Clicking in search of the U.S. Open with a remote raised above our matching bare feet, I paused, somewhat dutifully, on the image of Barack Obama. The American president had taped a one-minute preface to that Sunday's football game, one of several speeches he would make, live and on tape, to mark the fifteenth anniversary of the September 11 attacks. His remarks worked to soothe and reframe: the legacy of that day was "not one of terror and fear," said the president, "but of resilience and hope." Rather than alter the nation, the attacks "revealed who we are, and who we have the capacity to be . . . big-hearted people full of courage and optimism. On this fifteenth anniversary of a very dark day, that's the light that America continues to shine for the whole world to follow." We listened, squinting. I grumbled something about turning pure horror into a national win. My mother was silent.

"Where were you that morning?" she asked finally, as

though the question had just occurred to her. Six months had passed since she first mentioned Janis Jerome, three since our trip to Mexico. I told her I had been running in Mount Pleasant, a nearby cemetery. I often listened to the radio on morning runs, and heard the first reports come in during the eight o'clock news break. My mother told me she heard the same reports while driving downtown, on her way to work. She was at that time five years into her tenure as CEO of a federal government agency. Settled in behind her desk, in the heart of Toronto's financial district, she heard her employees start to scream. Within the hour she had called Ottawa, seeking the okay to evacuate her staff.

"They said: *Don't you think you're overreacting?*" My mother scowled at the memory. We were surrounded on the bed by the various foods I had delivered, in hourly installments, all through that day: a bowl of popcorn; sliced apple with peanut butter; the afternoon milkshake. I hadn't heard this story. All the downtown banks were evacuating, she went on. It was chaos, the scope so unclear. Ottawa remained skeptical. My mother gave the order anyway, and with the rest of her staff headed home. I can see her driving back uptown, alone, at midmorning, but when I try to follow her into her apartment, imagine the fear and sorrow she must have felt in those alien first hours, she fades from view. She abhorred disruption and unstructured time: the thought of my mother *at large*—sans action items and a to-do list—unnerved anyone who knew her. Though we lived only a couple of subway stops apart at the time, we didn't speak that day. I called my best friend in New York. I called my dad.

In a longer, more skeptical fifteenth-anniversary address, President Obama spoke of losses and wins, lives taken and saved, attacks suffered and prevented, justice flouted and delivered. He urged Americans to remember "the true spirit of

9/11," invoking again the idea that the attacks had served to galvanize a people "bound by our shared belief that I am my brother's keeper; I am my sister's keeper." Eight years earlier, Obama appeared to renew the American politician's lease on old-fashioned mythmaking. He loved to tell Americans who they were, and a critical mass of Americans loved to hear it. Speaking to the camera two terms later, hair grayed and jaw loosened, Obama appeared less successful as a visionary—a mythologist—than as a figure of myth. If some Americans still wanted to believe it, his signature message was more uncertain: "It's our diversity, our welcoming of all talents, our treating of everybody fairly, no matter their race, gender, ethnicity, or faith, that's part of what makes our country great." Another of Obama's assurances was more in keeping with its moment: "We'll stay relentless against terrorists like Al-Qaeda and ISIL," he said, looking more human each moment. "We will destroy them."

I MUST HAVE BEEN WALKING a dish in or out of the bedroom, later that afternoon, when my mother broke some news: "Hillary Clinton has *pneumonia!*" I stopped on the carpet. "Of course they'll be all over her for it," she added, turning back to the tablet screen in her lap. Scanning *The New York Times*, she read me the bullet points: having "overheated" at a 9/11 memorial service in New York, Clinton had collapsed. I groaned, folding a knee to the bed. My mother picked up her phone and checked CNN. More details. I dropped my butt onto the folded knee. Diagnosed some days earlier, Hillary had pressed on. "Clinton Had Pneumonia" the headline announced, and underneath: "See Clinton stumble."

We did. We saw her stumble. The footage shows Clinton

from behind, moving away from the memorial ceremony and toward a transport van. She holds her body stiff until the moment she falters, dropping into the arms of her aides at the van's threshold. *Oh God*, I kept repeating. The first woman to win a presidential nomination, Clinton was in the final weeks of her campaign. I replayed the footage. We looked for fresh angles, more versions. My mother and I agreed: this was very bad. Throughout the campaign, the language used to undermine Clinton invoked essential failures: she lacked *stamina*, the right look and temperament, the *strength* to serve. They had been calling her weak for months. Now the headlines had made it official.

"They shouldn't have let her go," my mother said. The doctors—they should have strapped her down, insisted Clinton rest. She was back on the tablet, scrolling through the comments. Never read the comments, I said. *Mmm*, said my mother. "I wonder if she's had it before," she murmured. "It's not something you get for the first time at sixty-eight."

Pointing and clicking, my mother was careful not to disturb the line in her right arm. The nurses had botched an attempt to insert an IV in her left, leaving a series of pansy-colored lumps. Nine days earlier, during her annual physical at a private clinic, the staff had ordered her to a downtown ER. In the previous two weeks, she had toured Scotland and flown to Montreal for a board meeting, feeling unwell but pushing through it. She was hospitalized and put in isolation until they could rule out tuberculosis; the eventual diagnosis was acute pneumonia. I arrived in Toronto a few days later, toward the end of her first week of IV antibiotics. She chose to spend the course's second week at home, her meds dispensed through an automated pump.

"Look at how *terrible* she looks!" Alternating between tablet and phone, my mother held up an image of Hillary Clinton taken shortly before her collapse. She appears ashen, her skin papery. Her eyes look glazed, peeled open. My mother exhaled, sighed, swore low and long. "I feel for her," she said finally. "That's the problem with pneumonia. It just kind of . . . *tricks you*." At the end of the bed my mother's toenails gleamed bright poppy; the nurses had offered their compliments. She swapped devices, tapped, scrolled. "'Bacterial pneumonia is preventable by vaccine,' someone wrote—that's not true!"

"Don't read the comments!"

"'Why isn't she in the ICU on a ventilator?'" My mother scoffed, shook her head. "So much misinformation." Frank entered the room to make his usual suggestion—that she get up. "I hope Hillary doesn't have to carry one of these things around," my mother said, easing to her feet. Frank held the pump attached to her PICC line with one hand and took her elbow with the other. Better to go for the twice-a-day IV hookup, then nothing would slow her down. "She could have someone follow her van with the meds: *Hit it! Flush it! Let's go, boys!*" Stooping forward, she inched ahead on Frank's arm. The pump made proper clothing impossible; she wore a short black robe with leopard trim. I watched their procession from the bed. As she passed it my mother urged me to straighten the Jack Chambers print, a watercolor landscape of London, Ontario, that hung on the wall opposite her bed. "It's driving me crazy," she said. "This one, too," she called from the hallway, then paused. "I must be getting better."

AS ILLNESS AND AS DRAMA, among human ailments pneumonia stands apart. In his catalog of acute diseases and their possible treatment, Hippocrates describes pneumonia as producing fever, pain in the sides, cough, and irregular sputum, often of a "blond or livid color." In his telling, even as it advances to suffocate its victims, pneumonia will respond to a systemic purge. A regimen of carefully formulated draughts, enemas, and barley tea may help draw the disease out through the bowels, urine, sweat, and sputa. The process is one of physical expulsion, exorcism, a turning out from within.

His suggested treatment for pneumonia is standard for Hippocrates, who prescribed purging and barley tea for a preponderance of ailments. "All diseases are resolved either by the mouth, the bowels, the bladder, or some other such organ," he wrote. "Sweat is a common form of resolution in all these cases." In his description of pneumonia, there is little resort to metaphor; he makes scant attempt to narrate or explain the disease, its nature, character, and tendencies. He presents pneumonia as he does all disease—as a natural part of life. His dispatch addresses the physician: if this happens, try this; if you see that, try the other thing.

Hippocrates wrote of pneumonia in part because he observed it to be among the most common and deadly of human diseases. "The ancients" knew it well. But in appearing to emanate from the body—specifically the lungs—pneumonia is an apt vehicle for Hippocrates's belief that all disease might be resolved through a process of emanation.

Theories of pneumonia varied over the centuries, but an emphasis on the patient's ability to physically overpower and expel the affliction remained a consistent feature of its description. In an 1880 article written for *The Lancet*, Dr. Octavius Sturges tells the story of Sarah F—, "a slight, pale girl of 18, engaged in laborious work as a biscuit packer, ill-nourished and neglected." Sarah went to bed well and woke up ill, presenting to Sturges "that assemblage of symptoms which so unmistakably betokens pneumonia," including fever, racing pulse, rusty sputum, pain in her side, and shivering fits. Fed a few ounces of sherry, after five days Sarah appeared to recover. But she quickly relapsed, growing sicker than before. More sherry; weeks of rest. Sturges wonders what he could have done differently. Should it have occurred to him, given the girl's "poverty and squalor, and seeing that she had little strength of herself to contend with pneumonia," that a quick recovery was implausible? Might more alcohol—judiciously prescribed—have helped? Maybe so; probably, yes.

Sturges's case history functions mainly as a jumping-off point for a treatise on the nature of pneumonia, perhaps the most common and mysterious of human ailments. "Let no one suppose that alcohol or anything else of this kind is necessary generally for the cure of pneumonia," he begins. "Let no one believe for a moment that the cases related from time to time of pneumonia successfully treated by this drug or that prove anything whatever." What can be known about pneumonia, according to Sturges, is that it comes on suddenly and arrests in the same way. Pneumonia, in fact, *wants* to resolve, or in any case to turn: "Its cardinal fact is crisis," a moment of climax in which "the lung is called upon to free itself," or perish.

In Sturges's telling, pneumonia is a far more compelling protagonist than poor Sarah F——, who recedes back into poverty and squalor without further note. He describes a doctor's wait for pneumonia to make good on its nature, achieve its crisis, and realize its "natural tendency to recovery." The doctor waits "in hope of this result—and very much in the dark, it must be confessed, as to any intimate changes actually in progress within the lung." The fear is that within that obscure chamber some damage is being done, "and that instead of a simple pneumonia, perfectly harmless to the lung except for the room that it takes, we may have a rapid dissolution of lung texture, a form of suppurative phthisis, in fact, necessarily fatal."

It is a strange and genial account, offered as the age of germ theory began its exterminating rise. For Sturges pneumonia is a disease "which has suffered, perhaps, more than any other at the hands of the druggist." He emphasizes the importance of food, rejecting "that old language of metaphor which speaks of pneumonia as 'sthenic,' as though we had strength to subdue instead of strength to provide." Starving a patient encourages her illness. Instead one must facilitate the "proper destiny" of lung-clogging gunk, which is "to disappear. All that is necessary for the process (or at least all that we know of or can in any intelligible way supply), is an adequate vitality on the part of the patient."

THE RELATIONSHIP of the lung to metaphor is a story of missed opportunity. The organ's mystery is perhaps too extreme for emotional analogy or sentimental graft. We don't know or feel anything deep in our lungs. The lung does not break with sorrow. We don't offer our lungs to each other, or up to the Lord. Our lungs are not the windows to anything, the seat of anything, the essence of anything. We feel no fire in the lungs. It doesn't take lungs to act with valor. Lungs vent us, we do not vent them. Metaphor surrounds the lung—we are forever breathing new life into this, puffing or beating our chests over that—but fails, or refuses, to penetrate it. In literature, if not in life, it is by attacks on them that we know lungs best. "Pneumonia" derives from the Greek word for lung. The lungs are vulnerable indeed, bearing constant exposure to the environment. As much as the senses, they draw in the world. Their work is transformative, dynamic; it acts on the world in turn.

If that work, at once basic and supernatural, is unromantic, or too abstract to lend easily to narrative, in its malfunction there is great pathos, and therefore potential for story.

Dr. Sturges's account of the impoverished factory girl and the lung disease that nearly toppled her was published on the far cusp of the Victorian novel's peak. Afflictions of the lung—pneumonia, tuberculosis; those sudden, fatal chills that sweep in off the heath—pervade the work of Victorian novelists, as they did many nineteenth-century lives. What Sturges's account makes plain is how fully popular notions of lung disease as metaphor penetrated even the most sober thought and advanced medical practices of the time. For Sarah F— to have succumbed would have confirmed a failure of will. With medical support she found the vitality—physical and otherwise—to prevail.

As Susan Sontag observed in *Illness as Metaphor*, if lung disease has represented a lack of physical and moral vigor—a fatal inability to hold the world in balance, within and without—it has also signified great piousness and purity, a higher plane of being. Either way, Sontag writes, "a disease of the lungs is, metaphorically, a disease of the soul." The body recedes, wastes, is consumed. The mind is preserved—indeed, the brow burns. A victim's suffering is frequently prolonged; a fevered climax will bring either death or recovery. In hopeless cases, drawn-out expirations provide a singular metaphor for life: the body slows; the system breaks down. For the period of her confinement, though the victim remains in the world, she is no longer *of* the world—a form of apartness, Sontag notes, in keeping with romantic ideals. Fantasies of tuberculosis, especially, offered "a way of affirming the value of being more conscious, more complex psychologically. Health becomes banal, almost vulgar."

The gaps that remain in our current understanding of lung

pathologies underscore a certain amenability to metaphor, and to story. Because cancer can strike anywhere, it is considered a disease of the body and not the soul. Unlike lung disease, Sontag writes, "Far from revealing anything spiritual, [cancer] reveals that the body is, all too woefully, just the body." Modern medicine has made a fine villain of cancer as scientists race to disarm it. But its operation in the body is generally just that: a bodily operation, often characterized in martial terms. Advances in the treatment of lung disease somewhat outpace our understanding of how those diseases proceed. A haze of mystery still surrounds their tendencies. The soundest knowledge is often the most intuitive. Some of the earliest and crudest mythologies of pneumonia were seeded with hairy molecules of truth: there *was* something in the air; you *can* cough up some significant part of your infection.

Pneumonia is no longer considered a disease but a cluster of infections, each with its own characteristics and requiring its own course of treatment. It bears no widely accepted, clinical definition, in part because the diagnostic method remains so diffuse. Where pneumonia is broadly suspected, antibiotics are broadly prescribed. The current metaphoric system of choice posits infected or blighted lungs as a sort of climate system, within which dark and enigmatic things *brew*. The identification of infectious bacteria in the lungs is still difficult and imprecise. Treatment remains focused on symptoms and metrics—the numbers. They may monitor oxygen saturation, hemoglobin, heart rate, and blood pressure, but even in a case involving severe lung disease, savvy equipment, and advanced facilities, for the most reliable markers of recovery, doctors will first observe how a patient looks, then ask how she feels, what she's eaten that day.

So close to some more sophisticated understanding of the

predicament he describes, Dr. Sturges falters. So sound in judgment and demurral, he stumbles in connecting and in failing to connect. I am thinking specifically of his assertion of pneumonia as perfectly harmless to the lung, separate from that organ's more serious afflictions. I am wondering how to present the facts of my mother's case, such as they are, without drawing certain connections, or resort to metaphor, appeals to meaning. Sontag again: "Nothing is more punitive than to give a disease a meaning—that meaning being invariably a moralistic one."

How might I write of my mother's body without punishing it, or her, in the same way she did, or appeared to do?

THE DAY AFTER news of Hillary Clinton's illness broke, my mother reported on her previous night's sleep. "I dreamed I was hitting a golf ball, and I hit it about four feet," she said. "It was horrible." The IV pump dangled at her side. Two words repeated in the mind of her dream self, or that of the dreamer, or both: *Oh shit, oh shit, oh shit.*

Having followed her parents into golf as a teenager, she gave it up on getting married. In her fifties, single again and finally able to afford a club membership, my mother was a golfer once more. Her seventieth birthday wish was for me to come and watch her play nine holes. After a breakfast of cake and mimosas, I strode barefoot across an absurdly lush course, standing clear as my mother teed off. In a visor and white shorts, her stance was confident. A viaduct was visible in the distance: the first tee stood atop a break in the landscape. My mother swung back and through; her club hung in the air. The ball rose to perform the world's longest jeté, landing out of sight. She played like a champion, like her mother, determined to win. She liked to repeat Rita's sole piece of advice when Frank came on the scene: just don't outplay him on the course.

The three of us were lingering in my mother's den when she mentioned the dream. We had passed the morning stacking, swapping, and revisiting various sections of the weekend paper. Having cracked open his laptop, Frank was soon frowning into its ten-inch screen.

"Frank, you're way too serious," my mother said. "What are you thinking over there?"

"You'll never know," he replied.

I knew: he was panic-googling. His first wife had died of lung cancer almost twenty years before. His second wife's ability to shape-shift had abetted the habits of denial she encouraged. By then we had all watched the cycle repeat, the way she could transform overnight from radiant hostess—fussing, beaming, fluttering from glass to glass—to a gray pencil sketch of herself, immobile and shivering on the couch.

That morning the question of my mother's breakfast, of how much and how well she ate, vibrated at the center of the room. Her weight had been in steady decline for years. Aware of the danger but fascinated, perhaps, by her shrinking form, through this process some part of her relished the thrill of buying smaller and smaller clothes. Some part of her may have enjoyed offering her baggy discards to other women, to me. Inquirers were ignored or coolly informed that her BMI remained within the accepted range. Interfamily back channels opened to strategize around the issue. I suggested an appeal to vanity, that we form pleas for better nutrition around words like "weak" and "frail," and not "thin" or "skinny." I once deployed the most radical tactic I could think of, telling her that the lack of flesh on her face made her look just like Rita. "I hope I have her longevity," she replied.

That particular jig appeared to be up. We had prescriptions and protocols and a diagnosis out in the open. As much as the illness itself, this made my mother miserable. She would handle it—she just needed, she said over and over, to get stronger. I shared in her misery. The sight of my mother not just sick but immobilized released something ancient: the sense of a shared body, of a space in which we could breathe together, beat back what we could finally confront as one. I extended my stay from two weeks to three, resolved to fix every meal, prepare her meds, fiddle with her breathing gadgets ad nauseum. Seeing her body thinned and sallow, I worked harder to add a layer of muscle to mine.

"Maybe we should check you back into the hospital for a few weeks," said Frank. "Let *them* get you back into shape."

"Maybe I'll meet someone there who's similarly inclined, and we can . . . *cough* together," retorted my mother. After a moment, her mind drifted to the memory of a woman she had observed at a nail salon some weeks prior, before her hospitalization. She was awful, my mother said. "So on edge. Berating the woman doing her pedicure—the water was too hot, then too cold. 'Don't put your hair on my feet!' she says. 'Would you like my hair on your feet?'" The memory unsettled her, as much for the rudeness as for the malignant ego driving it, trusting no one, tolerating nothing beyond her control. *Just one coat, this is taking too long*, the woman had hissed. *I can't be here anymore.*

"Is it time for a milkshake?" Frank ventured.

"*No*," my mother barked, flipping into her executive register. "Frank, you are not to be obsessive about my eating. That is *my* job. *I* will handle it."

"*We* have to get you back in good health," he said. "It's *our* job."

"It's *my* job," she insisted. "Ninety percent *my* job."

I told them they were both terrible at their jobs and turned to my mother. She had lost eight pounds, her arms and torso appeared suctioned to the bone. The day of her hospital release, I spent a frantic hour and several hundred dollars at a local grocery store, reeling through the aisles with a cart big enough to sleep in, piling fats on carbohydrates on proteins and more fats. On the second day of intensive feeding, after dinner, my mother puffed out her cheeks and asked if her face looked any fuller.

"I'm going to be like this," she said, re-puffing and ballooning her arms at each side.

"You're going to need a wheelbarrow for your ass," I said.

"That's right."

The hospital had given us their "super-shake" recipe, a blend of ice cream, whole milk, and protein powder. My mother's preference for my milkshakes reminded me of how, as a child, breakfast cereal tasted better when my father poured it into the bowl. "Michelle's not leaving until she teaches you how to make those milkshakes," my mother told Frank.

"I was thinking you could learn how to make them," he said.

"I don't think so. I lie in bed and you tend to me, that's the definition of being a patient," said my mother. "I rather like the role." A beat passed. The CN Tower twinkled. "Did I tell you about my dream?" Her face emptied. "I hit the ball about four feet."

HILLARY APPEARED TO RECOVER from her pneumonia almost overnight, and continued to campaign at full tilt. In debates with her opponent, Donald Trump, she was occasionally devastating and always supremely controlled. If she won them all, the public was reluctant to allow it. When she wasn't too boring and entitled a candidate, she was derided for her unchecked ambition and robotic drive. Her mastery of the issues, the task at hand, and of herself inspired as much offense as admiration.

Despite all this, aided by magical thinking and the modern sorcery of polling data, a significant portion of the country relaxed into the idea that Hillary Clinton would win, become the first female president of the United States. I didn't share that confidence. I left Toronto late that September, having sublet my apartment to spend six weeks in rural New York, where Trump signs dotted the landscape. Social media accounts I followed teemed with Hillary hate. Young women in my classroom bristled at her name. Alone in a rented Catskills farmhouse, I tried to write. Back in Brooklyn, on the morning of my fourth election as a U.S. resident without voting privileges, I was aware of having no party to attend that night, and of not throwing one myself. On election day in 2008, a group of schoolgirls in my building's stairwell asked me pointedly if I had voted that day. I told them I couldn't, but had volunteered for Obama's campaign. Eight years later, the same halls were quiet. Having tried to rally friends to volunteer for Hillary in Pennsylvania, I used their deflection as an excuse to focus on my work, punt the whole thing.

In the early morning after election day I wandered through a charcoal rain, covering my face with an umbrella, newly certain that the worlds we create are designed to tear open onto blackness. That in time we watch everything of value fall into that void. Back at home I wrote my mother, said how glad I was not to have a daughter.

"There will be a woman prez," she replied.

Timing

Remember what she said about
success and setbacks

You can't quit

Her political career is over

She's 69

She worked her whole life

And this is how it ends?

There could be no more
perfect repudiation

Or humiliation

Of her life's work

We're moving backward,
that's what is so dispiriting

But she was Sec. State and a
Senator and in the White House

No woman has got this far
before in US politics

She was the first woman to be
nominated for prez

And I believe she won the
popular vote

She tried

She took a risk

She stood up to them all

I have never seen anything like
it in my lifetime

If not a mother figure, for many women in their thirties and
forties, Clinton in 2016 represented a particular model of what
was possible. I heard from several who, like me, had passed the
previous night in a waking dream, moving in and out of consciousness, mixing return numbers with fantasy, half protected
from the truth and half engulfed by it. Perhaps Clinton could
not inspire a new mythology, and perhaps even her most ardent
supporters knew that. Some gap in our confidence had left Hillary Clinton too vulnerable to an old myth, and it devoured her.

I told my mother about a friend's struggle to explain the
election result to his four-year-old girl. He must tell his daughter H is a hero, she replied.

REUNITED IN MY MOTHER'S DEN that Christmas, we wondered
if there was such a thing as female leadership. My mother was
taking chipmunk bites of a ginger cookie, part of a care pack-
age from an old friend. This friend had been a rival to my
mother's least favorite boss, a woman at the bank where they
all worked in the early 1990s. Hired concurrently, the friend
and the boss were the bank's first female executive vice presi-
dents, and they hated each other. My mother cringed to recall

it. She once tried to intervene, broker peace in the name of getting things done. Eventually she grew fond of the rival; over the years their mutual respect bred a friendship. The boss remained only a source of bad memories.

Having interviewed for the boss's position, my mother agreed to join the bank as her direct report. She had had direct reports of her own by then. In one managerial position she had hired an outside consultant to work up a performance review, find out what kind of boss her team thought her to be. The results were crushing: they called her abrasive, demanding, more schoolmarm than leader. Too compulsive, a perfectionist. Hard on herself and therefore brutal on them. Number one on the recommendations list: "Develop more realistic (i.e. lower) expectations of yourself and others; be less tense." Ever the good student, my mother practiced smiling in the mirror until her cheeks ached. She tried and failed to tell a decent joke. She learned to ask about the lives of her direct reports and opened dossiers in which she recorded their answers. She lived then in a small apartment close to Toronto's downtown, her life a blaze of working days and nights. She had a big mortgage and no clue the trust company employing her was about to dissolve, along with Canada's entire trust industry.

Attending high school in London, I had dramas of my own. I knew my mother worked in finance, and that I no longer found that so impressive. She's a businesswoman, she runs things, I would say. And then: We have no real relationship. As though the two statements might be interchanged. While my mother mentored other women, instructing them on soft skills (how to manage a networking lunch with men made uncomfortable by your presence) as well as the tougher ones (how to ask for more money, command respect, recognition of your worth), I was hacking it out in the trenches: fielding solo the incoming barrage of inquiries from and about my body; facing alone the jeering of cafeteria goons at my small breasts and fat ass, confounded by the blend of loathing, shame, and pleasure their attention produced.

It came as a surprise to learn, some years later, that much of what my mother did amounted to a form of marketing. I had imagined her job in abstract terms, a matter beyond the scope of my interest but also my grasp. Marketing I understood very well. I knew it as a specific form of storytelling, hinged on visions of the future and refusal of the past. Which made some sense of my mother's skill in the field: not unlike her father, she worked in sales. She sold stories about the money and security you might have; about independence, prosperity, "financial well-being." A boss had christened her "Miss Next Steps," because she ended every meeting with a sort of corporate bugle call: *What are the next steps?* She loved her job. She loved *working*, solving problems, ordering and being obeyed. Not just work but the nature of her work gave structure to the world, a way to contain, analyze, enumerate; a box and a tick for everything. She loved it even more than she hated everything else in her life at that time. Her forties were amazing.

I have no memory of the first hospitalization. She had not yet started working for the bad boss when she was diagnosed with bronchiectasis, a lung disease associated with severe or chronic pneumonias. Bronchiectasis occurs most commonly as a subset of afflictions like cystic fibrosis and TB. My mother's case was unusual, having no primary cause beyond the infections that began in midlife. It was the name we learned that fall, the one she had held back for twenty-five years.

"I think she put several people in the hospital—I'm not joking," my mother said of the boss, still nibbling. "She made my life hell." She was tethered by a forty-foot cord to the oxygen generator that had arrived late that October. Powered electrically, the generator made a sort of astronaut of her even as it hemmed her in. My mother held out hope; she just had to get stronger. She had joined a pulmonary rehab clinic, but the first class made it hard to go back. Everyone looked so sick, she said, half dead. She was following instructions, within reason. She ate well and she didn't; she exercised and she slacked on her exercise. Mostly, she waited. For her body to respond, her lungs to clear, energy to return. The pattern required it: collapse and revival; illness and reprieve. "I always think I can beat it," my mother said that fall, as though the test were one of wills, mettle, strategy. Still, she was learning from her new boss, the nurse who ran the rehab clinic: "She's always saying you have to listen to your body." She repeated the phrase—*listen to your body*—giving her mouth a skeptical crook.

If the worst boss my mother ever had fit a caricature of that period—the *career woman*—the archetype of the single, childless, money-addled, work-obsessed shrew held no meaning for her. Her boss simply took to an extreme traits she encountered throughout her finance career. Like the string of men who preceded her, this boss refused to promote my mother, and following a major presentation humiliated her in front of their entire team. My mother resolved to move on, leave the private sector altogether. A "big five" bank CEO-ship for a woman was decades away. She didn't have that kind of time.

Talking with friends over that holiday, my mother's tone began to change. There were no more hammy retellings of her ER drama or shrugging off of a bug caught on the Scottish moors. She took their calls—summoning the big showbiz voice she reserved for phone conversations—but still refused most visits. Four months post-pneumonia, she could walk only a few steps before losing her breath. "Live in the moment" was another big rehab thing, and a tough ask for Miss Next Steps. Zen mindfulness remained elusive, but my mother became more prone to reflection. She returned to the obvious relationships, but also the people she hadn't thought of in decades, beginning with her former employees. She considered for the first time how she might have affected not just their working hours but their lives. A month earlier, she had pulled off one last board meeting, traveling by train with Frank to Montreal, gaming out each set of stairs. The first colleague to embrace her did so while gushing, in that sorry-not-sorry way of the workaholic, that she was fighting pneumonia.

That summer, my mother and the old boss had crossed paths for the first time in twenty years. Having spotted her across a restaurant, my mother resolved to stop at the boss's table on her way out. The boss gave a hearty greeting—too hearty, half drunk. They exchanged a few pleasantries on tiptoe. Then the boss asked that my mother lean in close: there was something she needed to say. Embarrassed, my mother demurred. The boss insisted, slurring into her ear that my mother was wrong to resent her. It wasn't she who had opposed my mother's promotion but the friend—the boss's old rival. My mother straightened. By the room's reddish light she considered this distant, familiar figure. The old fire sent a single lick up her spine.

"All that is so long ago," she said.

"Well, it is and it isn't," the woman replied.

I FIXED MY MOTHER A SMALL PLATE at a full table. It was the kind of holiday gathering she lived to plan and which in the offing her nerves often threatened to spoil. Gracious to the point of violence, she was the host guests urged to be still, sit down. *Relax.* That night she sat quietly, no longer buzzing, serving, fretting. Having ceded the head of the table, from her new position, next to me, she watched and listened and warmed herself in the clamor.

It was I who fussed, clenched, and turned cold. I worried she was struggling without her oxygen, pushing too hard, maintaining appearances at the expense of her health. I hardened against each cheery face surrounding us, the extended family shrieking and chatting, each one oblivious, it seemed to me, as they reached for seconds, refilled glasses, plied another dessert. Over the following weeks, my mother's dependence on oxygen became absolute. Across the next year, I would return to Toronto for at least a week each month, part of the effort to curb a gathering momentum, keep my mother's space travel in check. Ever more the astronaut—singular, indomitable, utterly dependent—her new role presented a punishing bargain: this room or the next dimension.

Approaching the meal's third hour, every new anecdote or burst of laughter balled my fists. My mother remained poised as I struggled to be still. My side of the battle underway between us favored the long view, caution, the fixing of people in time. At length I leaned in to ask, in as light and measured a tone as I could, if she was all right, not too tired. My mother reached for the hand resting in my lap and gave it a thump. She wanted to stay at the table.

# Seven

TEN DAYS BEFORE clutching my mother's hand as our ambulance raced into downtown Toronto, I marched up Manhattan's Fifth Avenue, chanting about democracy. The New York City chapter of the January 2017 Women's March that followed President Trump's inauguration marked my first mass protest. A speck in that day's human swarm, I knew I was not the only one learning to shout out in unison. Early in my American education, I wondered that the streets weren't burning every night. I wondered this mainly to the Americans I met, who so often spoke of politics with the professional spectator's blend of passion and detachment. A larger fatalism touched even the most radical-minded among them, meaningful change having grown rare enough to put its possibility in doubt. I found myself arguing with friends about the merits of public protest without having taken part in it myself. We didn't talk about money, it took me too long to realize, because few of them had ever worried about it. A friend once scolded a magazine intern for asking me, the lone freelancer at a table full of editors, what I did for health insurance. "That's like asking 'What's your net worth?'" he said, suspecting, perhaps, that I went without. But telling Americans I could not afford health insurance had become a minor pastime, if not a form of protest. They always appeared embarrassed for me, and I felt the same about them.

A few weeks before the Women's March, I had delayed my departure from Toronto, wanting to stick around for my mother's first follow-up appointment since her September discharge. I was convinced the respirologist would take one look at her and propose an intervention. Instead, Frank and my mother told me, he had listened to her chest, declared the pneumonia gone, and said he would see her in July. I left Toronto the next day, less furious with the doctor than with her bizarre deference to him. I wanted another opinion, a CT scan, *proactivity*. I wanted my mother to play herself in this story. A few days later, she mentioned a conversation with her rehab nurse.

What about?

The way forward

And?

I am going to take back control

And figure out how to keep
moving and involved

As I manage this next stage

I have been a patient all fall

Very nice

But I need to do more

Otherwise my world will get
smaller and smaller

The lazy way

That was never my choice
before so it shouldn't be now

Just takes will and courage

I asked if taking back control meant demanding more over-sight from her doctors. "All is on track," she wrote.

Meaning what

Meaning I am in control

She was admitted to the ER of St. Michael's Hospital a week later, the day she was set to fly to Florida. Her main complaints were lethargy and shortness of breath. After five hours they sent her home with a ten-day course of oral antibiotics. When I texted her about the Women's March a few days later, she said she wished she could have joined. I didn't ask if she meant march with us or simply walk—anywhere. That my mother was going to die, maybe soon, had felt like reason enough to shout my way up Fifth Avenue. But I gained from the march an expanded sense of what it means to *demonstrate*, the power of enacting for each other what collective action looks like, if not what it can do. In the week that followed I booked a car rental, packed a massive suitcase, and at the end of the month headed back up north.

It was as early in February as it is possible to be when a fire brigade entered the apartment, followed by two paramedics. Frank woke me to announce their arrival. Pulling on a bathrobe I found my mother strapped to a gurney in the foyer, her gaze blurred and breathing ragged. There was a scramble to locate the long list of medications to which she had become either allergic or immune. The lead paramedic's congeniality rode the line between crass and reassuring. He had slick brown hair and a barrel chest. "Your sats are *terrible!*" he crowed, pulling an oximeter from my mother's finger. She had refused the BiPAP, a positive pressure breathing apparatus whose enclosure of the nose and mouth made her panic. He agreed to go with high-flow oxygen prongs, but warned that with her saturation hovering below seventy a worsening of her condition left no choice: she was in respiratory failure.

"It's okay, Mom," I said quietly, taking hold of her foot. Hair askew, she focused in my direction. With Frank following in his car, she pressed her eyes shut as the ambulance juddered down University Avenue. Back in the St. Mike's ER, they lowered a portable X-ray monitor over my mother's chest and pumped more antibiotics through her veins. A nurse who exuded a rare blend of competence and sensitivity mapped out the various courses of action that a failure to stabilize entailed: BiPAP, possible intubation, a move to intensive care. Time collapsed, hours passed without passing: loud, windowless, and overlit, an ER is like Vegas that way. Together with Frank, I spent the night staring at the heart and oxygen numbers above my mother's bed. Would the one come down; would the other rise?

Seven years before, my mother and I had spent a day in the same ER. Unsteady on her feet that morning, in the bathroom she felt the floor give way. With Frank gone for the day, I was sleeping uncharacteristically late on the other side of the apartment. Naked on the floor, unable to lift even her cheek from the tile, she called my name for half an hour before a vague warbling sound roused me. Finding her there I stumbled for the phone, then paced and stood in the bathroom, asking questions, relaying answers, so focused on the unfolding story of my mother's body that she had to ask, finally, that I do something to cover it. For twelve hours she clung to the ER bed's railing, suffering from a freak inner ear virus that made her shiver and vomit. A man two beds away spent those same hours ranting, nonstop and in fantastic detail, about the insects inside his penis. My mother had been loyal to St. Mike's, on Queen Street just east of Yonge, since her first pneumonia hospitalization. Located downtown, close to the various offices she inhabited in those years, it stood at the stark intersection of the financial district and one of Toronto's most vulnerable populations.

Seven years later, watching my mother's eyes drift open and shut above the Optiflow device helping her breathe, for hours I willed Frank to step away. For almost a year I had dodged my mother's questions about what I was working on. I told myself there would come a right time, then made a hypothetical case for waiting until the book was finished. Along with much else, it appeared the latter option was disintegrating. I teach my students how to pitch despite having no gift for it. I turn cold in sales meetings, unable to tell things straight and unwilling to try. Bent on confession, when Frank finally went in search of coffee just before six I struggled to begin. Sitting at my mother's feet, the language went sideways in my mouth. What was it I thought I was doing, again? The few words I spoke hovered between us: mothers, daughters; legacy; feminism. My mother nodded, looking straight ahead, then turned to me with dim eyes. Weak as it was, her voice carried the low burn of resignation: "You were very angry, for a long time," she said. "And I'm sorry about that."

FOR MANY YEARS, my mother kept a photo of me in her living room, a close-up of my face in three-quarter profile, chin in hand, pinkie in mouth, breeze pushing through my hair. We were in Ixtapa, Mexico, a vacation my mother proposed as I entered my teens and she her mid-forties. Seated at an outdoor table, we had perhaps just passed a meal. I retain only a sense of the silence between us, its shock of purity and perversion, the agony and pleasure of sustaining it. I can see my mother deciding, with an air of bemusement, or possibly defeat, to raise her camera. In the moments before it was taken, I had ignored repeated calls to look her way, pose, smile. I looked to the camera without turning my head—no pose, no smile—wanting the terms of the exchange to be clear.

A trip to Mexico was the kind of thing my mother missed out on as a girl. I would be luckier than that, and lucky was exactly how I was meant to feel about being in Ixtapa. My confirmation had taken place not long before, at the exact moment I began to think my relationship with the Catholic Church might be near its end. I did as I was told, taking vows in the same church whose aisles I had tread, with all the solemnity a seven-year-old in a wedding costume can muster, to receive my first Communion. If baptism occurs at the will of others, confirmation is meant to ratify not just a Catholic's faith but her discretion. What the sacrament of maturity confirmed for me was a sense of capitulation, of having ceded to a suspect matrix the prerogatives—to create and destroy, mythicize and dispel meaning—that I prized more and more.

My first period arrived sometime between confirmation and Mexico. It was August; it was River Phoenix's birthday. Alone in the house, I decided to call my mother. Confidences fell outside our repertoire then, but I still cared enough about protocol to chance it. Having dug through my father's bedside drawer for the number, I placed a call to Toronto. My mother spoke in her office voice; we both strained to muster a sense of the occasion. After hanging up I marched to the home of my nearest schoolmate, a proud bleeder and second-in-command of a clique I was working to penetrate before we all entered high school. Here was an opportunity, a way to make myself known. There was some truth in my presentation as a hapless newb in need of guidance, if not supplies. There was contrivance too. As much as a change in status, I craved recognition of my lack—real and perceived—of maternal recourse. I wanted it known that if I was now a woman I was a woman with nowhere else to go.

I used to think my mother displayed the Mexico photo to embarrass me. It stood as evidence of her part in a familiar story: the suffering mother and her scowling, problem daughter. But in capturing something of the wordless, replicating chasm between us, the portrait now seems to me even more her image than mine. At thirteen I was done with family photos and their hedges. Having emerged from girlhood an academic star, as my mother had, I was through with perfect grades and grubbing for adult favor. I liked my friends, drinking, dancing, and making out. I liked Madonna. At forty-four, my mother was tired of returning to London, where she found the home she had perfected over many years encased in a cool, implacable shade of blue. She liked her job, respect, and diamond

# Michelle Orange

earrings. She wanted finer things, it seemed to me, than we could offer. To live not just apart but better.

Some years earlier, she had returned to London with a full-length coyote-fur coat. Modeling it in our living room—a special occasions–only space—she asked me to take her picture. Thick and fluffy, the fur was a heather of white, beige, and gray. I steadied the camera and turned it lengthwise, as directed, for a full-body shot. Pivoting in a made-up face and heels, my mother appeared both heightened and half swallowed. I understood the fur as a symbol less of new prosperity than perfect independence, the power to warm, protect, and lift oneself up. The coat was the future; our house and everything in it was perched atop a chill, receding floe. In the picture she appears sober and a little scared, wearing sacrifice like armor.

By thirteen, certainly, I believed myself finished with my mother's gaze, its confinements and erasures, the way it felt to be regarded as a figment of someone else's past. Her framing of my face, in the Mexico photo, is solid and square; the look I return to the camera is direct and unmistakable.

ON MY RARE TEENAGE VISITS to Toronto, my mother often sent me to Gerry for cleaning up. My nails, my hair—they were never right. An aesthetician with her own business, Gerry was tall and blond, reminding me a bit of Bets. Gerry called me "sweetie" and "my love." She held my hands. Sawing at my fingertips, she would praise my mother's stamina, her strength and sacrifice. And I would seethe, finding the whole transaction bogus: "beauty" for money; money for "beauty." An exchange of abstractions, a form of intimacy that proposes comfort but can't provide it.

In my giant combat boots and oversize clothes, I appeared to reject the beauty norms my mother observed with fierce discretion. In many ways I suffered more acutely in my relationship to those norms than my mother ever did. Perhaps because she *was* beautiful, according to the prevailing standard. But I don't think so. Questions that tormented me seemed for her long settled, if not beside the point: to be feminine was not an act of submission but a form of play; to look after one's appearance was both obligatory and a source of fulfillment.

"How did I first become conscious of what was always there—her astonishing beauty?" Virginia Woolf wrote of her own mother in *A Sketch of the Past*. "Perhaps I never became conscious of it; I think I accepted her beauty as the natural quality that a mother . . . had by virtue of being our mother." In *To the Lighthouse*, Mrs. Ramsay appears as a sort of universal mother, and so all through Woolf's novel her beauty inspires reverence. It is remarked upon so often and in such broad, absolute terms that the reader begins to doubt it. To what does all of this fussing praise refer? To whom is it really addressed? As Mrs. Ramsay is an abstraction to herself, my mother's loveliness had always been abstract to me. Others pointed it out straightaway, and I had to agree; I saw it too. If I registered her beauty, for so long it proved impossible to really take in.

Saturdays with Gerry formed the apex of my mother's week. Theirs was her most consistent relationship through her career-building years. The exchange between them was also more complex than I understood when, as a teenager, I submitted in loaded silence to beautification, to Gerry's mothering touch. The combination was new to me: my mother kept my hair cropped as a girl; I learned about makeup at preteen sleepovers. The shock of my own image in the mirror, after a friend offered to line my eyes for the first time, has never fully left me.

Atop a narrow staircase in a fancy Toronto neighborhood, Gerry often worked alone. She started her business in the mid-1980s, just as my mother arrived in town. In time she hired others, added services, began selling her own line of skin care and cosmetics. My mother was eager to support Gerry, an entrepreneur raising four children, in the same way she had insisted on contributing to a pension for Bets. The struggle to enter and perhaps transcend the middle class was the one she knew best; it touched her in a way other struggles did not. Rita, who never inhabited that class with the ease her daughters would, always found the resources to support her weekly wash and set at the salon. In style and careful grooming there was not simply vanity—nor enslavement to a beauty myth—but a measure of self-respect, an act of privacy and of restoration, a statement of persistence. Though it took place under the banner of beauty and at the risk of frivolity, across decades and in different ways for each of them, what transpired between my mother and Gerry was a matter of survival.

Years later, as their bond began to loosen, my mother and I stood beside a casket holding the body of Gerry's twenty-one-year-old daughter. A group of girls sat at the foot of the coffin, playing the Spice Girls' "Viva Forever" on repeat. The story we heard involved pills, a moment of black decision, then panic. She died on my thirty-third birthday. My mother asked me to accompany her to the wake. It had been fourteen years since Gerry buried her twin boys, infants who survived only briefly after birth. In the windowless funeral parlor her presence was awesome, enormous, deranged. A blur of motion, she spun from person to person, at one with a room seeking its axis.

Lodged inside ourselves, my mother and I stood slanted and dumb. At some point Gerry approached us, her eyes wild, and told my mother she looked fabulous.

IT SEEMED CLEAR the new antibiotics were working when, after ten days in the hospital that February, my mother's thoughts turned to a pedicure. I found an aesthetician who made house calls and booked an appointment for a few days post-release. This latest admission had doubled as a crash course in lung disease: a rotation of oxygen technicians, respiratory therapists, and physios offered advice. Though the drugs had an effect, the doctors disagreed on whether to call whatever was plaguing their patient pneumonia. The quest for a viable sputum sample began and for the next ten months never really ended. Her respirologist thought it was time—indeed well past time—to talk about transplant. I ferried meals to the hospital, shopped for food, and sent my mother links to movies and TV shows. In the evenings, after I left the ward with a dirtied plate from home, we texted. An old friend of my mother's had just lost her husband. I knew her and the friend to have been academic rivals in high school. Both went on to study Latin, Greek, and French, she wrote me one night.

Toughest stuff there was

I lessened my Latin and Greek
in yr. 3 and 4

In favor of?

More French

I always wanted to teach Latin

They took it out of ON
curriculum the year I graduated

And we went to NY

Sent me down a different path

The friend and her husband had both been teachers. When she heard about the former students who wrote and visited during his illness, my mother was inspired to reach out to her own favorite high school teacher. Young and vital, Sister Kathryn Ambrose had taught physics and history, my mother reminded me.

Most importantly she directed
our Cathedral girls choir

Climb every mountain

The hills are aliiiiiiive!

Yeah

The summer she visited her former teacher, two years earlier, my mother retold a story I knew only in fragments—the one about Jackie Boyle the choir girl and her moment of triumph. This time, the story centered on the sublime influence of Sister Kathryn Ambrose: as her student, my mother had won awards for physics and history, and sang in the girls' choir.

In grade ten the girls lobbied Sister Kathryn—successfully and in mild defiance of Catholic-school norms—to acquire the sheet music for *The Sound of Music*, which had recently made its Broadway debut.

We were walking in midtown Toronto, on our way to have our toenails painted, something I still did exclusively either with my mother or at her behest. "We would stand in a little line, with our hands like this," said my mother, stopping to clasp her fingertips together, over-under, elbows flared at her waist. "Or was it like this?" she said, drawing in her elbows and twining her fingers into a knuckle bouquet. In school, at fifteen, my mother felt safe: a class full of girls, a faculty of nuns, and nothing to do but answer questions, laugh, and sing out. The boys, the world—they could wait. That all came later.

It was late in the afternoon. The day's heat had eased, and with it the weight in the air. My mother had resisted walking to the nail salon; smog had begun to trouble her breathing. In fact she appeared revived in the street. She seemed to dance without dancing. We stood in front of my mother's old building, where I had slept on a pullout couch through three years of university. The few people passing curled around us with light steps. My mother backed into herself, chin raised, fingers locked: "And I sang, 'Climb every mountaaaain!'" This was the part I had heard before. "Our Peter Pan collars, our boleros, our saddle shoes, and those hands—I could show you pictures. It's documented." We started on again. Wearing my mother's pinchy leather flip-flops, I was conscious of slowing my usual pace, working to make it look natural.

"She'd always go—" my mother continued, raising both index fingers to the center of her mouth and pulling each one up and out. She continued through a half-crazed smile: "And we were like—'Oh, Sister! I want to be perfect, Sister! If I sing this song I'll be perfect, right? No? Oh . . .'" Her eyes cast down for a beat, then lit back up: "'I'm a virgin, Sister!'"

My mother told me that afternoon about her impending visit to Sister Kathryn Ambrose, who was then eighty-six and still living in Hamilton. "I want to tell her what she means to me," she said. I asked what the Sister did mean to her. The strange pitch in her voice turned to vehemence: "I'm going to tell her *I love her.*" I looked at her. "She lives at the Mother House," my mother added.

"The Mother House," I repeated.

"That's what they call it."

"But it's filled with Sisters."

"That's right."

"Who's the mother?"

"The BVM!"

*Blessed Virgin Mary.*

In my memory, the point of the "Climb Every Mountain" story had always been to make it known that my mother had an excellent singing voice and the bona fides to prove it. I can't recall her singing at home. I want to say she joined the hymns during Mass, but what I recall most about the services we attended as a family are my mother's silent acts of abstention. Shoulders back and gaze forward, she would remain seated as my brother, father, and I joined the Communion procession to the altar. At the height of my girlhood piety, I found this embarrassing. It spotlit what I felt to be my mother's determined separateness from our little group, which so rarely did things like attend Mass together. I wondered at her nerve, who she thought herself to be. The public moment of refusal fit my story so well I hardly needed hers. I did request it, though, and recall her reply as curt, forbidding of further inquiry. So many of my questions then seemed not just unwelcome but a form of interruption.

My mother's aunt Claire was another favorite from her youth. A devout Catholic, diagnosed with a condition that made pregnancy a risk to her health in the early 1970s, Claire turned to her priest about using birth control. The priest was adamant: to do so was a mortal sin, and would preclude her from participating in the holy sacraments, including Communion. Claire was bereft; the Church stood at the center of her life. But she had a family, growing children. She accepted her doctor's prescription of a birth control pill. In this she joined my mother, who began taking the pill after marriage and who after my brother's birth began to sit alone in her pew through the Communion ritual—as Claire had been forced to do.

During my mother's visit with her, Sister Kathryn expressed no regrets. Her life had unfolded according to God's plan. She asked only that my mother—who spent several teenage weekends at silent convent retreats and for a short time seriously considered joining the sisterhood—come back to the Mother House and see her again. My mother came to revile the Church's treatment of women and questioned the faith's more dubious mythologies: Why a *virgin* birth, anyway? But she never let go of the young Sister, or the ideal of fulfillment she had embodied: a grown woman who took pride in who she was and what she did. She represented also, perhaps, the hope of maturing into a world that would remain safe, well-defined, supportive of her needs and free of certain risks. I later asked my mother, during one of our texting jags, what she had told her former idol, how she described the difference Sister Kathryn had made in her life. "Inspiration to be your best self," she wrote, then slipped away.

In her 1959 yearbook, a photo appears of my mother the

choir girl. To the left of frame Sister Kathryn sits at a piano, what appears to be an entire tabernacle perched on her head. ("We thought she slept in it," my mother said of the sister's elaborate cornette. "We wondered how she swam.") Gathered around the piano, ten or so girls are shown singing or pantomiming song, leaning in toward their leader, gazing at or somewhere past her. Only one girl returns the camera's look, as though it were that of a secret friend. My mother stands apart from the interest of the scene, her body turned forward. In her Peter Pan collar and meringue curls she beams into the lens, smiling her prettiest pretty-girl smile.

AT NINETEEN, my mother sat down to record a bit of history, a story of beginning that itself required a prelude: "Almost an overwhelming desire to impart the story of a tender nascent love to the whole world compels me to take pen in hand this magic night of November 11, 1963 and begin."

Over nineteen handwritten pages, my mother's narrator addresses a reader who at times appears to be a general someone with a specific interest in melodrama, and at times is more clearly a second version of her. The style is urgent, self-reflexive, plush with romance. Set in the fall of 1962, following the narrator's arrival at university, the story is structured with scene and dialogue, action and reaction. The description is close, the tone polished. It begins with the narrator's introduction on campus to a handsome young man, and details the elaborate series of events leading up to the moment of their first kiss—where the story ends. Our heroine giggles; she demurs; blood thumps in her cheeks. She wonders if she should be coy and mocks her own high school prudery. She laughs when he laughs, working herself into a compatible mood. "By this time you can see I am no prose narrator," the author interjects on page three, having described a charming first phone call. "This is just a simple story—no frills, no artifice—simply a true love story."

Eight pages in, on their third date, while tucked into a local Italian joint the narrator and her suitor discuss "the educated woman as a wife and mother. Would she be content to stay in and take care of her children? Yes, I maintained." The suitor counters with the example of his own stepmother, who graduated from university in 1941, married five years later, had three children, and began the work in education that led to her term as president of the Canadian Federation of University Women. A woman with a degree, he argued, required more intellectual stimulation than domestic life could provide. "Neither of us really won," the young woman confides. "Although I hoped he believed me."

She floats home that night, singing "Moon River" to the October sky and musing about God's plan. What else could explain the appearance of this perfect stranger so soon after she left home, the answer to a sudden crop of impossible questions in the form of one gorgeous human and a set of skinny ties. Whether by providence or good luck, she felt herself finally opening up, "letting someone inside that closely guarded tabernacle."

My mother didn't mention her memoir that February, though it was among the papers she had asked Frank to retrieve from a storage locker. She did describe rereading her day planner from 1966, the year she married my father shortly after graduating from university. That September the newlyweds moved to Rochester, New York, where my father had landed a teaching job. Pre-marriage there were ticket stubs, nights out, studying, and vows to work for a while before settling down. Post-marriage, the twenty-two-year-old newlywed wrote at the top of each page what she had served for dinner that evening. She documented every nickel spent in a looping, deliberate hand. My mother felt at once sympathetic to and quite bored by her former self. "Such nice writing"—she sighed—"about absolutely nothing."

IT MUST HAVE BEEN A FLU that got me during our last Christmas as a family. At fifteen, I passed our holiday dinner in a private delirium, my request to stay home denied. Leaving my aunt's building, my mother, brother, and I stood silent in the vestibule as my father pulled the car around. In a moment my legs went wavy and my head lifted off my shoulders. I heard my skull bounce off the glass behind me, then my mother's voice. She was shouting, inflamed, as though the sight of me twisted up in my coat and Christmas dress were part of some ongoing plot to defy her. In the way of all mothers, she could sink my own name into the scruff of my neck. The sound was familiar but newly distant, unreal. A door closed and another flew open. Shadowed by her almost wild, agitated presence, I refused to look up, eventually pressing both palms to the ground.

A few years later, my mother returned to London in order to leave one last time. I found the exercise a bit silly. I found most things a bit silly at that point in my life. Having made a religion of mistrust, at almost nineteen I was ready to unleash its dogma on the world. It would not have surprised me to learn my parents had split years before. After maintaining with my father a ritual silence on the subject of their marriage, my mother drove to London to make an official divorce announcement, with me as her sole audience. We faced each other across

the same little-used room where a decade before my mother
had revealed she was moving to Toronto, then later modeled
the fur coat. This time, she appeared to want me to share in
her grief, a sense of the occasion's sorrow. But we had shared so
little. As much as the decor and the landscaping, this seemed
to me by her design. As far as I was concerned, the signing of a
few papers meant nothing. And meaningless things had come
to offend me in the private tabernacle where I lived. After a few
minutes my mother was silent.

*Is that it?* I wondered. Then said it out loud.

"WHAT DO YOU REMEMBER about your bedroom?"

By Valentine's Day, my mother's IV removed and latest antibiotic course over, a darker mood had set in. Death had receded,
for the moment, leaving a diminished set of alternatives in its
wake. Seeking distraction fodder, that morning I had brought
into her bedroom a section of the paper filled with updated takes
on traditional French cooking. She made a polite show of interest.
Then the question.

"What do you mean? My childhood bedroom?"

"Yeah."

I thought it over.

"I remember the yellow curtains."

"Yeah."

"I remember the big animals stenciled on the wall. A white
dresser." She didn't remember the dresser, which she had
painted in black lacquer and brought to Toronto when she first
moved. "I remember the yellow bedspread with white eyelet
and ruffles."

"The rattan headboard," added my mother. I had forgotten the headboard but then recalled the matching chair and toy

basket. "Do you remember the rocking chair, is it still in London?" No, and I didn't know. She had bought the chair at an auction, she told me, nursed her two babies in it. She asked if the lilies of the valley still bloomed by the side of the house, under my window. "I sprinkled a few seeds there and they spread, came in every April, maybe May. I could always get one good handful."

I tried to stay with her, in the moment—the past. It made her crazy that I couldn't remember those early years, all her perfect meals and holidays, the planting and decorating and vats of beans baked faithfully through the night. I had learned to cook watching my father: meat loaf, scalloped potatoes, veal cutlets, Chinese chicken wings, fried rice. I had assumed, with a mix of satisfaction and resentment, some part of the domestic burden she laid down.

"I loved those curtains, they were beautiful," I said.

"Cost a fortune. Yellow with the little white dots—organza, I think. Your crib was yellow too, with some orange. I had a whole scheme." Sitting at the end of the bed, I glanced at the paper: cassoulet, but new; tagine, but modern. When I looked up my mother's head was dropped, her mouth pulled tight.

"Mom."

She shook her head.

"What are you thinking about?"

She looked away.

"Sitting in the rocking chair." She turned to her lap and fought the memory some more. "I just don't understand how he could do it," she said finally. "He had everything. And then he cut down the magnolia. That was the last straw." I looked at her. It was true: around the time of their divorce, my father cut down the magnolia tree my mother had planted in our front yard. It had looked fine to me, but he insisted it was dead.

Arriving in Toronto three weeks earlier, I noticed first that my mother's bare feet were blue. She was propped up on the couch in her den, a look of fear and dismay in her eyes. The antibiotics were not working as they had; eight days with no uptick. Her doctor insisted she hang on, keep waiting. In bed later that night, bent almost in half over a meal tray, she was too breathless to eat. For two days I failed to call an ambulance, and she refused to ask for one. A whole world began to unmoor, its parts to intermix. The apartment, its furniture, her belongings—all appeared at once less real and more narrowly defined, props in a matrix on the brink of giving way. We felt ourselves becoming less real as well, more purely something else. If there could be no more denial, the atmosphere still coursed with disbelief. At the center of this new reality lay my mother, her body an intersection, a hub of metaphysical traffic. Like taking a deep, untroubled breath, her decades of planning had been a luxury whose extent was only now becoming clear. These were supposed to be the years of security and reward, of loving her husband, investing in friends and family; enjoying the money she had spared nothing to earn; taking the pills as needed and feeling better by day four. I had imagined a story unfolding as I saw fit, that would balance in a selected ratio the notional, historical, and personal; a story shaded at limited angles and to precisely crafted degrees by the prospect of my mother's demise. What could either of us do in the face of not just mortal illness but its tidal narrative force? Scanning the increasingly useless pile of French recipes on her bed that morning, my time playing interlocutor came to an end. Reborn as a dazed bystander, I accepted without question the expressions of a grief wholly unconnected to my father, the things he did or didn't do.

The night before, my mother had bottle-fed her two-month-old granddaughter. When my turn came to hold her, I grew unsettled looking into the baby's squinched-up face. She didn't yet favor my brother, or her mother, or her great-uncle Whomever. If no one could say exactly how, for what turned out to be the space of a single evening, everyone agreed she looked just like me.

# Eight

IN A FAR CORRIDOR of the respirology ward of St. Michael's Hospital, a series of watercolor prints lines the walls. Over a week of early-spring evenings, I accompanied my mother on a series of short, rehabilitative walks past the watercolors, each of which depicts a Toronto scene of a hospital board member's choosing. Her admission that March was the second in as many months. By then the sight of her using a walker, attached always to an oxygen tank, was less jarring. The nights we made it to the far corridor were good nights. On one of them I asked my mother which part of Toronto she would have the hospital paint in her honor. She ignored the question, intent on staying in motion. Her step was exaggerated, a sort of forward standing march. Her leg muscles especially had weakened from disuse. Her head had acquired what appeared to be a permanent tilt to the right.

I asked again.

"Oh," she said, and thought for a moment, then stopped. She wore charcoal-colored pajama bottoms made of light jersey and a lavender floral-print top, both brand-new. She had made a show of thanking me for them the previous afternoon, before her voice flattened. "I think I'll wear them for the rest of my life," she said.

I clung to small missions and minor offerings: rose-tinted lip balm, concealer, the tweezers she wanted. Some part of the burden of her hospital stays, and of this phase, was less about looking ill than the dissipation of those rituals that fostered consistency, self-care, a sense of control. For the first time in her life, my mother declined to be photographed. Those times she agreed the result was shocking: in photos she appeared as her old, relentlessly photogenic self. Even more than her beauty, her image had a will and persistence of its own.

"I guess the CN Tower," my mother said finally. Gripping the handles of her walker, she pushed on. I blinked, disappointed. The tower figures in so many of the watercolors. "I've always loved the CN Tower," she added. We continued a few steps as she thought some more. "But it would have to be from a specific angle. It would have to be the tower as you see it coming from London, heading east." In the hallway's bleak yellow light she cocked her head and dropped her jaw, affecting the awe of a traveler coming upon the mighty tower from below, from the west.

WE WERE NEVER STRANGER TO EACH other than when we tried to move in tandem. Walking the streets together recast our psychodrama as tragicomic dance. I blamed her, of course, specifically her habit of pitching toward me as we walked, veering into the modest bubble of space I fought to maintain. This kept me always on the diagonal, moving forward but also away, tracing long, irritated vectors in one direction and then back in the other. Sometimes I waited for her body to drift into mine, so I could answer it with a sharp check. Occasionally, when I couldn't take it anymore, I would jerk to a stop, startling my mother from what appeared to be a pleasant waking dream. "What," she would say, with a look of bright innocence. "What did I do?"

We had been locked in this exact dance, in the fall of my second year of university, when my mother went down. One moment she was there, walking Chicago's Michigan Avenue alongside me, the next she was bent over her forearms on the sidewalk. It was the kind of spill that left no clues. I spent a long moment turned back anyway, examining the curb. Up quickly, my mother swore a wounded oath. I asked, belatedly, if she was all right. Checking her clothes, her hands, her bag, she insisted we move on.

We were in Chicago over the October long weekend of Canadian Thanksgiving. I had just moved into my mother's midtown Toronto apartment. Our habits ensured minimum togetherness: she left for work before I awoke; I scheduled evening classes and made weekend commutes to London, just as she had. We had not shared a home in over a decade, and excluding my time in the womb had never lived as a pair. When my mother was the same age as I was that fall, she was a virgin preparing to marry, to leave her parents' apartment and a bedroom shared with her younger sister. After one year in the dorms, I appeared to be moving backward. The money issue was real: I had none, and part-time work was scarce. Their recent divorce had upended my parents' finances; the cheapest option seemed the most virtuous. I don't recall giving her a choice. I do remember thinking she could hardly say no.

Along with my adolescence, the mini-era sometimes referred to as feminism's third wave was just then coming to a close. For one slender, blessed, early-nineties moment, the girl everyone wanted to be wore baggy clothes, or femme drag, or whatever she wanted; women stormed a dominant cultural mode—rock music—and prevailed. Anita Hill testified before the U.S. congress about her sexual harassment by a Supreme Court nominee; Kim Campbell became the first female prime minister of Canada. That nobody asked me in those years if I was a feminist—that no one seemed to care—now strikes me as both a gift and a means to entrapment. I was free to pursue my own instincts on matters of gender, personhood, and equal rights, unburdened by cultural dogma, identity politics, or purity tests. I wrote stories about girls torturing their old Barbie dolls and a boy working up the courage to leave the house in his mother's clothes and makeup. I read the obscure zines, saw the relevant shows, screamed along with PJ Harvey, Hole, and Bikini Kill. No one told me marriage was a bankrupt institution, but I'd be sure to say so if it ever came up. I held many truths about who could do what, when, where, and how to be self-evident. To ride high on those truths into a world whose structural inequalities remained wholly intact is to understand your savvy youthful convictions as a function of whatever shelter you once enjoyed. Girls coming of age in the 1990s confronted in a particular way the limits they had sensed but were encouraged not to credit.

Unsure of how to proceed, on the brink of adulthood I entered an era of refusal. Finding solace in ritual elimination, each day I grew more certain of all the things I would not do. Negation and rage proposed their own model of selfhood: I would not marry; I would not fuck; I would not conform, identify, partake. I would hardly live. I would watch, read, and run. I would make myself a small, suspended thing, and wait. As a place of retreat, my mother's home proved ideal. The business of denial, it seemed, was our shared domain. In close proximity, our separateness could truly flourish, feeding on itself. As she reached her professional peak, I brought my life to a halt, squatting alone among her rooms full of lovely things. The shelter I took there was both real and provisional, dark but familiar, the kind of safety that can only be found in the shadow of the thing that bewilders you most. As my mother entered menopause, my period came to a stop.

The writer Caroline Knapp has described herself as "a classic heiress of feminism," a woman whose possibilities owe directly and indirectly to second wave activism. "And yet for all that," she writes in *Appetites*, "I remained somehow immune to its transformative potential, some sense of its transformative power never quite made it to the gut level." Having come of age in the late 1970s, Knapp felt the movement stall into irrelevance over the next decade. "The world had so recently opened its doors to women, it seemed, and then so suddenly stopped talking about what that meant, how it felt, what challenges it presented," she writes. "In the midst of the consumer din, feminism became something of an echo, a distant tick on another generation's clock." Through her twenties, Knapp wrote about women's issues, identified as a feminist, and was consumed by an eating disorder. "There you have it: intellectual belief without corollary emotional roots; feminist power understood in the mind but not known, somehow, in the body."

Knapp describes a scene in which, during the worst of her anorexia, she contrived to remove her shirt in front of her mother, to present as a kind of engraved message her clawed ribs and beaded spine. Knapp is careful to stipulate that her mother supported her unequivocally, never tried to steer her toward traditional models of femininity or harped on appearances. But when she thinks of her mother—an artist who would abandon her studio to feed her kids, "self-sacrificing and frustrated about it, and loving and angry, and full of passions that were never permitted to flower in full"—a guilty question looms: How can I allow myself to have what she never had? Emancipation has only intensified a woman's challenge to own and act on her appetites. Knapp writes:

> What may take even longer to work through—what nags and gnaws in more intricate and puzzling ways—is a deeper sense of unease; a vague disquiet that some-times feels like abandonment, sometimes like betrayal, and that springs, I think, from the territory of mothers, that plane of merging and attachment where knowledge of the mother is enlaced with knowledge of the self. That "other" we long to be—the one who'd emerge if we lost the right amount of weight or found just the right clothes, the one who so often gets lost under the relent-less focus on size and shape and appearance—is not a figure many women can conjure up from childhood; she is not deeply familiar or intimately known or felt at the core; a woman may have to invent her by herself. And in order to do so, she may have to leave something—or someone—behind.

Thinking of my mother and me in Chicago, I recall moments in images and images in moments: the baked potato that sat like a grenade on my dinner plate at the Pump Room; the sick-ening feeling of my mother's hand on my shrunken backside. Her voice as she said she always thought I'd look more like her. The sight of her folded over a curb several steps behind me; the uninterrupted flow of people going past. The two of us pressed together in the elevator of the John Hancock Center, our bodies rising and rising.

FORCED INTO THE SAME SPACE in a way we were not at home, in Chicago we shared a hotel bed. On the street we performed our awkward, quasi-tribal dance. In museums it was necessary to keep track of each other, to move forward and fall back, to seek the other's shape in a crowd. I found our museum visits exquisitely trying: the focus on money, taste, and performed response calls up a version of her—real or imagined—that frustrated a part of me. She adored the Impressionists, and Chicago's Art Institute was stuffed with them.

My mother's affair with French Impressionist painters peaked in her forties, as she began to cultivate in earnest a sense of her own cultivation. Life on her own made it more important than ever to have specific tastes, to know particular things, to stake claims that reflected well on one's sensibility and place in the world. In the stratum to which she aspired, intimate knowledge of painters like Edgar Degas, Claude Monet, and Édouard Manet was a basic point of credibility. I grew wary of her attachment to blurry, pastel scenes of Parisian street life, ballet dancers and park luncheons, apple cheeks and wildflowers. I wondered if my mother raved about them—hoarding postcards, prints, and coffee-table books—as a function of her new identity. If she had good or bad taste concerned me less than whether her taste could be believed. At the Art Institute I shook her from my shoulder, fled each hot rush of praise in my ear.

On the question of how a legitimate taste develops, a very young person is both the best and worst judge. A very young person has a vague sense of being shaped by cultural forces beyond her control—the times, the trends, the vagaries of exposure—and a complete immunity to caring. She cares least when she encounters an experience or a work of art that captures her imagination in part because it captures *her*. She agrees with the work, it agrees with her, and a momentary or more lasting synergy is born. The relationship is various: some part of her love of death metal, for instance, is rooted in the fact that all of her friends like it; or that none of them do. Claiming and being identified with a love of this or that is integral to the pleasure, to the experience of loving it. The very young person does not acknowledge or accept this, but she knows it. In time she will confirm what was sensed all along: passions take shape on their own terms, subject to circumstance, to internal and external pressures, and always to legitimate effect. Former passions embarrass for what they reveal, not because they were false.

My mother talked of the Impressionists as though no one had thought to love them before. The need they answered in her was genuine, intimate, and so was the attachment. His zeal for flower-scapes made Monet a favorite. She first visited his estate in Giverny, outside Paris, in the 1980s, snapping photo after photo of the gardens. She marveled at the recursive, obsessive quality of his Water Lily series, repelled by the thought of pondering one thing for decades but sympathetic to any mission so devoted to beauty, a world perfected and contained. In the bedroom she shared with my father, during the interim decade after her move but before their divorce, my mother hung a print of *The Plum*, Manet's melancholy portrait of a woman seated alone at a café, gazing over a glass of plum brandy. The woman wears pink, her dress and black hat trimmed with white; her right hand balances her cheek, her left a cigarette.

Her eyes are soft and full, perhaps with the recollection of great promise—a scene, a moment, a painting she once saw.

The model is Ellen Andrée, an actress who appears in a number of Impressionist works, including Degas's *L'Absinthe*, in which she reprises her role as a desolate woman slumped in a café banquette. With her hooded eyes, curved nose, and small, pursed mouth, Andrée was more striking than beautiful. Her aspect balances fineness and yearning with pride, solidity, and self-possession. In the Manet and Degas paintings especially, Andrée carries a certain knowledge of herself. It penetrates with self-consciousness the various roles she must play at once: the fading feminine ideal, the disappointed romantic, the woman as herself and as public spectacle, the muse. She appears, in other words, quite modern. Though she lived a notably independent life, the revolutionary aspect of the works that feature her and of Impressionism in general was apparently lost on Andrée. She preferred painters who favored the old ways: long brushstrokes, clean lines, formal compositions, classic subjects, an elevated style.

A century and more later, the Impressionists enjoy permanent exhibitions in the world's great museums. I see in my mother's passion a recognition of the way they reflected an essential tension in her life: between the pull of the traditional, the splendid; and the urge—the imperative—to see the world anew. The lushness, the colored light and romantic beauty that animates so much impressionist work bears with it an immense loneliness. The state of in-betweenness it suggests is at once sublime and untenable. At the Art Institute of Chicago a pair of rough, enigmatic Degas portraits of Andrée sit in the archives. We missed her on the walls.

After the divorce, my mother took the black-and-white portrait of herself, age twenty-two, that hung for decades above my father's dresser. She left *The Plum*. I spent the summer before our Chicago weekend starving and reading the complete Austen while sprawled on my parents' old bed, presided over by the painting's lonely, forsaken subject. It was, I thought then, a bit much. When I asked my mother about the Manet print many years later, she just shrugged.

"I felt like her at the time," she said.

WHEN SUSAN SONTAG ARRIVED in Chicago, in the fall of 1949, it seemed she had conquered her dread of leaving home, and specifically of leaving her mother. "How I long to surrender! How easy it would be to accept the plausibility of my parents' life!" Sontag wrote in her journal at fifteen. The more difficult choice—to enter the world, to become someone other than her mother—required a conviction Sontag couldn't name. "I can feel myself slipping, wavering—at certain times, even accepting the idea of staying home for college," Sontag writes. "All I can think of is Mother, how pretty she is, what smooth skin she has, how she loves me . . . How can I hurt her more, beaten as she is, *never* resisting? How can I help me, make me cruel?"

Sontag did leave, and for her single semester at Berkeley was close enough to home to make weekend visits. She describes one of those weekends with awe: "I felt in myself a further emotional emancipation from what I—intellectually—find flawed—I think I am finally free of my dependence on/affection for Mother—she aroused nothing in me, not even pity—just boredom."

Rather than an act of cruelty, for Sontag, leaving her mother, Mildred, was a source of exultation. After that first semester she resolved to move even farther away, enrolling at the University of Chicago, where she completed her bachelor's degree at eighteen years old. Within a year of her arrival in Chicago, Sontag met Philip Rieff, a sociology instructor ten years her senior. After three dates and two cheeseburgers, Rieff told Sontag he knew she was the woman he was meant to marry the moment he first heard her voice. Sontag was seventeen; they wed days later. "I'd never been called a woman before," Sontag said, reflecting on the event in an interview fifty years later. "I thought it was fantastic."

In the published diaries from Sontag's early life, mentions of Rieff are few. In the process of becoming that the journals document, marriage and even motherhood (Sontag gave birth to a son, David, in 1952) figure only slightly. Interspersed with and inextricable from her notes toward future work, reading lists, rule lists, word lists, aphorisms, and agonizing over various love affairs is Sontag's perpetual struggle with the question of her mother.

The liberation afforded by their physical separation, it becomes clear, was partial at best. Mildred emerges as Sontag's first audience, the first person for whom she performed, and whom she worked to please, amuse, seduce. In her diaries Sontag connects her intellectual tendencies and creative voice to her mother, the great love and unresolved drama of her life: "I wasn't my mother's child—I was her subject," she wrote in 1962. "My habit of 'holding back'—which makes all my activities and identities seem somewhat unreal to me—is loyalty to my mother. My intellectualism reinforces this—is an instrument for the detachment from my own feelings which I practice in the service of my mother." She reminds herself to write to her mother—three times a week; every other day—and resolves never to speak of her.

When she isn't complaining of the way her mother manipulated fealty out of her younger self—playing weak, unloved, and even bored to elicit from her daughter a ritualized devotion—Sontag associates her "compulsive monogamy" and fear of being alone with her mother's absence and neglect. Certain passages adopt therapeutic language as Sontag returns again and again to the question of who abandoned whom. Having achieved epic literary success, in 1967 Sontag the diarist combines her usual mode of self-inquiry with a first touch of self-mythology, the drafting of an origin story. Entering her mid-thirties, divorced from Rieff, and exploring her attraction to women, at a professional peak Sontag bemoans a "feeling of discontinuity as a person. My various selves—woman, mother, teacher, lover, etc.—how do they all come together?" She blames this incoherence on her mother's failure to nurture her as a whole person, her tendency to compete with her daughter rather than encourage her.

Mildred's beauty, in particular, boggled Sontag. It was the only of her mother's qualities she genuinely admired: "When I told her how beautiful she was, I really meant it. And I was so glad, so grateful to be able for once to say something to her I really, wholeheartedly meant." Mildred Sontag's beauty also represented a faulty and reductive model of womanhood, a trap for daughter and mother alike. Sontag describes a morbid fear of watching her mother age, become less beautiful. The loss implicates Sontag, who felt both ambivalent and proud of her own beauty, the former because it tied her to her mother ("I hate anything in me—especially physical things—that's like her"), the latter because it afforded her a certain status, a smoother passage through the world. For a pillar of her mother's identity to fall, Sontag observed, would signify a failure for the daughter who grew up believing herself responsible for her mother's survival. In 1967 she wrote of herself as her mother's "iron lung."

I was my mother's *mother*. My ultimate project: to keep her
afloat, alive. My means: flattery, unlimited statements of
how much I admire and adore her, and repeated rituals
of denigration of my own worth. (I confess, to her re-
proaches, that I am cold + heartless + selfish. We weep
together over how bad I am, then she smiles + hugs +
kisses me + I go to bed. I've gotten unclean, unsatisfied,
debauched.)

Sontag reflects on her tacit belief that, in raising a son,
she would defy the patterned dysfunction between a mother
who would keep her daughter a child—subject to her same
confinements—and refuse her the best possible launch into
the world. To realize herself as a woman and as a person, "I
would have a boy-child—David," Sontag writes. "I would be a
*real* mother. And no more female children. This was a fantasy
about getting out of childhood, attaining a real adulthood.
Also a fantasy about giving birth to myself –I was both myself
as the mother (a *good* mother) and the beautiful gratified child."

In other men—gay men—Sontag would find a path to her
own femininity. She saw her preference for the company of gay
men as in part a matter of recovering or exploring the feminine tendencies she had suppressed. "Everything 'feminine'
is . . . poisoned for me by my mother," Sontag writes. Were
there a chance her mother would do a thing, Sontag would not:
"If she liked it, I can't like it. That includes everything from
men to perfume, attractive furniture, stylish clothes, make-up,
fancy or ornate things, soft lines, curves, flowers, colors, going
to the beauty parlor, and having vacations in the sun!" Sontag
frames her attraction to gay male culture as a clever if unconscious strategy. She found "a back door to some of those things
by becoming close to a series of men who admire and imitate

'feminine' things. I accept that in them. Therefore I can accept it in myself."

In her thirties Sontag cultivated an interest in art nouveau. She came to enjoy flowers, let herself dance and love beautiful clothes. It was not a matter of embracing in herself the inexorable, the essential, the "feminine" (a word she habitually pinches with scare quotes), but of refusing to further deny a wide spectrum of experience and pleasure to spite her mother. If anything it was this process—and not motherhood, married life, or admitting a fondness for pink tulips—that made her a woman, a person in full. "How different I was until eleven years ago: no flowers, no colors . . . no lightness of any kind," she writes. "The only good was work, study, my intellectual + moral ambitions, becoming 'strong' (because my mother is 'weak')."

From age fifteen through her forties, in her journals Sontag is Sontag: striking, precocious, obscure, indulgent, astonishing, obnoxious, tender, contrived, audacious, discerning, dull, aloof, vibrant, stark, sensual. In part the journals document what is evident in Sontag's oeuvre, the moral and intellectual ambition she describes above, and which especially underpins her critical essays. The journals also reveal an essential source of that drive, well concealed in Sontag's work, and thus propose an uncommon primal narrative—that of a woman whose tremendous achievement was impelled and haunted by questions of maternal legacy.

Shortly after Mildred's 1986 death, Sontag published a rare piece of memoir. In it she claims Thomas Mann as a founding influence, and presents a teenage pilgrimage to his Los Angeles home as pivotal to her development as a writer, her personal and intellectual coming of age. Desperate to leave home, Sontag was "within a few months of my big move, the beginning of real life," when she knocked on Mann's door. His work had moved her, provided the model she lacked. In it, "characters were ideas and ideas were passions, exactly as I'd always felt." Having found a hero in Mann, Sontag set out on a kind of hero's journey of her own.

In L.A., she discovered that to meet one's hero is embarrassing above all. Sontag reframes the encounter's awkwardness (Mann was stiff in the role of mentor, speaking in aphorism and "sententious formulas") as central to its ultimately liberating effect. Thinking of it, Sontag writes, "I still feel the exhilaration, the gratitude for having been liberated from childhood's asphyxiations. Admirations set me free. And embarrassment, which is the price of acutely experienced admiration."

Sontag treats Mildred, who appears only briefly in the essay, with the opposite of admiration. She describes her "morose, bony mother" as a woman without appetites, the "peripatetic widow." Sontag's father, Jack, a furrier based out of China, died of tuberculosis when Sontag was five. Mildred, who was also involved in the business and spent a good portion of Susan's early years overseas, lied about Jack's disappearance from their lives at first, then amended his cause of death to pneumonia, which carried less stigma than TB. Her husband's death meant the end of their lucrative business and of Mildred's high-stepping life. Domesticity didn't suit her: on her own with two daughters, Mildred came to rely on alcohol. She moved the family to Miami and then Arizona in an effort to calm the young Susan's asthma. In Tucson Mildred met and married Nat Sontag, and the family moved again—to California.

In fashioning her creation myth, Sontag presents the burgeoning female artist's mother as a figure of no importance, to be cast aside with impatience and extreme prejudice. Yet it was a subject Sontag returned to compulsively in private. In her memoir, *Sempre Susan*, Sigrid Nunez describes Sontag talking of her mother so often, "and with so much feeling, that her mother would become almost mythical: a cold, selfish, narcissistic brute of a woman, who never showed Susan any affection, who never encouraged her gifted daughter, who appeared not to notice she *had* a gifted daughter." The themes of neglect and abandonment prevailed: "Over and over we heard it: *My mother never cared what happened to me. My mother was never there for me.* It might as well have been yesterday. A wound that never healed." Perhaps the artist Mildred helped forge was bound to erase her mother from her work. Better to trespass at will; knock on strange doors; cultivate models from a safe and admiring distance; give birth to yourself as a dispassionate intellect too rare and too pure to be denied.

Toward the end of her life, Sontag declared herself bored with the essay. Having encouraged what she described in a 2000 interview as her "insufferable moralism," the form as she conceived of it had become a sort of trap. In fiction she could be free, finally write with abandon. Nonfiction's sub-ranking in the literary hierarchy—an attitude that prevailed across Sontag's lifetime and which she shared—rendered her status as a titan of the genre a sort of booby prize. But Sontag is persuasive when she describes her disenchantment with the essay, which had powered her hero's journey to the center of the culture only to strand her there. The terms on which she defined the form were uncommonly strict; too rigid, finally, to complete Sontag's passage, and carry her home.

IN THE HOME she made with Frank, my mother hung no Impressionists. Her tastes evolved and clarified. She developed a love for the Canadian painter Mary Pratt and began collecting her work—prints and originals. Born in New Brunswick in 1935, Pratt painted what my mother called "homey stuff."

She texted me in a rapture on returning from a 2014 Pratt exhibition. A painting of a roast turkey—captured as it neared perfection in the oven—had brought her to tears. "Weird eh?" she wrote.

Funny how such simple things
can define generations.

A painting of a turkey made
you cry?

I said it was weird

Also another one covered in
tin foil

To be clear the first one was a
turkey roasting that was being
basted

I remember Grandma doing that

I mean it wasn't just a naked
turkey. I certainly wouldn't cry
at that

You can google it and see if you
cry

You just might

I . . . kind of doubt it

Really?

Maybe you had to be there

No, I don't think a turkey
would make me cry

It's really beautiful

During the talk that opened her solo exhibition, Pratt said
the work of other artists, including Canada's Group of Seven,
had no influence on her. Her vision derived from a more direct
and sacred engagement with her immediate surroundings. At
almost eighty Pratt was digressive and wry, telling practiced
stories plump with self-drama. Though she left her native New
Brunswick very young, of her origins she had no doubt. Though
her father's world of politics interested her only vaguely as a
girl, "what I was not naive about was color, and what I thought
was beautiful. I knew what I thought was beautiful. And it was
within the four walls of my mother's house."

High on the exhibit, my mother talked of writing to Pratt,
as she had done to Norman Rockwell. She was hurt when several of her artist acquaintances disparaged the show, calling
the work banal and Pratt a second-rate hyperrealist—a cheater
who paints from photographs. Like Chuck Close. Like Vermeer.
Like Rockwell. My mother asked me if I ever wondered why she
liked Pratt and Rockwell so much. I waited for her answer but
she claimed not to know herself. The question was genuine.

ON THE NIGHT OF the Dialogue on Women's Liberation in
1971, Susan Sontag rose from a clamorous audience "to ask a

very quiet question." Appearing slightly nervous and flashing her disarming smile, she objected to Mailer's earlier introduction of Diana Trilling as the country's "foremost lady literary critic." Sontag herself, she said, wouldn't want to be introduced that way: "I don't like being called a *lady writer*, Norman. It seems like gallantry to you, but it doesn't feel right to us." In response Mailer claimed he had only sought to be precise, to distinguish Trilling as "the best *in kind*." The audience hissed. Rearing back in her chair beside Mailer on the dais, Germaine Greer wrapped her arms around her head.

In her address earlier that night, Greer had sought to dismantle what Mailer was there to represent: the myth of the great male artist. She described first encountering this myth when, as an aspiring teen poet, she read Freud's description of the great artist as a man who "longs to attain honor, power, riches, fame, and the love of women." She understood instinctively that men—especially men who are artists—are loved for their achievements, but "all too soon it was very clear that the female artist's own achievements will disqualify her for the love of men, that no woman yet has been loved for her poetry." Where Sontag's objection hinted at a vested interest in the established order—who gets to be serious, unmodified, enshrined—Greer wanted to burn the whole thing down. Rather than a competing female or gender-neutral mythology of the artist, Greer envisioned a revolution whose effect would be, in part, to make art "the prerogative of all of us." She further suggested that a post-feminist future is by definition post-mythology, even post-individual. The artists of this future will work "as those artists did whom Freud understood not at all, the artists who made the Cathedral of Chartres, or the mosaics of Byzantium—the artists who had no ego, and no name."

The crowd cheered.

Elsewhere in the same speech, Greer invoked Sylvia Plath, repeating a popular legend about Plath conceiving her best poems in the kitchen, while baking bread. "She was such a perfectionist," Greer muttered, to mild laughter. "And ultimately such a *fool*," she spat, to uncertain applause. That night and across the decade that followed, it appeared many avowed feminists had no idea what to do with the foremost poet of their generation.

Sitting in the Town Hall audience, Elizabeth Hardwick was that spring preparing an essay on Plath, an artist whose fate and themes she would argue are intertwined, "and both are singularly terrible." Hardwick resists the impulse to read the American-born Plath's suicide in her London flat as a womanly tragedy, or any conventional sort of tragedy. Rather, in Plath's work suicide is the means to "a grand performance . . . an assertion of power, of the strength, not the weakness, of the personality." Unflinching and free of sentiment, Plath "always seems to be describing her self-destruction as an exhilarating act of contempt." The poet's tragedy is "completely original," a story without straight lines, lacking history or precedent, out of time and distinctly of its time, as Plath seemed to be. It resists settled opinion, as Hardwick herself makes plain. "I don't see the death as a necessity for the greatness of the work," Hardwick wrote in 1971. "Quite the opposite."

Three years later, prepping the essay for inclusion in a book of collected works, Hardwick revised her position on the relationship between Plath's suicide, her work, and her legacy. Believing the author alive and well while reading *Ariel*, Hardwick argues in a previously unpublished passage, the poems are still excellent, even genius, "but they are obscured and altered. Blood, red, the threats do not impress themselves so painfully upon us." If Plath's suicide was not essential to "the passion and brilliance of the poems, nevertheless the act is key, central to the overwhelming burst of achievement."

> To imagine anyone's taking his life as a way of completing, fulfilling, explaining the highest work of a life may appear impudent, insulting to death. And yet is it more thoughtful to believe that love, debts, ill health, revenge are greater values to the human soul than creative, artistic powers? Artists have often been cruel to others for what they imagined to be advantages to their work. Cruelty to oneself, as the completion of creation, is far from unimaginable, especially to a spirit tempted throughout life to self-destruction.

One senses a response to Greer in this, and to what Hardwick saw as the (implicitly feminist) "sentimentalization of [Plath's] own ungenerous nature and unrelenting anger." In Hardwick's imagining, Plath is merely human, nobody's victim, and hardly a fool. She is also the roaring, mythic creature Greer once wished to be, though the transformation required that Plath leave her own husk behind. In the guise of a corrective to the metaphors, allegory, and bathos threatening to consume Plath, Hardwick put forward yet another story, one that held the great poet above the worldly concerns of romantic abjection, misogyny, and women's domestic oppression. In Hardwick's rendering, Plath is above all an individual, independent of history, subject chiefly to her genius, representative only of herself.

Greer ended her talk with the revolutionary vision of a collective of nameless, egoless artists at work. Cutting through the cheers that followed with the sort of precision strike he seemed to manage despite himself, Mailer dismissed the notion of an arts and culture improved by communist ideals: "The means you offer—and in fact that Women's Liberation offers—to go from here to that point where we will be artists all, belongs to a species of social instrumentality that I call *Diaper Marxism*." Greer's answer to the loathsome hegemony of the Great White Male Artist, who for centuries has squatted fat and well-fucked at the center of the culture, was to dismantle the very notion of individual greatness. Different versions of this idea colored mid-century feminism, which in its fight for equality sometimes trafficked in theories of equivalence. As though it were necessary to see men and women—or anyone and anyone—as no different in order that they might be treated the same.

Greer prevailed at the Town Hall less on the merit of her ideas than on the force of her personality. As much as anything else, the moment called for a swaggering ego, a goddess, an individual—and she appeared. In an essay published a few months after the event, Greer recalled her ecstatic reception, a moment that formed the pinnacle of her influence and power within the feminist movement: "Why did those people applaud, I wonder," she wrote. "For they cannot have accepted what I said."

IN THE WEEKS BETWEEN her February hospitalization and the one that followed in March, my mother got hooked on *Call the Midwife*, a BBC series about a 1950s-era cohort of nuns, nurses, and midwives in London's East End. The stories of intrepid women working to support each other proved an addictive comfort, plus she knew all the songs. She had begun fantasizing about a movie she could watch all day and night, a world into which she might disappear. Debilitating tension headaches and severe neck pain now struck each morning, a result of her constant struggle to breathe. Often it was mid-day before the headache cleared, leaving her spent for the day. "Everything looms so large," she texted me one of those nights. The thought of the next day's rehab session filled her with dread.

Takes me so long to dress

I am such a wuss

                                   I'm sure it feels overwhelming

                                   Be patient with yourself

                                   You're not a wuss

                                   You're extremely tough

I feel so vulnerable

Like a cold could do me in

Like I have no reserve

                                   Well we have to build that up a bit

And when I'm resting I feel I should be exercising

                                   It's a balance, you need to rest and you need to exercise

Those are your two big tasks

I wish I had a magic wand

Sharp chest pains brought her to the ER two nights later, where a CT scan revealed a clot in her right lung, and another possible pneumonia. She had one IV for blood thinner and another for a new antibiotic; nebulizers became part of her daily therapy. After two weeks shuttling between wards a bed opened in respirology, where she belonged. Soon after my arrival in Toronto, my mother asked that I send an email she had drafted on her laptop at home, a note to her golf cronies announcing her medical leave from the club's summer season. The language was discreet, allowing for the possibility of her return. She had given me room to opt out of that month's visit, saying I needed to write, but we both knew I would come. As had become her habit, in the hospital she mobilized, blasting emails all day, organizing, giving orders, making plans. Her role as the principal around which human and other resources were gathered twitched a fallow instinct back to life. In those weeks she told me the story of her boss at Canada Trust, the crack about eating bonbons, the executive with the huge college ring.

At St. Mike's one evening I asked about her second long stay on the same ward almost twenty years before. Having just signed on as CEO of a newly formed federal savings and investment program, she had spent the spring and summer launching a massive sales campaign. Pitching bonds and treasury bills as the good citizen's way to save, she focused her efforts on women and youth. Described as a "single mother of two" in a magazine profile titled "The New Bond Girl," she smiled gamely above a fanned-out stack of bonds; she wanted "to make savings weird and cool" to kids. Then minister of finance and eventual prime minister Paul Martin sometimes joined her on the road during her months of cross-country travel. The campaign took a toll; a virus lingered. I wondered whether she finally went to an ER, or made a doctor's appointment, or was carried off in an ambulance. She couldn't remember. "But we raised five billion!" she said, making the squinty face of someone laughing at her own joke.

I couldn't remember either. I spent the same year organizing my time around third-year university classes and the ongoing punishment of my body. When they weren't ruining my life, the disciplines I imposed on myself—running for hours each day, restricting food—felt like perfection, a way to force freedom and control into a viable balance. Isn't that what a person must do?

I made one visit to St. Mike's that fall, bearing magazines and candy. I remember corridor walls the color of decay and a tiny private room. Looking more sheepish than unwell, my mother insisted she was fine, a few days on the right drugs would clear things up. We were clumsy together. I didn't stay long. When she noted my tan skin, odd for mid-autumn, I reminded her I was outside—running—for half the day. Before I left she asked for help getting to the toilet, and I sensed embedded in the request a wish to lay out before me what we had tacitly agreed to ignore. I wore a short-sleeved shirt—too small, no coat—for the same reason. I owned little then, and aspired to less, going through winter in only a windbreaker and cheap oxfords, as though even protection from the cold expressed too vulgar a need. Clinched together, we shuffled a few feet to the bathroom. The weight of her arm on mine was unnatural; I was seized by a strange fear of our hands touching. Despite looking more or less like herself, she was feeble, unable to stand on her own. As she took hold of the bathroom railings I saw she was naked underneath her paper hospital gown, which hung open at the back. Had no one brought her some clothes? Hadn't I?

On the subway home, the full weight of a force I had been outrunning through the streets of London and Toronto came to rest on the back of my neck. It traveled down my spine, folding me forward, and settled in my chest. For the length of the ride I sat in my body as I had not for several years. I sat in the world, unbridled, and with my head in my hands began to sob.

# Nine

THAT SUMMER I received a summons, via text, to my mother's bedroom, where I found her sitting up in bed with her legs extended, one under the covers, one on top. She asked me to search her closet for a black leather portfolio case and watched as I pulled it out, then placed it on the bed, across her lap. It was evening; the bedside lamp had turned half the room a yellow gold. Together we considered the leather case.

"It's Bottega Veneta," she told me. "I bought it in a consignment store in Yorkville for five hundred dollars, it must be at least twenty years ago." She stroked the woven leather and asked what I thought. I said it was beautiful. "It always made me feel special," she said, then searched for a better word: "bulletproof." "I would carry it into meetings, under my arm, like: *ka-pow*."

Our visit had not been going well. The promise of summer, when Toronto's roads clear and the city quiets, intensified my mother's sense of confinement. Spring had brought enough respite to make plain how limited her new life would be. My arrival had been delayed by a bout of what I insisted was bronchitis. After about ten days, what started as an un-usually bitter cold led me to the nearest ER, where my report of growing sicker each day and more breathless at night drew faint concern. I had no fever and my lungs sounded clear. "My mother has end-stage lung disease and no one knows why," I told the ER doc. "Please just take the X-ray."

I arrived in Toronto to find my mother's anguish grown thick. After a handful of lilacs caused a violent coughing fit, flowers were no longer allowed in the home. A shower spent her energy for the day. Along with the air hunger, severe muscle pain continued to grip her body. In the mornings she hung her head as I stood massaging her shoulders. The magic-escape-hatch fantasies grew more elaborate: flying carpets, spar-kly wands. *"Boom."* She waved an imaginary wand over me. "You're a princess." Then wanded herself: *"Boom!* You have a perfect lung." In her neck bands of sinew rose and fell under my fingers, playing a nameless tune. When I pressed on a thumb-size knot she groaned and spoke into her chest: "I promise in my next life I'll be a better mother if you make me well."

She obsessed over her pulse oximeter, the numbers it re-turned. Frank and I took turns running to the compressor outside the bedroom—jacking her oxygen up to six liters, then down to four, then back up again. A portable, personal electric fan required constant adjustment. An actual cowbell sat on the floor beside her bed. Her bed pillows multiplied, often supple-mented by rolled towels. The more baroque their arrangement, the worse the day at hand.

"Ask me anything and I'll answer," my mother had said as we sat at her den's round table earlier that day. Outside the window, the CN Tower's lance tip flickered behind a veil of passing clouds. "Go ahead, I'm still compos mentis. Ask me." She was slumped in her chair, her folded hands on the table.

My questions that week had mostly to do with what I could make that she would actually eat, whether she was ready for her next walk, or nebulizer session. Focused in that moment as in all others on the minutia of daily survival—of maintaining the ground we still had—rather than answer it I wondered what her invitation might mean. My mother continued looking at her hands. "I'm tired of this," she said in a small, high voice. "I want to go back to being a person."

The portfolio case was a crowd-pleaser, she told me that night—even men made comments. "I always told myself, you get to have one of everything in this life," she said. Even the very fancy things: Armani, Movado, Chanel. In her experience, having one settled the question of having one. That was enough. I didn't ask: Enough of what? Enough how? The relief of seeing her in a peaceful state, almost relaxed, was intense. She ran her hand along the zipper with a coy look. "It's a good case for a manuscript," she said.

"Hm," I said.

"A *man-u-script*."

"Hm."

"Would you like something like that?"

"It's gorgeous," I said, performing an appreciative inspection, turning the case over and tracing its fine leather ridges. It *was* beautiful; too good for me. I didn't want to carry it out of the room, away from her.

"Take it. Use it in good health."

"Are you sure?"

She said she was.

IN JAMAICA KINCAID's 1985 LYRIC NOVEL *Annie John*, across eight slim chapters the titular character, a young Antiguan girl, ages from ten to seventeen. Early on, her mother's love makes a sort of paradise for Annie John, who lives enfolded in its safety. But the daughter's adolescence brings a cooling of her mother's heart. A shadow enters their relations. They become obscure to each other, possessors of a corresponding darkness that seems to operate outside their control. The narrator describes the tension between herself and her mother this way: "I could see the frightening black thing leave her to meet the frightening black thing that had left me. They met in the middle and embraced."

Their bond remains occult, its beatific harmonies replaced by the threat of mutual obliteration. When the narrator is fifteen, *Annie John* becomes a ghost story. Having been branded a slut by her mother for talking to young men in the street, Annie John contemplates the wooden trunk in which her sixteen-year-old mother packed all her belongings when she left her parents—and their island—at sixteen: "At that moment, I missed my mother more than I had ever imagined possible and wanted only to live somewhere quiet and beautiful with her alone, but also at that moment I wanted only to see her lying dead, all withered and in a coffin at my feet." At dinner that night her mother's presence appears doubled:

> Out of the corner of one eye, I could see my mother. Out of the corner of the other eye, I could see her shadow on the wall, cast there by the lamplight. It was a big and solid shadow, and it looked so much like my mother that I became frightened. For I could not be sure whether for the rest of my life I would be able to tell when it was really my mother and when it was really her shadow standing between me and the rest of the world.

A mysterious illness envelops Annie John at sixteen. For three and a half months she lies prone, her senses distorted, the world reduced to a rolling, hallucinatory tunnel. Time collapses; it rains nonstop. The novel shifts again, into earthly transformation myth. Having shaken off her illness as abruptly as she succumbed to it, Annie John is taller—taller than her mother—and speaks in a different voice. She emerges from the dark cleansed of a long list of homely desires—particularly for her mother's care, her cooking, her cadence, her touch. She resolves to leave, and at the novel's end is alone on a boat bound for England. In an instant, "The whole world into which I was born had become an unbearable burden and I wished I could reduce it to some small thing that I could hold underwater until it died."

THE SUMMER AFTERNOON when a power failure blacked out much of Ontario and the northeastern United States, I was in my final week of work at a provincial public broadcaster. Having been hired as an assistant two months before graduating from university, I went on to write for kids: web copy, game copy, educational programming. In those years I left my mother's couch and moved into my first apartment. I directed and produced and at least once played a cowgirl for an on-air skit. I traveled. I got monthly massages, all reimbursed by my benefit plan. It was a top-of-the-line low-stakes job, complete with iMac and lime-green ergonomic desk. I spent five years there, alternately passing time and plotting my escape.

It was an absurdly bright day for a blackout. Hot and blinking, most of working Toronto filed into the streets. With colleagues I lingered outside our midtown office. A homeless person directed traffic at Yonge and Eglinton. My mother, I knew, was aboard a Toronto-bound flight from Ottawa when the grid went down. My belated acceptance into a graduate program at New York University made the summer a shitstorm of logistics and bureaucracy. For the three-week interval between leaving my apartment and moving into the Brooklyn place I had sublet sight unseen, I was back on my mother's couch. After an hour or so of nervous bar patio toasts to whatever had just happened, I left my coworkers and joined the mass of people moving south on Yonge Street. Passing Davisville, then Mount Pleasant Cemetery, I turned right on St. Clair. Stepping inside the apartment I called for my mother. We appeared on opposite sides of her bedroom doorway at the same moment: standing stark naked, she told me to take off my shoes.

My mother made her first solo trips to New York City early in her working years. When she wasn't imagining a parallel life in Paris, she dreamed of living in New York. She returned from one of her trips with a poster of James Jebusa Shannon's *Jungle Tales*, a cozy bedtime scene which she framed and hung in my childhood bedroom. In the painting a mother, her face obscured and hair swept into a dreamy bun, reads to two rapt, nightgown-clad little girls. More than the image, the poster's origins, stamped across the bottom, enthralled me: "Metropolitan Museum of Art, New York City." The words had a painful glamour, even more elusive than the mother's face.

During a high school drama class trip to the city, I strained to hide my desperation from my peers, for whom little more than Times Square fake IDs appeared to be at stake. At sixteen, my inchoate desire—to become the artist I suspected I might already be—merged with a vision of New York. I worked my way up to confessing all of this to my mother, in much the same halting, mortified way I had asked, a few years earlier, for my first bra. She made it clear, in both cases, that my wishes were just that. About New York her doubt was laced with pique, as though any greater aspiration stood in rejection of the considerable advantage already accrued to me. Rather than aligning, it seemed our respective hungers for the world would exist in direct competition. Still in its first flower, my mother's was an ambition unto itself, its borders well-defended. Perhaps she recognized the flaw in my thinking, the confusion of escape with freedom, a place with personal accomplishment. Perhaps she saw in my drive to set myself apart, to acquire a vague yet certain status—to win—the long shadow of her own endeavor. Perhaps she confronted with sadness and some disgust the possibility that the most powerful tradition in which we shared was not our own.

For the moment, being on my own left me nowhere. I chose to postpone university, turn west and head for the coast. I cashed in my savings from a series of part-time jobs and sold a freshwater-pearl necklace my mother gave me—a sort of junior version, I thought then, of something she might like. She had made presents of other pieces through the years—a mini–gold signet engraved with my initials, a garnet ring—gifts whose meaning I tried and failed to appreciate. Intended to convey a sense of shared value—a wish of some sort—the jewelry came to represent our mutual disappointment. What I got for the pearl necklace didn't cover my ride to the airport.

My ill-fated exercise in rebellion squared away, the next fall I found myself enrolled at my parents' alma mater—with tuition of a few thousand dollars paid as a perk of my father's tenure—and installed in one of the two all-female dorms on campus run by nuns. My mother, who had lived in the other, proposed a trip to New York for the semester's first long weekend that October, just the two of us. It was a gift, and I was grateful, but our tour of New York's greatest hits had the feel of a consolation prize. Trekking through her itinerary, from the Met to the Brooklyn promenade, I had the sense of my mother standing between the city and me, both arms outstretched: keep it moving, the image said, *this is my dream you're passing through.*

We lit candles the first night of the blackout. On her balcony, my mother joined me for the only cigarette I ever saw her smoke. The endless paperwork, planning, and goodbyes had left me raw. Unsettled by her office's closure, my mother began placing calls at dawn the next morning. Sprawled on the couch that still bore my body's imprint, I woke to the sound of her voice—the one that dropped two steps, going flat at the bottom and sharp on top. A headhunter had advised her, during an early 1990s jobless stint, to speak in a lower register if she hoped to be taken seriously. The result was a flinty chest voice whose baseline marked most other people's top volume. Her big rounded tones and displays of lung power seemed to reach full expression on the telephone. During our years together the especially thunderous calls often brought me to her doorway, where I would make various "what gives?" poses as she continued shouting into the middle distance. I don't know what to make of the degree to which her authority sounded, to me, like anger; and vice versa. The admission is inconvenient. It is fair to say she had authority, and she was angry. Perhaps there is no connection. For her and women like her, perhaps the connection was inevitable.

Keeping her home and its belongings in order focused my mother's natural restlessness. If meticulousness was a moral good, it was also a means to constant frustration. I sometimes wondered if she chose white carpets as a measure of her own virtue. It was a test I failed throughout my student days. She complained bitterly of my lack of respect for the space she had worked to claim. I resented what seemed to me a condition of her perfected home: that my presence remain hidden, its evidence neatly stowed away. In this way, through my early twenties we remained locked at opposite, equally untenable ends of the question of how to live. I outfitted with my mother's old living room furniture and a single place setting of everything the three-hundred-square-foot studio I eventually rented for nine hundred dollars a month. To build an altar to my own loneliness, I had all I needed. My mother had forged her redoubt as a tribute to self-sufficiency and good taste, but also in accordance with a deeper instinct: that a refined, civilized existence would either conjure meaningful attachments or substitute for them.

In those years she threw a party to celebrate paying off the condo, inviting a dozen female friends. Dinner was served on her exquisite new china set; wine was sipped from fine crystal. At the end of the meal she stood at the head of the table and lit up her mortgage document; the other women applauded as it burned. I smiled too, pleased by my mother's triumph but aware that despite having spent three years living there, the apartment felt no more like home than the feral room of my own to which I returned that night.

Back together at the condo, in the weeks before my emigration, we restaged our old battle on more ultimate terms: both of us still lonely, frightened, suspecting we might have it all wrong. That first blacked-out morning, my mother followed her early calls with round after round of home inspection, the kind of ritual that takes hostages. Watching her whisk from room to room, a relentless blur of dissatisfaction, stirred a mean old ghost behind my ribs. More than I could remember needing anything, I needed her to stop. We faced off in the guest bathroom, where I found her muttering as she scrubbed at the vanity countertop. My face soap, she insisted, was causing her expensive soap dish to bleed color onto the marble, in the way of a not-so-expensive soap dish.

It felt so good to pack my bag, to fulfill the sense I had, in my mother's unusually bothered presence that August, of an almost carnal act of expulsion. She loomed as I pounded my clothes and her old bedsheets into a massive suitcase. Heat shimmered at the window, looking for a way in. The air we breathed was cold and dry. She was yelling, all her voices blending together, about advantage, and gratitude. She didn't think I knew what I was doing. She did not want to have to worry. I kept pounding, grateful for the feel of it, the power to act, and the familiar silence to come.

Within an hour I had checked into the closest hotel with a working generator, blowing a chunk of my moving budget. A week later, the grid restored, I packed a few relics from my mother's first Toronto apartment into a rented minivan and left the country alone. I abandoned the glass dining table whose successful purchase at auction she had taken as a sign, almost twenty years before, that she should stay in Toronto, continue on her path.

Rita's letter nearly beat me to my Brooklyn apartment. That first New York year especially, we were devoted correspondents. Having crossed a line that held great interest for her, I was rewarded with a steady line of chatter and movie ticket stubs, each one bearing a two-line review. Divided by a border and five hundred miles, we grew closer than either of us were to my mother. In her late eighties then, Rita drove herself to the Cineplex several times a week. Her meal updates, movie reviews, and the crisp American twenties she enclosed with each letter were unexpected treasures. Sitting in class, on the N train, in Washington Square Park, at the west-facing window of my Park Slope flat, I replied without fail.

In those same months my mother met Frank; the next spring they were engaged. Her first CT scan in four years revealed increased scarring in her lungs, the usual nodules and granulomas but also some lesions her doctor couldn't explain. She took notes on her office letterhead about mycobacterium avium complex (MAC), a bacteria that leads to infection especially in those with lung disease or weakened immune systems. MAC is in the air, the water, the soil; for most it poses no problem. "Very common," she wrote. "Not going to die; or shorten life." She filed the notes away in a folder much slimmer than the ones she had recently opened to contain her plans for a new life, a new home, a new wedding dress.

The next summer, I crashed back into my mother's apartment for a few weeks. My first ten months in New York had yielded little more than a grisly love affair. One evening she left the small dinner party she was hosting and came to the door of the guest bathroom. Her knock took me by surprise, as did the readiness with which she joined me on the floor, where I wept for about twenty-eight years. My mother put her arms around me, and was quiet.

"You're tired," she said finally. "You need to rest."

THE TIMING OF MY ARRIVAL in the United States seems ideal in that it could hardly have been worse. Two years before, a month after the 9/11 attacks, my mother and I rode into Manhattan like pilgrims from a distant past. She had offered to join my rebooking of a solo trip originally scheduled for a few days after September 11. That October we peered out the taxi window, crossing the East River into the upper Fifties, where the streets were hung with flag after American flag. In a gilded shop window beneath one of them sat a toilet that appeared to be made of gold. My mother shook her head, murmuring about the fall of Rome.

Rome fell again and again in the years that followed. For a period of time it was unclear whether this progression was unique or I had simply not been paying attention. An early life spent backstroking through American culture, media, and cereal had sparked little interest in the nation's history, its systems and mythologies. We weren't taught the great American writers. Despite years of watching affiliate channels out of Erie and Cleveland, I could not locate those cities on a map. For much of my childhood I imagined the White House somewhere south of Vancouver. Some part of this apathy must have sprung from a position of relative privilege: I grew up white and middle class in a free, peaceful, progressive country. We didn't need to look elsewhere for a dream of democracy, plurality, and self-determination. We looked to the United States in part because it never looked back.

The outsider knows America first, if not best, as a feeling. For Canadians especially, bound up in that feeling is the shame of unrequited energies, of remaining unseen. Visits with my American cousins gave this sensation a worldly presence: to me they appeared fed by confidence, grown from it like beets in rich soil. They beamed with the same easy purpose my mother noticed when, as a freshman, she encountered her first Americans on campus. You could spot them at a distance—the ones always belly laughing, signing up for everything, forever leading the way. Canadians recognize the qualities that offend us—hubris, love of money and violence, a certain high-spirited oblivion—as the same ones that can make Americans so much fun. The attraction is itself a source of annoyance.

It must have been different when my paternal great-grandfather sailed from Calabria to the shores of New York in the nineteenth century's last decade. For him, perhaps, America-the-feeling was a purer form of knowledge, one whose imaginative heft relied on a vast set of unknowns. To be American was to find specificity in broadly defined ideas: freedom, courage, happiness, success. His first experience of America-the-place was that of expulsion: having headed west, to Utah, he returned to Italy after work in the coal mines made him ill. It was on his second passage through Ellis Island that he decided to try Canada, where he eventually settled, opening a corner grocery in Northern Ontario. He sent for his wife and grew a family: two boys and two girls. The boys were educated, became doctors. My grandfather resisted his community's tendency, encouraged by his father, toward insularity. He would not trade greetings in Italian, or favor members of the tribe. Where his father was a peasant from an old country, he would speak a new language. But like bodies in too-shallow graves, familiar lines resurfaced: when two of his own children married Americans, his wife could not contain her grief.

Arriving in New York a century after my great-grandfather, I found a nation chasing the same feeling that had attracted me and my ancestors; a people adamant that it still meant something to be American, despite rabid disagreement on what that might be. This confusion was not native to the United States, or to New Yorkers, but an essential feature of the new millennium. The greater the scale of a collective belief, the smaller and sharper the fragments of its ruin. I staked an apartment, claimed a neighborhood, traced the contours of the city with my feet, but never shook the sense of having entered a place that no longer exists. This seemed at least somewhat a personal failure, a function of my own imagination's decay. Having finally planted myself in the soil I believed basic to my survival, I poured the better part of my energy into a vortex that threatened to whittle the significance of any physical space—of place itself—down to the chair I sat in and the device in my hands. If the city could not resolve or reward or otherwise provide a point of focus for my ideas about America, it was in part because I wouldn't let it. The more I understood how little I understood, the less I trusted the forces that had bent the shape of my life in their image.

Still, the city wrapped me up. So much so that the 2004 reelection of George W. Bush came as a rude and vivid shock.

I spent that first decade, especially, feeling both stranded in this abstract new world and pitched in a desperate struggle to stay. Success meant hanging on, resisting banishment, flying blind and backward toward a sense of home. Even more than my friendships, work brought me closest. I was nowhere more settled or more fused with my surroundings than when I was seated at my desk.

In the years after I scored a green card and before illness rooted her in place, I watched my mother move like a woman betrayed through the newly reopened Whitney Museum. She had little love for modern art, but the Whitney was a hot ticket that spring she and Frank came to town, and it was what we were going to do. From floor to floor, Willem de Kooning to Agnes Martin, she searched; she stood; she shook her head. In skinny jeans and a white spring jacket, she appeared to squint with her entire body. "Fraud" was the word of the afternoon.

Having left her native Antigua for New York City as a teenager, Jamaica Kincaid changed her name and began to write. "Clearly, the way I became a writer was that my mother wrote my life for me and told it to me," she once told an interviewer. "I can't help but think that it made me interested in the idea of myself as an object. I can't account for the reason I became a writer in any other way, because I certainly didn't know writers." The notion of a mother writing her daughter's life and telling it to her could hardly be more foreign to me, yet as products of a sort of opposite experience, Kincaid and I wound up in much the same place. Pacing through the Whitney, I grew protective of even the pieces that bored or embarrassed me. The museum's narrow white chambers felt like shelter one moment and in the next another form of constraint. In flashes I saw them as my mother did: a monument to art—of the clever but unbeautiful sort, adorned and codified by disgusting sums of money—rather than its habitat. Within the hour I was miserable, fighting wave after wave of defeat.

Frank eventually found me on the bench beside Chuck Close's massive portrait of Philip Glass. He mentioned a recent CT scan, new shadows on my mother's lung. It might be more scarring—it might be nothing. It might be something else. We were in the habit of sneaking such exchanges by then, smuggling and trading information like arms dealers. Down the hall I saw my mother, a figure in a scene of people and paintings and string installations, as she turned to head toward us. What more could I do? When was the next scan? What was the nature, the point of this indignation? If not here, where was art supposed to go?

THE BOTTEGA VENETA BRIEFCASE was one in a series of bequests that began the previous Christmas, when my mother presented me with a two-page story she had written that fall. It was a stroke of inspiration, she told me, that may have had something to do with the internet going out that day. The story, "Reflections on a Golden Bracelet," which she typed in bold font and tucked inside a gift box along with a bracelet she often wore when I was young, begins in the mid-1970s, with my mother's thirtieth birthday and my subsequent birth. She describes the period as shadowed by her sense of having slipped from the center of my father's universe: "I was in deep denial then . . . constantly and consciously trying to make things work. At the same time, unconsciously probably, I began building my independence." Three purchases serve as early markers of that process, beginning with a car: she went to the dealership alone, negotiated the deal, and took out a loan. "It does not sound like much now, but then it was huge—for me and for any woman I knew. Some of my friends still did not drive in 1975." Next was *Diego Sleeping*, the Jack Chambers print that hung in my parents' bedroom and then above my mother's bed in Toronto. One of several Chambers pieces she collected, it marked the emergence of a personal aesthetic. More than the purchase, the act of curation mattered: "I had little confidence in much else in those years."

Third was the bracelet. She had saved for it, determined to own something lovely. At Birks she chose a box chain of oblong, eighteen-karat gold links. She would wear it at every special occasion "and feel so proud." It was her only "good" piece until the diamond earrings in her forties, the ones she upgraded with each promotion. The time had come for me to have the golden bracelet, she wrote, "with all the love and meaning it had for me as a young woman." The story ends with a maxim, and a more general, second-person address: "Don't wait for anyone else to give you what you want, or need. You are perfectly capable of getting it yourself and it will have equal or more meaning for you. Love yourself always, and stay independent in spirit."

The story of my mother's relationship to things was one I thought I knew well. Equally familiar was the image of her emptied out at thirty, at the mercy of two little vampires. Any complaints I made moving through those same years, on my own in New York, prompted reminders of how good I had it by comparison. After a first, nervous skim of "Reflections on a Golden Bracelet," I refolded the pages and put them away. But it was impossible to turn from the bracelet, which I couldn't have described from memory but knew intimately on sight. Classic at a glance, the chain alternates smooth, tri-sided links with round ones bearing a faint, stippled imprint. The effect is a pleasing balance of old and new, delicacy and the suggestion of rigor, of something bold. The bracelet draped beautifully on my wrist, a gilded frame for the hand that is so like my mother's it seems a subtle witchcraft, a sort of trick.

# Ten

IN THE SPIRIT OF THE SEASON, my partner and I were fighting. Each day that autumn, it seemed, another high-profile man faced high-profile allegations of sexual harassment, misconduct, or abuse. And every night the rest of us had to find a way to talk about it. Conversations between men and women especially often stretched across a high wire. Willing or unwilling, it appeared we still lacked a common language, a way forward. Instead we watched each other. Women grew familiar with the dance performed by certain men: shock, then horror, and finally guilt over their own rather obvious innocence. In private spaces, public forums, and text bubbles on tiny screens, these men made elaborate theater of tending the line between them and the rest of this mess.

It was a moment of rage and relief, triumph and alarm. Having watched a searchlight sweep the darkness of a gendered world with pleasure, a woman might be dismayed to see the same light flood her life, casting her father, her lover, her mentor into shadow, if not doubt. She might understand the reduction of a man to his outline to be unfair, an impulse as hard to justify as it is to fight. She might feel for the first time an urgency to assume her own outline, to lead with a status she has always held at least a little suspect. She might accept the imperatives of progress—the role of generalizing in the war on generalization; othering in the name of equality; claiming an identity to destroy its power to define—and despise them anyway.

My mother was avoiding her p.m. meds routine the October evening that I slumped nearby, firing text after text my partner's way. Stationed in her den, she and I were each bent over our phones. Propped on one elbow, under the table where she sat my mother's left leg bobbed its nervous rhythm. On the couch next to her I was clenched near in half. The drone of the oxygen compressor down the hall enhanced our silence. The scene, the meds, my regular presence—all elements of what we had been instructed to think of as our new normal. Doctors used the phrase to reframe my mother's steady deterioration, to chapter off—if not normalize—the slow unraveling of her life. At this point, her team assured us, frequent hospitalizations were to be expected, not feared. Her ideal oxygen saturation now fell between 89 and 93 percent; anything higher and her lungs would trap excess $CO_2$. Along with flowers, perfume and candles had been forbidden. Often deployed as a palliative, "the new normal" suggests a more hopeful sort of progression than it generally describes. Hearing it made my mother flinch— the new normal what? As much as her ailments, she complained of a maddening sameness: days that melted together; hours distended by the constant fight for breath. Nothing felt new, least of all the succession of normals breaking like dominoes. The phrase's deceptions are obvious: each lowering of our expectations brought us closer to my mother's disappearance. But no one is above a good con, and we accepted this one with the understanding that in the end it would shred to irreparable bits the very concepts of newness and normality.

I threw the phone aside. Looking up, after a tired pause my mother asked what was wrong. I wondered myself. It had something to do, I thought, with the proprietary nature of grief, the question of whose it is to feel, and why and in what measure. It had to do, I told my mother, with feeling compelled to fan my partner's forehead as each grim new story rolled in, to play comforter, tutor, and audience. It had to do with the way his response seemed to push mine aside; his refusal of any spectrum that joined him and an accused rapist; the something so vast and pernicious it implicates him, me, and everyone goddamn else. It had a lot to do with the claim of perfect rectitude I heard embedded in his bewilderment. *Who knew? Who could have known?* Was I supposed to agree? Commiserate? Offer absolution? I spluttered words to this effect as my mother nodded, appearing thoughtful. Though we read the same appalling daily digest, the reports didn't send her reeling through her own history. She didn't tell the story—one I heard later, and not from her—about a presentation she once gave to a group that included the president of the bank where she worked, one she prepped for weeks and carried off without a hitch. Knowing she had done well, after wrapping up she lingered where she stood at the conference table, awaiting acknowledgment, perhaps a few words of praise. The president rose in silence, along with everyone else, and began to file out of the room. He leaned in close as he passed my mother, so only she could hear. "You smell *great*," he purred.

She didn't tell me, either, about the doctor who assaulted her during a physical in the weeks before she and my father moved to the United States. They went together to see the accredited physician, an older man. During her private exam he told my twenty-two-year-old mother to draw down her gown, then moved out of sight. I imagine the skin of his hands cool and papery as he cupped and fondled her breasts from behind. My father told me the story in the wake of my own green-card physical: my mother emerging from the exam room disoriented, mortified, unsure of what had just happened. The memory stirred in him a vestigial, indignant sense of his own impotence. When I asked her about it, though, my mother appeared perplexed, at once detached from the story of a young woman's violation and open to the possibility that it had in fact happened to her.

I withheld as much the night we sat together, giving the lock on the vault of my own abuse another spin. Buried elsewhere is the experience of telling: of a livid eleven-year-old convening her abuser and her protector to make a few things clear; of the simple, scornful denial that blanketed the room more swiftly and fully than she would have believed possible, right up to the moment that it covered everything.

We left aside, naturally, the men in our family with public records of gendered violence, the one who almost killed a woman and the other who did.

When my mother finally spoke it was of being chased across a field at seven years old. A boy was trying to kiss her, she said, and would not quit. She beat across the grass in a cold fury, he in a hot one, and on it went. She went hollering to her teacher, made a big to-do. I had a story like that: the boy who cornered me in our kindergarten class, the kiss he nailed to my cheek, the tumble I took rearing backward. The decision to file a stern complaint. I can picture us, thin-limbed vessels of righteousness, sure of our recourse. I can see our reddened cheeks, fingers pointed one way and faces another, tilted up at the women in charge. As with all the other wrongs righted in this exact way, it seemed with proper acknowledgment this one too would dissolve in the evening's bath. Yet there my mother and I were decades later, comparing twin imprints, a hot sting rising in our cheeks. I was reminded that evening how often it is that when women talk about men they confront almost directly the rages and disappointments wedged between them, the ancient ocean of things that remain not just unsaid but impossible to say.

MY MOTHER DIAGNOSED my first pneumonia over the phone. Thirty-two that summer, I had brought home from Scotland a cold that kept changing shape. Bored by its persistence, I would dress and go about my morning, then wither each afternoon. By evening the words on my laptop screen had sharpened into 3D relief, the letters beginning to sizzle. My chest hurt. My sinuses went solid in my face. At night, my body burned. I turned wet in my sheets.

She had been tracking the cold. When after a couple of weeks I sent an email that mentioned a resurgence of my symptoms, she called to ask about chest pains, cough sounds, night sweats, then demanded I head to an ER. The next morning, turned away from the nearest urgent care clinic for lack of health insurance, I made a slow, uphill trudge to Brooklyn Methodist Hospital. "My mother thinks I have pneumonia," I told the ER doc, eye roll implied. The part of the daughter harassed by her mother's care was unfamiliar but pleasing to play. I peed for a pregnancy test and posed for my X-ray like a criminal against a gray wall: hands up, front and back. In an exam room the doctor pressed a stethoscope to my ribs. "Your mother is right," he said.

Packing an inhaler and a week of antibiotics, two days later

I flew to Las Vegas. The man I was seeing considered pneumonia insufficient cause for a change of plans: just get here, he said, and I'll take care of everything. What was a lung infection compared to his suffering without me? It was early, overheated going between us. He was supposed to be the better choice, the one to carry me away from another preposterous affair. Of the unavailable men I seemed to prefer through my twenties, two had impregnated their wives with a second child during our involvement. The second time around even a moron could spot the pattern, and a moron did: the marriage faltering under the pressures of new parenthood; the man believing himself more cheated than cheater; the woman steeled against heartache and indignity; the younger woman feeding from an ill-gotten source, sure she is not the one being duped. And then the cluster that grows and grows: organs, bones, layer upon layer of sinew and skin. Twice I stepped into the blank outline that had dominated my girlhood, shading my understanding of womanhood and power. Both times I wound up longing only for the wives, the mothers—their stories, their forgiveness, an endless study of their faces.

My previous stay in Vegas was also my first. Seven years earlier, my mother had invited me to tag along on a business trip, share the free hotel room. Men were everywhere in my life then, and nowhere in hers. Our suffering over our respective situations was roughly equal. We did no gambling. I wandered while my mother worked. Wherever I went, men handed me promotional material for the porn convention in town. I sat among an Elvis impersonator's audience of four. I plotted several stories I would never write and bought a slinky dress I have still not worn. I discovered that getting lost on a single strip of road is not only possible but easy to do.

My strongest memory of that trip involves my mother's

personal laptop, the first one I had ever seen. Staring into it, at an email offering to publish my cold submission, I felt certain, in the way that was still possible then, that my life was about to change. If I did I don't remember telling my mother, only running to the lobby and placing a pay phone call to my dad. On the casino floor nearby stood a martial formation of slot machines, row on row; beyond them, a series of openmouthed storefronts. The soft denim blue ceiling was stippled with semi-convincing white clouds. Clutching the receiver with both hands, I strained to hear my father's voice, one ear pressed to the phone and the other to the breast of a wilding, many-hearted machine.

On my return trip I won big. At my boyfriend's urging, I played the slots. Standing beside a faded TV host on a game show stage, I tried not to pass out. My fever rose; the night sweats returned. I couldn't stop winning. The weaker I grew, the greater the returns. With each win my boyfriend got more quiet. We had once shown up for a movie date in matching Harvard Business School shirts—mine a gift from my mother—worn with matching irony. He also wrote, and was regularly showered, it seemed to me, with pallets of money. In my world only bills fell from the sky, including a giant one forthcoming from the hospital. He had just moved from one cushy fellowship perch to the next; I was freelancing in six different directions to make rent. On the night I shared a prize-laden stage with a young woman in a bikini, he thanked me for winning "like a man." I gave him half the money, bought us dinner at the Wynn. He asked why, when the TV host asked where I was from, I had said Toronto. I wasn't sure. I had lived in New York for four years by then. The more American the context, perhaps, the more Canadian I tended, or wanted, to feel.

In Vegas I went on two of the most ill-advised runs of my

life. First down the strip at four in the morning, before an early flight back to Toronto with my mother; later with a case of pneumonia. Both times I ran in a sort of controlled panic, growing disoriented and stopping often. Sensing a trap in the act of escape.

I FLEW TO SEE RITA several weeks into my pneumonia recovery, shortly after her relocation to Nova Scotia. She had an apartment in the independent-living wing of a residential facility close to her younger daughter, Jeannette. My mother and I met in the Halifax airport. In the year or so since the onset of Rita's depression, I had learned something of her history with mental illness, the hospitalizations and shock treatments; the weight loss and silencing of her famous volubility. I continued our correspondence, sending newsy updates in the old style but not expecting a reply.

Gripping the chair that offered her only safety, in Halifax Rita appeared both resigned and defiant, unable to live but unwilling to die. Our visits made witnesses of my mother and me; more than anything, it seemed, we were there to not look away. In turn Rita was riveted to our presence, which appeared to bother but also intrigue her. On her solo visits, Rita often greeted my mother by asking when she planned to leave. Excluded from the tension between them when we were all together, I would find myself oddly at ease. While Rita sat vacant, my mother would flutter with industry: doing, making, listing. Occupying herself—with the laundry, the groceries, the state of the good silver. The trimming and arranging of the flowers she brought ate a reliable half hour. Red roses were Rita's favorite, but she loved them all.

As a child my mother often picked wildflowers to cheer

Rita up. During one of her afternoon rambles, she entered the grounds of a Toronto convent with her eye on a fat lilac bush. Only six, she stuffed her fists with flowers as a pair of nuns approached, then made a failed attempt to disappear into the bush. She was caught a second time way east down Queen Street, at the juncture where the city once dissolved into woodland. Finding a paradise of white trilliums, she piled her red wagon high. Because it is rare and also Ontario's provincial flower, confusion has long reigned about whether and where one is allowed to pick a trillium. A passing woman scolded my mother, as the nuns had. "They're for my mummy," she protested each time, which was true. But for the length of those recovery missions, the beauty of the world belonged only to her.

The bad weather and flight vagaries a trip to Halifax involves became central to the experience of visiting Rita. A blizzard once stranded us at my aunt's apartment overnight. For the allotted time we had again maintained a faithful cheer, offered our presence, and relieved Rita's burden not at all. That night my mother and I sat on the pullout couch where she slept, listening to the wind and watching the windows cake with snow. I was glad for the extra time, bemused by the predicament. My mother was fending off a meltdown, checking and rechecking flights on her phone. Whatever had carried her through the previous two days was threatening to give way. She turned to me with widened eyes and spoke from low in her throat: "I have got to get out of here."

That weekend we had lingered at my aunt's table, where Rita joined us for a Sunday brunch. Despite her apparent vacancy she had followed the conversation closely, answering occasional questions on point. Before dessert was served, she rose to use the bathroom alone, something her daughters had not seen her attempt in many months. The dishes cleared, we were talking about keepsakes when my mother mentioned the pair of diamond stud earrings she had purchased on first moving to Toronto, and that marked her early years in the city. She found a jeweler she trusted, she recounted, and with each promotion and new job she returned to him to buy herself an upgrade. Over time the earrings got bigger, blooming in what for my mother became a meaningful succession. Describing this ritual she brightened, fine feeling textured her voice. Something about the story worried me; my hands slid from the table and took hold of my seat. She was a few pairs in the year of her business trip to San Francisco, where during an evening out she removed the earrings and put them in her handbag, only to forget the handbag in a cab. At this point in the story—the basic facts of which we all knew well—my mother's voice went soft and her eyes glassy. The rest of us looked elsewhere, embarrassed by her show of grief, if not a sense of our implication in it. It was less plausible, then, to consider the earrings part of my mother's attempt to establish a new life, to give herself what was missing: a sense of tradition, of things earned, cherished, and passed on. Unable to meet my mother's eyes, I turned to Rita, who looked ahead, her expression even more blank than usual.

WHEN I WAS TWENTY-ONE, my mother suggested I sit for a professional photographer, as she and Rita had done at that age. I would be glad when I was older, she told me, to have been immortalized in my youth. I resisted at first: by then the thought of posing for a camera gave me a morbid jolt. It had something to do with my mother, I knew, but also with a more general and growing dread of being caught, documented from without, trapped in whatever ironclad testament my image might provide.

This attitude inverted the one that came before. In child-hood photos I appear thrilled by the camera, delighted to find myself in any moment warranting its presence. I also obsessed over old family albums, spending a portion of my visits to Rita's apartment ritually unloading the photo-stuffed bottom drawer of a turquoise dresser. "I *never* look at those," she'd say, appearing both pleased and dismayed to see me back on the living room floor, puzzling through the same scrapbooks and envelopes. "But I keep them for you." By her seventies, Rita would happily pose for pictures, having shed all interest in what they represented, in the place of any one version of her along a larger spectrum. She was indifferent to the future and uninterested in the past; her self-sufficient existence comprised a complete, present-tense story. I never saw her lift a camera to her face. In the best photos of her from that period, she is alone and away from home. I once gave her a photo of us taken when I was six and she was in her mid-sixties. Her response, the way she flinched to see it, was my first indication of the depressions that pocked her life. "I can't look at that," she said, pointing to her image, the congealed expression she wears in lieu of a smile. "You can see how sick I am."

Her final silence enlarged Rita. The rooms she inhabited seemed to bulge with her presence. Shortly before she moved to Halifax, my mother took Rita to St. Peter's Cemetery in London, where they visited Latham's grave. Both of them forgot the way. Rita's silence through a chain restaurant meal afterward vexed my mother, who at one point started to choke on her food. Rita kept chewing, said nothing. She found it hard to talk, she said in those years. Rather than the words, she lacked the energy to arrange them out loud. She waited for respite, flow, the return. Did she know herself best this way, as a creature of limbo? Was her current predicament as recognizable as the grimace she wore beside her six-year-old granddaughter? Even if it persists for decades, can a state of suffering ever be considered normal?

If illness and the silence that long surrounded it were familiar to her, Rita bore her affliction in a posture of resistance. The image that returns to me of her final years is that of a ninety-five-year-old woman in an easy chair, small and mute, having breached a new century against the odds. She is stubborn and still waiting, gaze forward, toes pointed to the floor.

In the end I submitted to the photo shoot my mother proposed, just as I took the trips. She paid for a makeup artist and booked me in with a Toronto studio. I suggested black-and-white, offering an old image of my father's mother for reference. We'll make sure you look beautiful, the photographer assured me. I doubted it, but sat as still as I could, swiveling and tilting on command. When the contact sheets arrived I stole crooked glimpses at my own repeating face. The most flattering shots were the least familiar, and all of them revealed some unbearable quality of being twenty-one. Something about their number and minimal variation belied my sense of the image's absolute power, row on row of obedient poses giving plain form to pure evanescence. I couldn't picture any one of them framed and hung, third in a line of women; proof of existence, if nothing else. And so none appeared. I never showed my mother the sheets. I told her the project simply hadn't worked out.

WE WERE TEXTING about a friend of mine who was married, pregnant, and considering a job in a distant city. My mother asked if they were in love and I said I thought so. The money wasn't an issue; she would hardly make enough to pay for childcare. The husband would move with her, maintain the work that was their main support by flying to a satellite office each week. My mother was skeptical: Why risk something so rare for a job?

True love is everything

Everything

I stared at the screen. She typed on: for her a good marriage would have made all the difference. A loving home life and a little work on the side would have been enough. I said I didn't buy it: motherhood had bored her. She was already restless. Her true fulfillment—if not love—was in work and the recognition of her work. My father made us think she left for her career, she said, that she didn't care.

> I don't think he did that

> But isn't it true? You wanted a bigger career.

I needed to get out and support myself

After ten years out of workplace

So yes some is true

What I really wanted is a loving husband and kid

And a little work for variety

I don't know

I had it all but it evaporated

> Don't you think if you'd had
> that you would have wanted
> more?

Not much more

Not MBA more

Not move to another city more.

My mother inquired often about the money in my bank account, the number of my writing assignments. She had opinions about the length of my hair. True love and its relative currency had pretty much never come up. Finding marriage as inconceivable as I did at twenty-two, the age my mother posed for her wedding photos, seemed a matter of my good luck. The idea wasn't on or off the table but floating in some parallel dimension. I now see this as partly my mother's doing: intentionally or not, her example flouted the notion of romantic love as central to woman's existence. That this conspiracy has long been passed between women affirms its wild success. "You're smart, make something of yourself," Vivian Gornick has recalled her mother saying. "But always remember, love is the most important thing in a woman's life." It surprised me to learn of Rita countering news of her daughter's professional coups with questions about her suitors. I never heard her talk that way. Rita's letters and fresh greenbacks seemed to trumpet my ambitions, my lack of interest in a settled, partnered life.

Though I wonder now if she bristled to hear herself described as *independent*, as I do. If she objected to the misapprehension, believing it more accurate to say she didn't handle disappointment well, and sought above all not *independence* but to be free.

Two weeks before she died, appearing on a talk show in the summer of 1974, "Mama" Cass Elliot claimed to be done with marriage. She was into cohabiting, a preference she acknowledged might shock even women her own age. Her generation was bridging the gap between old and new, Elliot noted, which meant "half the women are evolved and half are liberated, and half will *not* be liberated." She would not be sad, she said, if her then-seven-year-old daughter refused to marry. The show's host wondered what Elliot's mother, Bess, made of all this. Fifty-eight-year-old Bess, seated in the audience, smiled a downturned smile in round-frame glasses and a short-sleeve print dress. "Well, I think it's dynamite," she said to a crash of applause. "I'm just jealous that I'm not living now."

Sometimes a story begins before the language exists to tell it. Bess and Rita's generation watched their daughters converge with a revolution. For some that beginning posed the threat of not just severance but obsolescence. What did it mean to live now, have it all, or at least have more than your mother did? Was a portion of Elliot's generation not liberated or unliberated but somewhere in between, and would they pass on to their daughters some smaller or larger fraction of that divided freedom? Janis Jerome suspects her parents will be less accepting than her children of her big career move: "If I take this job it might be harder to explain to Mom and Dad," she says. "They tend to see me as the dutiful, home-loving wife and mother. I think they would have great difficulty adjusting to me living in another city, away from the family. I'm not sure what they would think."

Several years away from widowhood and her own self-rule, Rita scorned her daughter's decision, perhaps seeing in it some garish expression of her own will to independence. It is tempting to look at Rita's early depressions as a turning inward of that will—the establishment, in lieu of other options, of a lonely island, where nothing and no one was needed or welcome. Either way: independent women, everyone knew, could not contribute, and therefore matter in the world. Less free than they might seem, they lived on hills, and only for themselves. Between the two women there was a clear winner—could her daughter not be content with all she had? Stung by Rita's reaction, rather than confiding the doubt in her marriage my mother put her head down, determined but ashamed, and on her own. If she was able to unleash and ride her anger out into the world, she did so unallied, having neither solicited nor enjoyed her mother's support. Confounded by her mother's depressions, my mother would point to Rita's perfect physical health. Rita remained bewildered by my mother's physically punishing turn in the business world. Each woman held the other responsible for their differences, which seemed to be a matter of wanting and doing too much, or too little; of wanting and doing at all.

Rita wrote me shortly before her final depression set in. In between mentions of a recent dinner with my mother, her upcoming Alaskan cruise, and "feeling a little down," she made an unusually blunt and personal observation, in line with the general downturn of her thoughts. "Jackie is not a great one to talk to me," she wrote. "Her life is so foreign to mine." Her frustration was mournful, the observation sadder for its generic, reflexive quality. It appeared to me mother and daughter never had so much in common as they did in those years: Rita had a man in Toronto whom she saw when she felt like it, a strong golf game, and a full slate of social and travel commitments. They had both experienced marriage and romantic love as obstacles to the self; had each sought and won autonomy at great cost. Still, a breach persisted, the sense of my mother's life not extending from Rita's but standing in rejection of it, canceling it out.

Eventually, my mother's life would expand as Rita's diminished, a growth that appeared rooted in having found with Frank a rare balance of independence and attachment. If I questioned intimations of her sacrifice on the altar of love and family, it was a gift to watch my mother defy the romantic abstractions that had warped her early life. It was more than that to bear witness to a love she was finally free to define for herself: it was everything.


EARLY ONE WINTER MORNING, my phone shuddered on the bedside table. In a staccato burst of texts my mother was describing a dream she just had, in which a strange woman she found in the kitchen of our London house said my mother had given her a key. My father was there, playing dumb, denying everything. They were both younger, in their forties. Then Rita appeared: though much older and slurring her words, she stalked the linoleum like a prosecutor, producing incriminating photos and a stained bedsheet. Panicked and humiliated, my mother insisted she drop it, that nothing was wrong. The whole thing ended "like a business case," she wrote. Like: What the fuck are you going to do now?

Sometime after she earned her MBA and before she became Janis Jerome, my mother ran into Rita in the parking lot of the hospital where she had just undergone a tubal ligation. In the wake of another hospitalization for her depression,

Rita was receiving outpatient treatment. The women played down the surprise, exchanging tight hellos. Neither spoke of her reason for being there. The encounter was brief but cordial. A bystander might not have guessed their relation, or sensed the skein of longing that bound them, tangled in that moment on the stretch of asphalt between their feet.

# Eleven

THE DAY I TURNED UP PREGNANT, I texted my mother first. Coming off another hospitalization, she was increasingly opposed to the idea of bimonthly admissions as a way of life. For her, decline could only be an ongoing disaster. "Decline," in fact, seemed the wrong word. Her body was a riot of activity: the effort to breathe now burned twice as much energy; her heart beat out a wild, punching-bag rhythm. The constant filling of her lungs with mucus required varying methods and degrees of violence to get it out. Her psyche, too, suffered constant paroxysm, grappling for a vantage that allowed for any kind of future, a version of herself she might recognize. The struggle for air was also a fight to reset the clock, leave this endless, spongy moment and reclaim the delusive relationship with time that is the first condition of any life considered "normal."

I snuck in the news between updates on her day. "Oh my," she wrote. After a pause she asked whether I had strong feelings, if I wanted a baby. I understood that I was pregnant in part because I had no idea, the subject had never come up;

and in part because although I bled each month and habitually dressed the part, I remained unsure what it meant to be a woman, whether I qualified, or cared to. My new normal involved a strict preoccupation with those questions, and a related, more casual relationship to risk.

Rather than provide an answer, early pregnancy upended my sense of time, carving from each day a distinct panel in a frieze with no clear parameters. Attuned to the passing seconds, the new pangs and twinges rewiring my body, I entered into an interminable series of calculations—the two weeks before I could see a doctor felt like decades; nine months was way too soon, next spring moments away—which seemed to continue in my sleep. My thoughts returned inexorably to my mother, and my work. How would I manage? Where would I find the energy, the money? Why should these questions be so difficult? What does a woman do?

I watched YouTube videos of young women documenting their pregnancies, the many things no one told them. I watched other videos, of dogs welcoming infants into the family home, licking their soft-spotted heads, guarding, mothering. Disinclined to pets, my mother expressed pity for my dog, but more so for the predicament of her kind. "Awful to be so dependent," she once said. When I tired of the baby videos I watched a few more. I avoided direct confrontation with my finances. I noticed an unconscious ticking of my head, from side to side. I conducted an intricate dance with my partner, who was scared and equally unsure how much energy the question merited, when we might treat it as more than rhetorical. Eight weeks? Twelve? I purchased prenatal vitamins in one browser tab, refreshing in another the schedule of a nearby abortion clinic.

In this period I came across a 2012 study out of Ontario's Queen's University. Along with the subtitle, "Interpreting the

Evolutionary Roots, and Future, of the 'Childfree' Culture," a few of its key words called my name: legacy, leisure, parenting drive, meme transmission, female empowerment. Undertaken by the biology scholars Lonnie W. Aarssen and Stephanie T. Altman, the study begins by noting a much-noted trend: women in developed countries are, on the whole, having fewer children. Popular explanations for this phenomenon often frame it as a matter of culture. A turn toward greater leisure, a self-focused lifestyle, and an increasing emphasis on personal freedom precludes the raising of hungry, greedy, selfish children. The authors wonder if there might be an evolutionary explanation, whether the decision of a growing number of women not to reproduce could be rooted in their genes.

As human consciousness evolved, they explain, so too did our attraction to legacy, the desire to cheat death, to leave something behind. Evolution selected for our subscription to the idea—or fantasy—that we "live on" through our children, that "the transmission of one's resident 'memes' into the future will confer an enduring legacy of the 'self.'" Nature would accept species propagation by any means necessary. As a side effect of this, there evolved a legacy drive that could be satisfied through gene transmission (where a sense of legacy derives from having kids), *and/or* meme transmission (where that same sense derives from achievement, the endurance of one's works and ideas). In a sort of evolutionary blooper, selection failed to distinguish between those who viewed their children as personal accomplishments and those otherwise accomplishment-driven individuals who happened to forgo children.

For much of human history, this was not a problem. In all its forms, *legacy drive* was expressed chiefly through the behavior of men, and men "historically have had widespread freedom to engage in both leisure and meme transmission through personal accomplishments, without compromising gene transmission." In other words, it has always been possible for men to have children *and* to satisfy their drive to succeed, to leave a legacy of thought *and* deed. At no point has it been necessary for men to choose between the two.

Women, by contrast, were long denied the means for any relationship to legacy. Whereas historically, "most men who became fathers did so only because they wanted sex or wanted to leave a legacy . . . most women who became mothers did so also largely because men wanted sex or wanted to leave a legacy." A woman's relative desire to produce offspring as a legacy or to experience motherhood was of no consequence in both practical and evolutionary terms. Those men who preferred not to procreate were free to express that choice, and selection in turn had the potential opportunity to disfavor the genes that might influence those preferences. "By comparison, for women historically, the same freedom and potential were essentially negligible."

Given the chance, across the last century, to pursue both leisure and a sense of legacy derived from accomplishment, and having gained some control over their fertility, the study contends, women encountered a conflict between the two drives. For the first time, women could express a desire not to have children, and/or a preference for memetic transmission. In turn, selection had the opportunity to favor or disfavor those inclinations.

To pursue the question of whether a woman's decision not to procreate might have genetic roots, the authors surveyed just over a thousand people, mostly university students, and—if only because higher education demographics now skew female—mostly women. They asked participants how many kids they wanted, and to rate, on a scale of one to five, the value they assign to things like financial wealth, fame, a successful career, and meaningful innovation. The authors found a negative correlation between a woman's desire for children and her interest in accomplishment-based legacy: the more children a woman claimed she wanted, the less desire she expressed for fame; the fewer she wanted, the more interest she had in pursuing innovation, new ideas and discoveries. In the men's responses they found no such correlation.

If the survey's results yield few surprises, the study soars in its interpretation of the data. A dramatic twist is buried in the second paragraph of the concluding remarks: Women are having fewer children, the authors propose, in part because they have "inherited genes from female ancestors who were not attracted to a life goal involving motherhood, but were nevertheless forced to endure it." The descendants of those women "can now freely realize the lifestyle and . . . goals that their maternal ancestors wished for, but were denied because of patriarchal subjugation."

In this scheme, lowered fertility rates are not only a female-driven trend, but the expression of a silent, ancient rebellion; a generation of wombs empty but for the avenging fists of our mothers, and their mothers, and so on. The authors warn that this moment is an aberration: if the expression, at last, of woman's desire for memetic legacy should curtail fertility, nature will quiet that expression; if selection has only recently had the opportunity to favor the presence of a parenting drive in women, the course is obvious. If and when nature can select for a woman's wish to procreate, *it will.*

Sometime between a first, exhilarated reading of this paper and my subsequent, closer scrutiny of it, the cluster inside me grew silent and slipped away. On a screen I saw ghost traces of a semicolon, embryo, and yolk sac; the right size but inert, just shy of a question mark. The medical term is a "missed" or "silent" miscarriage: although my body still believed itself pregnant, I knew, even before the ultrasound, that I was not. The doctor sent me home to wait, a stretch of days that proved worse than the purge itself. Were we in league—my body and myself, my body and that of my ancestors—or worlds apart? What had been missed, or settled? I found the whole experience aggressively devoid of meaning. Mostly it delayed my scheduled trip to Toronto, where I was again due to help feed, bathe, dress, and amuse my mother. Where I would eventually stand over her, still bleeding, and with cupped palms beat a percussive rhythm against her back, trying to draw the sticky poison, like a serpent, from her lungs.

To perform a proper chest percussion, each hand must hold a rounded shape, palm curved and thumb tucked up against compacted fingers. The tighter your dome, the harder you can strike the patient without hurting her. Doing it right reveals the sound and feel of a lung's more solid parts: the *thwack* becomes more of a *thok*. The aim is to break up the mucus, set the patient hacking into tissue after tissue. Lung physios brag about volume, measuring gunk in quarter cups. "It's like a dream, right?" my mother said one afternoon, lying curled on her right side to expose her ribs. "You can whack me all you want." I had to be coaxed into really going for it, but when my hands were right and the impact sufficient, my mother would make a satisfied noise. Many unthinkable things had grown commonplace over the preceding year, but I never got used to that sound.

The Queen's study appeared to me at once fantastical, spurious, useful, destructive. Another story, told in a strange language, to dubious purpose. Another tragedy in which women emerge as both victims and villains, destined for a brief stint as hero, only to be cast back on their bodies, their free will a delusion—doomed to overpopulate an already bulging planet. The young women in the legacy drive study claimed a desire for children that far exceeded the concurrent lifetime fertility rate for Canadian women. To explain the disparity, the authors suggest the young women may have been conditioned to believe they *should* have or want a certain number of kids. In time, the legacy drive inherited from their mothers would emerge, and they would have one child—or none—instead of the imagined ideal of two. Either that or nature has already set about correcting the last century's aberration, and is selecting for those women with a strong mother drive.

More than either scenario, or the data that inspired them, I was struck by the moment of decision: hundreds of young women speculating about their own future choices, in the name of science. In the survey's hypothetical space there is safety, containment, freedom from consequence. It asks only that respondents agree to its terms, reduce themselves, sit alone at their laptops and attempt to articulate, on a numbered scale, the wants and ideals of a person they haven't yet become. I think, of course, of those students who circled numbers in some parallel classroom, interlopers in the closed, speculative world of Janis Jerome, a woman forever on the point of decision, destined foremost to submit to the judgment of her lessers, the cohort after cohort tasked with predicting her fate.

"WHAT DOES A SICK PERSON DO?" my mother asked the day I arrived with a suitcase full of medical-grade Maxi pads. We were to spend the first week of my visit alone, giving Frank a badly needed break. They were experimenting with home-health-aide workers, and it wasn't going well. Bags set down, in my mother's den I found a young woman at a loss, unable to help

---

Michelle Orange

her breathless, agitated patient. In the bedroom lay my mother, exhausted by the aide's questions, the stress of managing a new hire.

She had a general way with medical and hospital staff. I had watched her work to connect with an array of nurses, the oxygen and physical therapists. She strove to a degree that surprised and moved me to be a good patient, amenable, deferential, at times, to a fault. I also came to worship the nursing and support teams, but navigating the larger system posed a constant challenge. The effect on my mother's condition of humane, competent treatment was profound; gaps in that care had an equal but opposite consequence. They could crush her morale, make it literally harder to breathe. As much as anything, seeing that difference radicalized me. Especially when a lack of beds left her bouncing around the hospital, I embraced the role of righteous advocate, hunting the wards for whomever had failed to check on her that day.

"You can play innocent," I said when my mother worried before one such rampage. She had been stranded for days in a chaotic step-up unit; I had arrived direct from the airport. "Just shrug and apologize for your bitch daughter from New York." She liked that: we had a plan. Having tracked the doctor down, I complained of my mother receiving no physio on the unit and only one of two prescribed antibiotics, finishing with a mention of the empty beds I had spotted two floors down, on his ward. I turned to my mother, who was cued up with a bashful smile: *I'm so sorry, my daughter is from New York . . .*

At home the role of patient posed a bigger problem. If the prospect of hospitalization made my mother miserable, negotiating dependence within her own domain proved impossible. By the fourth or fifth admission, it was clear she felt safer on the ward, relief from the existential burden of illness proving at least as potent as the focused treatment of its symptoms. The presence of a hired caretaker, who she dismissed for the length of my stay, only increased that burden. Alone together, we faced the spiraling of my mother's needs. Some days they overwhelmed us both. Entire mornings passed in deliberation of whether and how to attempt a shower. If it was agreed to, we might reach the edge of the bed only to sit there together, our feet planted and shoulders squared to the wall, for another two hours.

Such went our twelfth day together. Morning having given way to early afternoon, we were seated on the bed and facing the bathroom. After a long silence, finding it too hot my mother asked for help out of her robe, which she pressed to the front of her body. Worn and hungry, I found myself incapable of the patient cajoling that had made me a better helpmate than anyone would have imagined. I needed lunch, and would again have to forfeit the single hour allotted for my work. Forty minutes passed. When she signaled, I stood and moved to adjust the oxygen compressor, just outside the room. My mother called to my back, ordering a nearby pair of her shoes put away. I turned and reentered the room. "*Please*," I said, bending to pick up her flats and looking her in the eye. "I'm not the maid."

The comment, I knew, betrayed a central tenet of our new normal—that the use of my body as an extension of hers remain unspoken. Stricken, my mother demanded another pill. I brought it with some water and rejoined her at a further remove on the bed. More time passed; she began to weep. I moved closer, putting my hand to her bare back and listening in silence as she grieved—for the woman who mastered every task, got so much done in a day. The minutes again went liquid, collecting in buckets that poured into bigger buckets, letting off a heavy vapor that clung to the walls and filled our lungs. The effect was primitive, sucking all pretense from the room. I had only my frame to offer, next to hers, for as long as it took.

Eventually my mother admonished herself: stop, pull it together. To some extent her orders just externalized the litany of self-commandments that had always shaped her days. To a different extent, it seemed to me, the nature of her illness caused my mother to confuse being loved with being obeyed. At length, she rose on my arm to begin a thirty-second shower's intricate protocol. Wrapped in a robe and several towels afterward, she baby-stepped back to the bed as I wrangled the oxygen cord behind us. "I did it," she said, working to recover her breath. "Great job," I replied. Staring at the floor she repeated the words—"Great job." What they say to little babies. She shook her head. "Life is a circle," she said, nodding as if in recognition of a thing she had long evaded, the enemy that had crossed the street to position itself directly in her path.

At night, or propped in the shower, I hid myself. As if observing from a distance, I wondered that a person could witness real torment, sustained at such length, and find a way to live with it. It was quite a thing to imagine. That my presence often seemed to help enhanced a larger sense of failure: like my mother, I wanted to believe that if I could just arrive one more time, at the correct angle and in the right light, she might be freed. Never surer of the need for meaning, I had never been farther from its possibility. Our days together made their own answer to the old questions, clear and vital as my mother's fight, the feel of her embattled body in my hands.

Some nights I wondered about Jack Jerome, and whatever happened to him. Did he relocate after all, take the better job? Did he choose well? Was he (1) Successful in career? (2) Successful in marriage? (3) Successful as a parent? Did Jack Jerome ever ask himself whether he was any of those things? Did the questions plague him at night such that he couldn't breathe? Did he ever wonder how he might have scored, in his professional prime, on a seven-point scale between cold and warm? Caring and uncaring? Selfish and sharing? Submissive and dominant? Ambitious and unambitious?

Did he spend his working years driven to the point of collapse, and did his body retain the scars? Did he burn out, triumph, divorce, prevail? Did his life transcend, negate, exceed the hypothetical, and was the price of this transcendence his containment in a limited, physical form? Was he forced to reckon with the fact that not only did he have a body, he *was* a body? Did he question that idea as he watched a body much like his own—that of a father, friend, lover—weaken and fail, even as its spirit rose and clarified? Did he fantasize about a new body, of replacing its decay with a crust of gems and pearls? Did he promise his son that in his next life he would be a better father, if only the son would make him well? Did he wish to wake up from the nightmare of illness, and wonder if it was possible he had dreamed the rest of life?

Did Jack Jerome ever weep on a summer morning for being trapped inside, desperate to stride free, walk in the sun, be a person again? Did he indulge his child's suggestion of a meditation exercise to help calm him at night, and did it raise in him the memory of picking wildflowers for his mother, of standing under the tree boughs—tethered yet fully alone? And did he feel again the anointing play of sunlight through the leaves, the patterned heat on his face?

# Twelve

BY THE END OF THAT YEAR a palliative care doctor was checking on my mother each week. We were urged to greet this development without too much alarm, assured this most recent new normal was not about dying but improving the patient's quality of life. The doctor had started my mother on what he called "baby doses" of liquid morphine, intended to relax her airways and ease the increasingly brutal coughing fits.

We were supposed to be celebrating: after an eleven-month wait, my mother had been listed for a double-lung transplant, having nailed every test even as her body entered a new stage of failure. Her enthusiasm for transplant was never more than faint; the hope offered by surgery was counterweighed by risk. The wait-listed are subject to incredibly strict regimens of food, testing, drug therapy, and physio, intensifying a core injustice of lung disease by holding the patient even more responsible for her condition. The transplant candidate must be gravely ill yet strong enough to survive a colossal ordeal. Rather than buoy her spirits, news of my mother's addition to the list seemed to trigger a spiral: within days she suffered a partial lung collapse; the transplant team didn't notice her plummeting weight. Twice in the week after her release from the hospital, she asked to be taken to the ER. Both times she was sent home after being told, in essence, to calm down. But it wasn't just anxiety building: it was $CO_2$ narcosis, a toxic saturation of carbon dioxide that before killing the afflicted can make them quite mad.

I arrived late in the day before Christmas Eve, after a ten-hour drive out of a snowy disaster movie. In her bedroom I found my mother wedged into a fortress of pillows and rolled towels so elaborate her backside sat midway down the bed. During the palliative doctor's visit that morning, her list of concerns was topped by the fact that she saw her mother's sunken face in the mirror. An aide sat by her side, recording morphine doses and handing her a non-rebreather mask when she asked, which was often. Though it raised her saturation, the extra oxygen ultimately added to the $CO_2$ her lungs were too damaged to clear, worsening the crisis. How long would it take, she had asked the doctor that morning, if I gave up now?

The apartment was chaos. Frank and Jeannette, who had been with my mother for the three weeks since my last visit, appeared frayed and bewildered. When I attempted the usual presentation of food and gifts at my mother's bedside she barely registered my presence. Anxious about crowding, she had arranged for me to stay with a friend nearby, in the building where we had lived twenty years before. Setting aside the rebreather mask, she bent forward on her hands in what I recognized by then as the tripod position, a posture of distress. She raised her head to ask that I fetch her checkbook from a nearby bureau. With difficulty she wrote out a check, tore it from the stack, and placed it between us on the bed. Seeing the row of zeroes—fifty thousand—I asked with forced calm what was going on.

"I want you to have some of what is to come," she said.

"*Mom.*"

"I worked hard for it," she added, her voice sharpening. I looked at her. "People say: 'Oh, I worked for my family,'" she continued, as though rejoining a parallel conversation. "Bullshit! You did it for *you*. You did it for *yourself.*" Her shoulders formed sharp points beneath a thin black top. I was supposed to have a better life than she did, she said. Better than both my parents, though my father had more growing up, in terms of *things*. Invest it, she said, between quick, shallow breaths. Save for when I was her age. The room was dim, the curtains pulled but for a six-inch sliver. Despite a morbid allergy to clamor, Mercy sat fast at the bedside. I stood and put the check somewhere I couldn't see it, like a lie I had told and was hoping to forget.

THE PALLIATIVE DOC returned Christmas morning. My mother's oxygen kept crashing. I felt sure a new infection was afoot, that she needed an X-ray, perhaps another admission. He didn't think so, prescribed more morphine, and left. No one had yet mentioned the possibility of $CO_2$ poisoning. She slept for hours. That afternoon I arrived with shortbread made from Rita's recipe, my mother's favorite. She accepted a morsel, and after two hours broke off from that morsel a crumb. She was too weak to hold a cup. She wondered if it was Christmas and I said it was. We sat alone that evening, as we had the night before. After a long attempt at a meal of stuffing, mashed potatoes, and cranberry sauce, my mother lifted her head to ask what I was thinking about most "in life." I smiled and shook my head, turning the question back to her.

"You and your brother," she said, her eyes narrowed. "Money, whether you'll have enough money."

"You don't have to worry about that," I said. "I will be fine."
She looked intrigued.

"Really? You're going to be fine?" She turned away. "You've done more for me than I did for Rita," she said finally. "I know it's so tough. The paradigm is all turned around." I studied my hands, the oximeter on the bed. One of the few times I had clipped it to my own finger over the preceding year I got a perfect reading, and felt the urge to hide. "You're very beautiful," my mother said, studying me.

"Okay."

"Why did you never think you were beautiful?" I closed my eyes and held them shut, then stood to refresh her water glass. As I set it beside her a few minutes later, my mother lifted her head again. "I'm going to go at the right time," she said.

"What does that mean?"

"I don't know."

"When is the right time?"

"I don't know."

In the ER two days later, I found my mother contorted on a gurney, her mouth pulled down and to the left in an unnatural grimace. We were alone when a resident from the transplant team came by to say my mother would be removed from their list, ten days after being put on it. "We're *very worried*," the resident said, making a *very worried* face. A few hours later, a miserable Irishwoman stomped into the ER and with a hand in each coat pocket announced to the wall behind us that my mother had trapped too much carbon dioxide and would not survive. In the meantime she would be admitted to respirology, where a high-flow apparatus would ease her breathlessness and make for a more comfortable death. Transplant testing had confirmed the rest of my mother's body was strong, but she had lost ten pounds in ten days. I had arrived to find Frank despondent and my mother floating in and out of consciousness. After Jeannette and I convinced him to go home, the two of us flanked the bed.

"The Boyle girls are together," Jeannette assured her sister. But I have my father's name, and each of them had kept that of the man they divorced. "Meunier girls!" Jeannette amended, invoking Rita's maiden name—and ultimately that of another man. Having spent much of her adult life wishing out loud to die, Rita felt differently at the end. But my mother was ready, or at least she was through with being a sick person. "I don't think," she said carefully, "that anyone should feel this bad, for this long."

Hours later, I staggered out of the hospital into a slanted wall of snow. The cold was ungodly, the compliments of the season replete. The contrast of bedlam and stillness, black and white, dizzied the sky. Fighting to move forward I heard myself cursing: *I hate this city; I hate it so much.* The words repeated, an old passion doubling, unfettered. I set it free and filled with rage. Toronto the dread, frozen, sterile, *void.* Why Toronto, again Toronto? The place where I'm always headed and forever trying to leave. What do I want with a piece-of-shit town that has never wanted me?

I was very angry, for a long time, and she's sorry about that.

"NO BODY EXISTED less for me: none existed more," writes Simone de Beauvoir near the beginning of *A Very Easy Death*, her 1964 book about her mother's final days. As a provocation the sentence rivals—and stands in direct relation to—the more famous opening gambit of *The Second Sex*: "Are there women, really?" Beauvoir writes of her mother, Françoise, with cool fascination, alternating between character analysis and close descriptions of Françoise's decline from cancer. Where she must reckon with her mother not as an abstraction but a ravaged body, the philosopher's habitual detachment frequently gives way. Eventually even she seems to notice: at the end of *A Very Easy Death*, she wonders why her mother's death affected her so deeply, as though her opening observation had not made the answer plain.

Beauvoir had not expected to be shaken: "Generally speaking, I thought of [my mother] with no particular feeling." The maternal alienation she experienced as an adolescent only deepened with time. Beauvoir had no interest in emulating a woman who had been "taught never to think, act or feel except in a ready-made framework." After Françoise placed her in a convent school, Beauvoir for some time considered becoming a nun. When she began to move away from the Catholic faith, which sat at the center of her mother's life, "the silence between us became quite impenetrable."

As death loomed, however, Beauvoir spent days at her mother's bedside, "renewing the dialogue that had been broken off during my adolescence and that our differences and our likenesses had never allowed us to take up again." In one scene, Beauvoir's sister, Poupette, asks Françoise if she has regrets.

Maman laughed and said, "I always say to my grand-nieces, 'My dears, make the most of your life.'"

"Now I understand why they love you so much. But you would never have said that to your daughters?"

"To my daughters?" said Maman, with sudden severity. "Certainly not!"

Their conversations were welcome but limited in scope. It is the sight of her mother after a brutal surgery, "her face the color of wax, her nose pinched, her mouth open," that undoes her. Beauvoir shed no tears when her father died, and expected to greet the loss of her mother with similar stoicism. "I had understood all my sorrows up until that night: even when they flowed over my head, I recognized myself in them. This time my despair escaped from my control: someone other than myself was weeping in me." The image of her mother's twisted mouth—the humility, hope, distress, and loneliness the daughter saw in it—dissolved the differences between them: "I had put Maman's mouth on my own face and in spite of myself, I copied its movements. Her whole person, her whole being, was concentrated there, and compassion wrung my heart."

*A Very Easy Death* is a curious book, at once moving and austere, intimate and aloof. For all the time Beauvoir spends describing Françoise, the portrait feels narrow, obstructed, not just shaded but compromised by a powerful, unmetabolized bias. Though it presents a critique of medical ethics and overtreatment, and poses familiar questions about freedom and choice in the face of the existential void, the book stands as a primarily feminist text almost precisely because Beauvoir didn't intend it to be. In the most startling passages, she brings to bear on her mother's already prone figure the full power of her intellect and authority—in brief, obliterating displays of fury. She admits having kept her mother ignorant of her diagnosis, her status as a dying woman. Beauvoir notes with approval that Françoise, a woman whose "whole life turned on religion," showed no interest in prayer or sacrament across what she didn't realize were her final weeks. Contemplating an old picture of herself and Françoise, Beauvoir delivers a blow through her tears: "I am so sorry for them—for me because I am so young and I understand nothing; for her because her future is closed and she has never understood anything." In demonstrating the violence of the breach between the two women—the same rift she is mourning and struggling to resolve—Beauvoir is most plainly a daughter.

Those moments when I didn't believe her narrator were for me the most moving of all.

Françoise is frightened by her daughter and tells her so. No longer subject to her mother's anger, Beauvoir recognizes it as a result of having been forced to live against her own appetites, subject to "out-of-date ideas." As a child, her mother's body, her heart and her mind "had been squeezed into an armor of principles and prohibitions. She had been taught to pull the laces hard on herself. A full-blooded woman lived on inside her, but a stranger to herself, deformed and mutilated." Born in the twentieth century's first decade, Beauvoir had some greater chance of converting her own fury into fuel. But she does not claim a heritage of anger. She describes instead a reckoning of bodies and a bequest of carnality, a passion for living thwarted in the mother's life but well-expressed in that of the daughter. Perhaps one is not so far from the other— anger and a woman's love of life often share an intimate relationship. That Beauvoir should attain any sense of legacy was a result of her mother's death, and its only gift: the loss freed her to see the connection as well as the severance, the mutuality and interdependence.

In her mother's death, as well, Beauvoir experienced some part of her own. And what would she leave? Shortly before her mother died, Beauvoir published *Force of Circumstance*, the third volume of her four-volume autobiography. In it, she describes her partnership with Jean-Paul Sartre as "[the] one undoubted success in my life." The two shared no children; Beauvoir expressed a passionate skepticism of motherhood. As Adrienne Rich writes in *Of Woman Born*: "The twentieth-century, educated young woman, looking perhaps at her mother's life, or trying to create an autonomous self in a society which insists that she is destined primarily for reproduction, has with good reason felt that the choice was an inescapable either/or: moth-erhood or individuation, motherhood or creativity, mother-hood or freedom." At the time Rich published those words, Beauvoir—who readily associated herself with socialism and existentialism—had only recently agreed to call herself a femi-nist. More than two decades after the publication of *The Second Sex*, she noticed that not much had changed for Frenchwomen. In that book, she had rejected feminism out of a belief "that the problems of women would resolve themselves automatically in the context of socialist development." That had not proven to be the case, even in socialist countries. "I am a feminist to-day," she said in a 1972 interview, "because I realized that we must fight for the situation of women, here and now, before our dreams of socialism come true."

The apparent contradiction between her philosophy and her personal life had been well noted by then. "It was no matter of chance that I chose Sartre; for after all I did choose him," Beauvoir writes in *Force of Circumstance*. "I followed him joyfully because he led me along the paths I wanted to take . . . This does not alter the fact that philosophically and politically the initiative has always come from him. Apparently some young women have felt let down by this fact." They shouldn't, Beauvoir suggests: freedom means freedom to choose. True autonomy may well lead a member of the feminist vanguard to consider a relationship with a man to be her greatest accomplishment.

Still, she maintained an aversion to marriage and mother-hood, and was firm in her decision not to bear children. "In fact, when I consider the relationships the women I know have with their children, especially with their daughters, they often seem dreadful to me," she said in 1973. "I am genuinely glad to have escaped that." If the movement demanded a broad reconsider-ation of the roles of wife and mother, Beauvoir's language—she frequently referred to childrearing as a form of enslavement—was extreme even for the time. Though, as with her partnership, she frames the matter as one of personal freedom, on the question of motherhood especially Beauvoir appears less than free.

If only in death, in the natural course of things, all daughters become their mothers, and sons their fathers, and so on. But death itself is altogether common, and few things are more rare—difficult to secure, maintain, transmit—than a fruitful heritage. For Beauvoir, questioning certain traditions—of authority, oppression, misogyny, bigotry, religion, economic exchange—was a way of life. Progress so often occurs in the overthrow of those legacies that thrive on passivity, and our lesser natures. Chaos so often results when the entire concept of legacy is torched in the name of progress. As Beauvoir faced the loss of her mother, there came a flow of notes, from both fans and detractors, about her recently published book. The latter tied her fear of death to her renunciation of the Catholic faith. The former offered comfort: death would never erase her; she lived on in her works. "And inwardly I told them all that they were wrong," writes Beauvoir in *A Very Easy Death*. "Religion could do no more for my mother than the hope of posthumous success could do for me. Whether you think of it as heavenly or as earthly, if you love life immortality is no consolation for death."

"HOW DO YOU KNOW?" my mother asked from her hospital bed. Dipping back into consciousness, she had found me in tears.

"How do I know what?"

She closed her eyes.

"How do you know you're going to be okay?"

"I'm going to be okay. I'm just going to miss you."

She opened her eyes. "You got to live your dream," she

said, with a slow-breaking smile. I mirrored back a smaller, less persuasive smile, unsure it was true, that it was me she was talking about. "Are you happy about it?"

"I'm not unhappy about it."

In the three days following her admission, the extremity of my mother's suffering had eased. As her morphine dosage made a steady rise she began to want things: chocolate, Jell-O, McDonald's, ginger ale with lots of lime. Most of all she wanted butter pecan ice cream, a reminder of her mother, and her mother's mother. The food wars were over. We would provide without comment as much or as little of whatever she wanted. She would no longer be prodded to leave her bed, for any reason. There were no more IVs, no way to check her sats. She asked to be put in her own clothes; she could hold a glass again, reach for the call button at her side. She was still dying, they told us, but the present crisis had passed. Several times she had to agree not to treat the next pneumonia, which would hasten the end. One evening she asked for sushi, but after a few wolfish bites began to feel sick. "It looks so good," she sighed. "I just want to shove it all in." A third nurse had just noted our resemblance, prompting my third attempt at a wan smile. "You're so cute," said my mother after she left. "You're like: she's dying, what are you trying to say?" I wanted to tell her she was still beautiful. Earlier I had spread balm on her flaking lips, and lotion across her brow. "You're going to have a one-man show by the end of this," she added. "I swear."

As we gathered around her on New Year's Eve, my mother roared. None of it made sense: she had been so tired, but now she was less tired. How would this work? What did it take to die? "I must be in some in-between stage," she muttered after a last wave of grief. "I'm moving through something."

The next day we sat alone again. She asked for a story—a

long one. I tried the one about the mistaken flower delivery in Mexico, but it fell apart in the telling. When she asked for a song instead, I hummed the nonsense tune I sing on Mercy walks. In rehab, where singing is taught to help support posture and breath control, my mother had tried to master Leonard Cohen's "Hallelujah" and "Rainbow Connection." Some years before, I had watched her perform her first karaoke number: "Where the Boys Are," by Connie Francis. It's the title song of a 1960 movie starring twenty-one-year-old Dolores Hart, an actress who three years later abandoned a publicity tour in order to enter a convent. I sat beside my mother on a living room couch as her voice began to carry, thin but high and clear, her commitment dragging me square into the moment. My mother was in another moment, and she was there alone. "Where the Boys Are" is a ghost story, a presumptive elegy; it's the sound a dream makes in the face of implacable odds. A stillness fell as she nailed the finale, one with the song, safe in its pocket:

> *Where the boys are, where the boys are*
> *Where the boys are, someone waits for me*

Her transfer to the palliative care unit on the fourth floor of St. Michael's Hospital offered further relief. Seven months earlier, we had visited the ward after an appointment elsewhere in the hospital. My mother had insisted we stop in after learning a former bank coworker was there, a woman she didn't really know. Worried for this woman's privacy and annoyed at having to draw any closer to death, I waited out the visit in the unit's communal kitchen-slash-lounge. In January I remembered a nurse from that day—the earnest, deliberate way she directed us, as though kindness itself was a language she often found herself extending to non-native speakers. The staff was uniformly tender and solicitous; from the start their attention filled my mother up. On Tuesdays and Thursdays the music therapist came, a sort of human jukebox who honored near every request, including Kermit. My mother began taking daily Communion. She had greeted Pope Francis's welcoming of the divorced back to the Communion ritual with a smirk, but now it was I who looked askance as the chaplain entered, and who remained silent during their recital of the Lord's Prayer. We brought lunch and dinner at her request, preparing soft-boiled eggs and grilled cheese sandwiches on the unit's kitchen stove. A pneumatic mattress eased the pain of a pressure wound. The Optiflow mask kept her oxygen stable. She was more comfortable, her coughing fits quelled with breakthrough hits of morphine, but more general debilitations overtook her without warning.

The average stay on the unit is ten days. On my mother's fourth night, I watched her whiten and turn gray, then ask for my hand. Feeling disoriented, she asked the nurses to move her to the bedside, where I sat, and curled into my shoulder. "I don't want to leave you," she said, beginning to cry. "I think about you all the time."

"I don't want you to go either," I said, feeling a surge of the amazement that so often crowded out all the other things one might be less surprised to feel. Expectation itself became a thing my mother and I considered from a remove, a relic of some other life. In this new place, only surrender to each moment made way for the next one. Only very close attention kept the horror away. Our knees were lined up, hers pared to the bone. Her feet felt like lead, she said, before asking that I join her in a Hail Mary. Still astonished, I agreed a first and then a second time, starting over when she said I was going too fast. Her ninety-two pounds felt much heavier propped against me, her head a boulder on my neck.

"I was looking at old photos last night," she said. "There was one of you dancing when you were little, at Christmas." It would have been taken in those years when the adults put a record on after dinner to watch me do my beastly thing—a four-year-old in full dervish. My mother returned to the image often through the years, as if to remind us both of the riotous, free-limbed child I used to be. I never told her I have always felt myself more a dancer than anything else I could name. I never considered what those nights might have to do with it. "Do you remember the tree we used to put on the balcony, with the white lights?" she said. "We thought we were so affluent, we had two trees."

"We had a lot," I said.

WE PASSED those early days believing death close by, a sudden fit or bad night away. I took a teaching leave, remained in Toronto. Members of my mother's respirology team began to drop by, looking skeptical: Was she sure? Why not just try to get up? Their questions felt cruel, reviving the pressure that had so afflicted her. We got to know Vicky, my mother's gentle, middle-aged roommate. Still mobile, she had an inoperable tumor on her spine. Vicky had recently moved from Barbados, where her adult son lived, and knew few people in Toronto. She did her own laundry and chatted with the nurses in the hall. She brought back a stuffed electric-blue shark from the nearby aquarium she visited with classmates from her social work program. Having approved a room visit from Mercy—if she could pet her too—Vicky appeared in the doorway fresh from the shower the day I brought the dog in. Spotting Mercy on my mother's bed, in a T-shirt and towel Vicky steered toward us with a look of hungry purpose, one hand holding the towel at her waist, the other outstretched. She stroked her the way people who know dogs do, talking of the ones she'd had back home.

Leaving each night, I stole extra looks at my mother, stunned in those moments by the sight of her merged with this new landscape. After two weeks she agreed to receive a friend or two. One day I arrived to find her back on regular nasal prongs, relieved of the mask that had kept her alive. She manned her iPhone all day, fielding opus after farewell opus from her friends, the women she had mentored. When she requested a haircut I arranged for a stylist to come. She asked for a gin and tonic and for a picture to be snapped of her raising it up, Mercy sprawled at her hip. Another long interim moment fell open, different from the one before. As suddenly as they emerged, my mother's stories slipped away. She slept more and dreamed less. She wrote letters to her granddaughter. She immersed herself in movies and TV series, recounting plotlines in wondrous tones and precise detail. She lay besieged by unlikely memories, including that of a peanut butter soup she once tried, early in her courtship with my father. She wept to remember how lucky she felt, at eighteen, to live in a big city, dine at a strange restaurant, taste such good food. She urged me to enter the real estate market with my inheritance, finally acquire an asset—to buy a home and to do it alone. She chose readings for her funeral and catering for the reception. She lingered over her obituary. Months before she had asked that I draft one to have ready in the event of a transplant. I agreed, and did nothing. In palliative she asked again. I agreed, again, and sat down to write. As assignments go, it was more unnatural and less awful than I had feared: there was strain but also relief in finding two hundred words that might say everything but mean nothing, as the form demands.

The changes my mother requested were minor but several:

a full name here; standard etiquette there. We settled on a paragraph of maximum expedience and minimal flourish. She chose an accompanying photograph—from her second wedding—and dispatched me to find it. Still she revisited the obituary, unsure we had it right. Further, ever finer requests for revision arose in tandem with each waver in her condition, such that the reappearance of that same, tortured document in my inbox—with instructions to reorder two clauses, adjust one last comma—made me tremble.

She suffered a finance colleague she hadn't seen in many years, who one afternoon appeared unexpected, unwelcome, and demanding to be *caught up*. She attempted to satisfy this woman with an account of her predicament. She ventured that the diagnosis of her lung disease was twenty-five years old, that smoking and genetics were not factors, that she was otherwise healthy. She pleaded a game, persuasive sort of bewilderment. When I added, despite myself, that the cycle began with a series of pneumonias she sustained through her peak working years, she turned to me, her bright expression flickering, and said, "Well, that's true."

She savored floral ecstasies: the magnolia at our London house; the nasturtiums grown from seed in pink Georgian Bay rock; the calla lilies that waved along the roadside between Nice and St. Paul de Vence.

She considered her obituary, the whole and then each line. She felt satisfied, and let it be. She frowned, and found it wanting. She sent it back to me, crisp in her directive:

"Let's review one more time."

# Thirteen

IF SHE WAS ILL-SUITED TO THE ROLE OF PATIENT, as a dying person my mother was legend. I left Toronto after a month, half suspecting she might wait until I had gone. But it was Vicky who turned in the ensuing days, who began to refuse food, keen in pain, and who at the end scrambled for her shoes in the middle of the night, determined to go home. Vicky whose fine, dulcet voice I first heard rising from behind the curtain that divided their shared room. The day after her admission, my mother and I watched a *Call the Midwife* episode that ended with a loud rendition of "Sealed with a Kiss." Over in her bed, Vicky joined the first chorus:

> *Yes it's going to be a cold, lonely summer*
> *But I'll fill the emptiness*

Two days after her death, I arrived to find Vicky's bed still empty. A chart posted in the hallway detailed ward protocols:

the number of hours a family is allowed with the deceased; the schedule on which a new admission is made. Despite the drugs, Vicky's death had been painful, lonely, and chaotic. My mother's witness of it sheared away whatever illusions had crept into her own vigil. We had yet to fully appreciate that the only thing worse than having one dying person in a room is having two.

That weekend, my mother asked for breakthrough after breakthrough of the morphine delivered under the skin of her upper arm via automated pump. Her baseline dose nudged higher. She had picked her favorite staff, preferring the best problem solvers and the aides with the fleetest touch. The thought of returning home appalled her. She made a habitat even of the much smaller shared room to which she had been moved by my next visit. Her portion of the space measured eight feet across and not much longer. I was horrified—*Not here*, I thought, *in a fucking closet*—yet my mother showed no alarm. Coming and going, especially, I fought off a terror we no longer seemed to share: of being trapped. I had to admit her unlikely radiance, entertain the possibility that freedom might look something like this. A greenhouse of cut flowers surrounded her, the garden whose tending she directed twice a day. Roses, tulips, lilies, and hydrangeas appeared in constant rotation. A family member continued to prepare her every meal. The urge to shove it all in faded; it appeared she had time. The situation's terms grew more obscure, submitting bite by bite to the adaptations that routinize the worst of life.

Our visits acquired ritual. Each time I felt a stab of shock to find her hidden in the same tiny nook, body prone and eyes bright. Arrival meant gossip, gifts, and menu planning; then food shopping, special meals, new shows, heated card games. Some vestigial twinge had revived a taste for gin rummy, which she associated with her father. I kept the trips short and frequent; we agreed on light goodbyes. There were no more tearful scenes. I stopped taking notes. There was nothing to do but face each other and feel time pass. As my mother continued to waste, I redoubled my efforts to grow muscle, stay fit. I felt square in my body as I had not since the age of ten. Some weeks another visit was a miracle; some I cursed all the way to Toronto, a deadweight dragged by taxi and plane and another taxi back to my mother's side. As winter gave scant, grudging way to spring, like a wayward student I worked to fathom her suffering one more time. She remained as unwell as a terminal patient not yet actively dying could be. For every hour passed in peace, I spent two more watching her nod off, or weather various bodily furies. Would the ordeal's extravagance finally amount to something, or was its nothingness the point? Which was worse?

When the predicted pneumonia failed to materialize, my mother wondered too—not what it all meant but what she was meant to do. She kept such thoughts from me, diverting her guilt and worry to the staff who had erected around her a scaffolding of care. One result of her persistence was the appearance of a second butterfly clip on her arm, this one delivering subcutaneous doses of the powerful sedative midazolam. Assisted death was not my mother's preference and not an option at St. Michael's, a Catholic hospital. The doctors raised instead the prospect of "palliative sedation," describing it as a sort of voluntary coma, one they could use to hasten a weary patient's exit. It reminded me of the Irish respirologist's casual suggestion that we remove my mother's high-flow mask: she would suffer, yes, but it would speed the whole thing up.

Up to that point, the Canadian system's limits had been plain but unsurprising. Palliative patients who wanted to die in their own room paid extra; the facility was run-down but the nursing staff exquisite; the food, of course, was gross. We soon learned that although patients are admitted on the basis of having an estimated max of six months to live, after three the hospital will seek their eviction. Early that spring, the resident known for his cool-guy socks and ooze-y bedside manner announced to us that the ward would have to let my mother go. Her gift for dying looked a little too much like living, and that was to be done elsewhere.

This too we put out of our minds. The unit could not eject her until a bed in a longer-term facility opened up. Incredibly, my mother's timorous, Dublin-born roommate also had no plans to die and no place to go: a fresh round of tests had revealed her terminal cancer diagnosis to be mistaken, but the old woman's children had already closed out her home. And thus the shitty hovel at the end of the hall acquired a singular light, one I focused on each time I passed through the ward's main doors and veered right.

With spring came a period of revival; the season had always been not just her favorite but her best. Her movements now had a hypnotic, druggy slowness, but her mind was sharp, her mood consistently serene. We plotted new pajamas—a chic, floral print—and a cache of makeup. If certain higher-ups resented my mother's stamina, I wondered at the nurses and aides—most of them women—who were as tender on the hundredth day as they had been on the first. With their patients they developed as a matter of course the kind of intimacy most people are programmed to avoid. Despite almost two decades of Catholic school, until I saw them in action month over month, I had not fully understood what it meant to be called, to do work that could rightfully be considered divine. This despite the extreme tenuousness of their schedules and job security; the budget cuts that reduced from four to two the number of nurses assigned to the ward's ten beds. Some of the staff confided in my mother, and she in them. They responded swiftly to her calls, never diminishing her concerns. They took heed of her professional advice and genuine joy in her more successful bowel movements.

She wrote me after a bedside Mother's Day celebration:

Why do these things have to
end?

Not fair

Need more

Me too

I hope I am not too demanding

I just don't want it to end

In palliative my mother's lifelong flair for paradox reached its peak: giving up had extended her life. In a state of total dependence she acquired unprecedented authority. A river of class A drugs left her clearer, more herself. Every tenet of identity stripped away, she was never more individual. Having plunged to the center of herself, she emerged a communal being. Limited by her body, she became a sort of nexus: potent, fluid, a creature of myth. Her surrender to a need for mothering mothered me in turn. It fulfilled and instructed the daughter in us both. The reckoning I had sought and abandoned amounted in large part to this, a leaving aside of what each of us was not taught, the ways we were left—the "accurate and radical" analysis of the modern mother-daughter breach, as Adrienne Rich wrote, that assumes "consciousness knows everything." She allowed me to bring her pleasure, in my person and via plates of shrimp, tubes of lip gloss, boxed cupcakes. I allowed myself to take that pleasure in. The more banal the shared activity, it seemed, the more profound its yield. Together we watched a derby, a royal wedding, a championship round of golf. Apart we gossiped about fallen men and red carpet looks. My phone pinged the morning after a famous Manhattan costume gala:

Madonna. Ugh.

She gets spookier as each year
passes

Just can't imagine what her
vagina looks like

???

On my mother's seventy-fourth birthday, that June, we cut a cake covered in sugary spring flowers. The next week I left for France, a trip I had booked shortly after her palliative admission and imagined taking in her memory. My mother insisted I go, but I felt sick in the car to the airport: leisure travel of any sort had never seemed more pointless. Waiting in the terminal, a photo of my mother taken earlier that day appeared on my phone. She was wearing her granddaughter's princess crown, wielding a glowing scepter, her smile broad and skin luminous. To the extent that it showcased her beauty, the image took its place in the running chronicle of her years as cherub, ingenue,

Pure Flame

bride, young mother, cultured traveler, corporate leader, bride again, and blissful retiree. It also captured something altogether new. Though I regretted especially the severing of her time with Frank, when I looked at my mother I saw someone who had lived with a vengeance, wringing out each day. I saw that her anger had ensured it. It was an anger that in many ways set the course of my life, the flame by which I had lived, toiled, and sought my own reflection. It was the teacher I fled and ran toward, the message that survived every absence. It was, finally, the example whose realization in my own life proved a tremendous relief, a way out of my thoughts and into the world. I don't burn like her, but pure and plain enough to light my own way.

That January, as she helped me plan the tour of southern France I would ultimately take with her buzzing in my pocket, a text or photo away, my mother asked often enough to read what then existed of this book that I eventually agreed. The project was in tatters anyway, a ghost of a ghost of the more elliptic, impassive document I first envisioned. I had wept at least in part from uncertainty while promising my mother, as she lay close to death, that the book would be a gift to her. As her requests for evidence of this multiplied over the weeks that followed, I sought out the few scenes I had sketched by then in which we both appeared—attempts to capture the light that finally sparked between us—and from Brooklyn sent on a few strategically chosen pages. Lying across from Vicky, my mother read with increasing disquiet a description of mother and daughter walking in midtown Toronto, her favorite nun, the perfect choir girl. Who was this trifling, silly person? How had I gotten such important things so wrong? Did I really imagine she never sang—just because I didn't hear it? She bristled to see herself depicted in the grip of lung disease and not her brilliant prime. She read again, then one more time, her disappointment turning to alarm and finally a low, bleak simmer. Her tone over text was subdued. Maybe her feedback would prove useful. Everyone has their own truth. But to be a true story, she wrote, this one needed work.

It was, of course, a huge mistake. The indictment I feared, straight from the source. Even in a favorite memory of mine my mother saw an expression of daughterly anger, the drive to warp and diminish, if not destroy. Perhaps she was right: it angered me that my happiest moments with her dated back just a few years. My resentment of her illness implicated us both, magnifying our shared habits of self-containment, self-punishment; self, self, self. It seemed pointless to claim my mother's fury, given how long and how fully it has claimed me. But among other things it was that anger urging me forward, free of malign intent—free. I couldn't say then how I longed for my mother to credit a rage of mine that was not about but *of* her, to see it as an ally in my own life and in hers, in whatever story I might choose to tell about us both.

AFTER SIX MONTHS, having acclimated to a total daily dosage of morphine that would kill a person in one shot, my mother decided to rise from her deathbed, and walk. As the summer heat set in beyond her window, she pictured herself sitting by the condo pool, watching her baby granddaughter splash and swim. The vision persisted, discrete but specific, until she wanted nothing more or less than to make it so. She would not reenter her home: just hospital to pool, then back. Goal set, she succeeded in taking a few steps on her first try, earning hosannas from the staff and a dedicated physio slot. She had not gone this long without a crisis in the two years since her illness turned. Despite doing no physio, no nebulizers—despite doing nothing at all—the presumed pneumonia hadn't come. Though we had applied to one of the city's two longer-term palliative facilities, the wait list ran several months. St. Mike's had needed her out in April; by summer they were ready to get creative. A new doctor appeared, tall and atypically sunny. "She's my hero," he told me early that July, as my mother wobbled past; the ward had never seen anything like it. *She'll pay for this*, I thought, watching her pivot her walker at the end of the hall for another lap, her eyes locked with mine.

I had arrived from Brooklyn by car, exiting the expressway into Toronto's downtown. After parking and walking Mercy through the patch of green space across from the hospital, I stumbled upon Frank and my mother, who was enjoying her second venture outside. She had been granted permission for these outings, to feel the sun and breeze, watch the people flow by. Dressed and eager for her next haircut, she wore an expression of caution and amazement in her wheelchair. At her feet I unloaded gifts marking our French itinerary: a Gordes T-shirt and eggcup from Èze; Provençal dresses for the little girls in her life. A beautiful young woman passing by had stopped earlier, my mother told me, to tell her and Frank what a lovely couple they made. She seemed to ripple with the pleasure of this encounter, awed by its pure kindness.

In the days that followed, the grinning doctor reappeared bearing a flowchart, a naked overture to his resident MBA. The chart proposed my mother's transfer to an inpatient rehab program, a path for her return home, perhaps back onto the transplant list. It presented her with a decision. For months she had insisted that she would move only if absolutely necessary and only once, to another palliative space. But as we faced each other that week, a fog set in: she studied the flowchart, its boxes and arrows and clean predictive logic, producing it for every visitor's inspection. The thought of her cast back onto her illness—and into an indifferent, porous system—disoriented me to the point of vertigo. My mother appeared similarly helpless, applying the old tactics of logic and negotiation to a bargain that surmounted both. The proposal's ambition was bitter and vast: she would have only six weeks to progress from terminal to functional, ready to return home. The unlikely idyll of spring and early summer fell away, reexposing the impossible choices, the calamity from which we had taken refuge. The other likely outcome of six weeks' intensive rehab was my mother's hastened death. "It's a moonshot," said the doctor, still smiling.

Hope returned, clad in black. We spent the ensuing days alone together, the forces of will and circumstance prying apart what they had so recently fused. The divide grew a new fracture when my mother announced her decision to accept the challenge, apply to the rehab; her immediate acceptance into the program opened it wide. She asked to be weighed for the first time since entering palliative, turning to me like a child in the stunned moment between injury and meltdown when the scale read eighty-six pounds. Within hours she developed a crippling heartburn that would persist for weeks. A month later, the day before her discharge, a man arrived to clean from her windows the layer of grime we had hardly noticed for eight months. Early the next morning we waited at the elevator, my mother bundled onto a gurney and flanked by two EMTs. The unit's doors flew open and a nurse ran toward us, gushing last goodbyes. My mother returned her emotion, urged her to eat every second. We were silent in the ambulance, watching the city fall away through the back window.

At the rehab a daylong procession of medics and clinicians

appeared to collect their new patient's history. Few seemed to grasp her situation: the program's range of need was broad enough that some patients walked unaided, or without supplemental oxygen. None were fresh from eight months of hospice care. She needed a different mattress, drugs they didn't have on hand. All the numbers we had abandoned—sats, heart rate, white blood cells, oxygen liters—reappeared to dance a fierce jig before us. The perfume and flowers that had reentered her life in palliative were re-exiled. She was there to work, each new face told us, and work hard. If she couldn't manage they would kick her out. "What is all this morphine!" a hulking Russian doctor cried, looking at the discharge notes. "It is crazy so much morphine!" My mother remained composed. My jaw felt close to fusing shut.

THE PNEUMONIA DIAGNOSIS came within two weeks. In the hospital nearest to the rehab, what had been considered a death sentence months before was treated rather casually: a short course of antibiotics prescribed by a doctor unfamiliar with her case. I didn't scramble to Toronto. More than stamina, I was losing the plot. My encouragements acquired an imitative feel better camouflaged over text. The sense of madness that returned that autumn was compounded by my mother's sudden fluency in the language of hope and avowal. She began to talk and plan big, coaching and admonishing herself, setting ever tougher goals. The daily schedule was intensive, the risk of ejection high. Somehow she gained five pounds, sucking back the gluey drinks she had refused a year before. I suffered another miscarriage, telling no one. My relationship fell apart. Arriving that September, I contemplated from one more threshold my mother's changeling silhouette, framed by a picture window.

Tense and distracted, she proved hard to engage. The rehab had weaned her from the drugs that kept her calm, her airways supple. We didn't talk about the extra time gathering between my visits. "You look *well*," she said one afternoon, sounding at once admiring and forlorn. "*Strong.*"

I spent a temperate weekend morning buying flowers and sweets for her den, the only room she wished to enter during a pilot visit home. She had resisted the exercise, fearful of crossing back into territory she had done battle to cede. Her poolside vision had not come to pass. Instead a permanent discharge date loomed; we had no other plan. Frank had been busy repopulating the apartment with the equipment he had divested that winter, and then some. We both retreated into panicked resignation, our expressions vacant and communications vague. We wore the same gray look as he wheeled my mother into the den and settled her onto the couch. The vibe was minimum fuss, lightness at all costs. Frank and I sat silent for a few minutes, snacking with false ease. My mother appeared almost weightless atop a pillow designed to reduce pressure on her backside. "I feel *good*," she decided, turning her head about the room with wide eyes, then to the CN Tower, cut with platinum sunlight into the horizon. Minutes passed. In a tone of soft recognition, she looked onto her beloved dining room, adding: "This is a beautiful home."

Several discharge dates came and went in the following weeks. Issues recurred, followed by more antibiotics. My mother's request for further treatment at her native hospital was brushed aside; everyone agreed she was just anxious about going home. In fact my mother had grown intent on her homecoming, hiring an aide to assist and cook meals and a physio to come five days a week. With each setback, her planning intensified. The rehab doctor treated her with an impatience that bordered on menace. *What do you think they can do for you at the hospital,* he hissed, inches from her face, *that I can't do here?* All through October, every new problem met the system's corresponding gap. After coughing up blood for several days, her sats grew volatile, crashing without explanation over a weekend. That Monday, her next discharge date, she was finally transferred to St. Mike's for more acute care. I spent the preceding days in a separate misery. A string of messages arrived as I sat in my Brooklyn apartment, staring dully ahead.

I am hanging on

You have to too

You have to be strong

You have to be tough

Start to write something

I am here for you

Talk to others about this

That's a mistake I made

I kept too much inside

Very bad

Cry your eyes out

It's very sad

But then you'll hit the
angry part

ARRIVING ON HALLOWEEN, two days after her scheduled transfer home, I headed to St. Mike's respirology late in the afternoon. The nurses wore black cat ears. Even before entering the
room I noticed my mother's eyes, which appeared mismatched,
bruised, slightly out of place. The doctor on call had just performed an aggressive bout of chest percussion. They were treating for pneumonia, another IV. I didn't know it then, but she
had refused the high-flow apparatus that had saved her life in
January, afraid of disturbing a recent cauterization to treat her
violent nosebleeds. Slumped at the bedside with a computer in
his lap, Frank had been there all day. Up close my mother's
eyes struck me as having a new, more concentrated shade, one
that matched her periwinkle gown. Her lids were swollen, her
pupils contracted to tiny dots. The room felt dark and slanted.
But no worse, my body insisted as I took it all in, than the other
rooms, the other very bad times.

Her greeting was muffled behind the oxygen mask. Arranged by the bed sat the markers of medical exile: meds and
inhalers stuffed in a cardboard bedpan, phone, two travel
bags—toiletries and makeup. A dish and spoon from home.
Frank rose and stood at the foot of the bed, ready to end another vigil. Calling up the last of the day's optimism, he leaned
forward and told his wife he thought she was improving. She
lifted her chin for a long look, gave a sharp nod, and was silent.
Out in the hall, nurses were seated at their various monitors,
marking changes, updating charts, recording minutiae. The

one noting the arrival of her patient's daughter would later note the same daughter's departure.

It was just us then. I sat at the bedside, my mother's hand limp in mine, pulled in a familiar way between retreat and the radical focus that so often seemed all I had left. It was worse than I thought: in some far corner I tallied the immediate plans to be dissolved, the resources needed to weather another low. When my mother spoke it was of her own plans, her voice thick and cut with betrayal. "I did what they wanted," she said, stopping for breath. "Everything they asked." She fought to keep her head up. "I went off to rehab like a *good soldier*, I sat through all the classes, the exercises. I hired people, I lined things up."

I had stayed away five weeks. We remained in constant, blooping touch, news of her condition, her triumphs and laments arriving on the hour. But in that time I blew up no nursing stations, hunted no doctors from my Brooklyn living room. I lay down the bitch from New York. I had a class to teach, a life to hold intact, bounded, separate. Looking at my mother now, it was clear whatever I had done I did in anticipation of this moment. Pitched back onto herself on the bed, she talked of losing ground every moment, the hard-won pounds of flesh and weeks spent fighting. She reeled to think of it: her goals, all her goals. The darkness in her body reached out for the darkness in mine.

I fled to gather dinner from the Eaton Centre: cartons of acorn squash soup and butter pecan ice cream. She ate the ice cream first, pushing determined spoonfuls under her mask, then attempted her breathing exercises. I rubbed her feet, too hard at first, then brought the two cups—one full of water, one for spitting—and put paste on her toothbrush. She complained to the nurse about a band of discomfort tightening across her lower abdomen; we decided on a laxative drink. She asked for a vitals check: no fever, normal sats, blood pressure ninety-two over fifty-five. *That may be normal for you*, the nurse said as I blanched, doubting it, doubting everything. *Let me check your chart.* At some point I produced from my bag the latest in a line of coveted baby-pink lipsticks, a minor but reliable source of cheer. Watching me open it my mother flinched and turned away. Raising it up past her nose she considered with effort the pristine, sculpted bullet. Then passed it back to me.

In the hall a resident introduced herself. Young and fervent, she had not yet learned to treat family as a job hazard. Having opened with a stilted history of my mother's case, she declared the previous two months of antibiotics to have been a waste of time. The current cocktail, however, was the right one. Things would lift, she said, peering up at me—but my mother had to want them to. I felt unshowered and out of practice, like I had left the right questions somewhere between Syracuse and Buffalo. In two years, a doctor had never sought me out. Some patients give up, she added, that's their choice. But my mother's cursing as they beat her about the chest was encouraging: anger is a sign of life. Her X-rays already showed improvement. It was a recruiting talk: the young doctor was inviting me onto team recovery. Focused on clearing the lungs and nailing the current interaction, she made no mention of high-flow oxygen, or $CO_2$ narcosis, what builds up in the veins.

Hearing a report of this conversation, my mother sneered. All these doctors with their hot dog drugs, the bespoke cocktails no one else would think to try—and none of them work. She caught her breath. "It's enough, it's too much—for everyone." I said she needed rest, that she was right to be upset. But that the doctor had made a decent point: anger means you're still in it. My mother considered this. I tried to feel something other than fraudulent, hollowed clean.

"I don't know if I'm still in it."

She would sleep, she said, and think more tomorrow.

I left her there, our rituals complete. As I pulled on my coat—her coat, she noted correctly—she asked for the day planner in which she kept some cash. I watched her work to pull out three twenties, the airport taxi fare she always insisted on covering. I had driven that day—we had talked about it—but said nothing then, folding the twenties in half and slipping them into my wallet, crossways against the American bills. Across the room I unplugged her phone, with its tulip-laden screen, presenting it as a sort of parting gift. Until morning. There had been so many; I don't remember our exact goodbye. My mother began typing the first of three emails as I stood at the elevator, watching the nurses stuff candy into plastic cups. *At St. Mikes vs home*, she replied to one relative. *Getting tired. What is the answer?*

In bed at the apartment I studied a photo a family friend had passed on: my mother from behind, her head turned in profile. Her back is strong, her neck straight. Her smile is relaxed and soft; she doesn't see the camera. She is older than me but still looks young, unblemished. I tried to wipe out that night's flashing images, the strange bruised eyes, her plea for relief, that I might take it all away. I was refusing even then the knock that would wake me just past three that morning, the forces conspiring to carry me back down the city's spine, to her side. Setting her picture down, before sleep drew me under I sent my mother a single red heart. There was no reply.


I HAD NOT PACKED for a funeral. I wore my mother's clothes that day, and for months to come. I never had such fine things. Her things. Though I wore the silks and cashmeres naturally enough, the greater passion for them remained my mother's, a matter of thwarted inheritance. If not her means, her good taste bound her more directly to Rita, whose relationship to personal style involved pleasure and expression but also the subverted order of things. A woman found in style a way to make the world submit to her body, to wear it exactly as she pleased.

I find the world a little less worth wearing. Each room stands poorer. I attempt to fill them up again, first in all the old ways—searching my own mind and beyond for meaning, context, hidden constellations. If their comfort is gone, certain habits remain. I turn over the same stories, prod the flesh of a nameless old beast. I collect and try on like brushed-leather boots the various selves lost, found, and discarded in my mother's house, arranging them in straight and broken lines. I return, eventually, to the ways my mother taught me, the things I learned despite her teaching. I reenter the rooms we shared, scouring for evidence and finding only two bodies, facing each other. I recover the sensation of bequest flowing free and electric between them—a twofold charge of lament and exaltation, burning love and fierce resentment. An attachment bound by the need to hold its extremities in balance, to keep each other in view for as long as we could.

As I write, another spring is coming in. I never cared much for the season. Springtime brought not relief but impatience, the suffering of its same maudlin rites—of renewal, fecundity, florid display. New life, maybe, but the death of thought. I would bend my gaze around spring's closed purview of sign and metaphor, sure what mattered lay just beyond. Half a lifetime passed indifferent to the sum of its passions, the fury of each rebirth, the fearsome effort of a single bloom. I feel a great many things about to change.

# Acknowledgments

I am grateful to Jin Auh for her belief, guidance, and tenacity. Thank you, Emily Bell, for keeping the faith, and much gratitude to the team at FSG, especially Jackson Howard, Julia Ringo, Chloe Texier-Rose, and Na Kim. Thank you to the friends and family who lifted me up throughout the writing of this book, and to the students who challenged me to do and be better. Thank you, sweet Mercy. Thank you, Wil Hylton and Liam and Sylvie Hylton, whose love and brilliant light helped ease a dark passage.

*A Note About the Author*

Michelle Orange is the author of the essay collection
*This Is Running for Your Life*, named a best book of 2013
by *The New Yorker*. Her writing has appeared in publica-
tions including *The New Yorker, Harper's Magazine, The
New York Times, Bookforum, McSweeney's,* and the *Virginia
Quarterly Review,* where she is a contributing editor. She
teaches in the graduate writing programs at Goucher
College and Columbia University.